THE GRANDEUR THAT WAS ROME

Augustus

THE GRANDEUR THAT WAS

ROME

by J. C. STOBART

4th edition, edited and revised by
W. S. MAGUINNESS
and
H. H. SCULLARD

BOOK CLUB ASSOCIATES
LONDON

This edition published 1971 by
Book Club Associates
By arrangement with Sidgwick & Jackson Ltd

Made and printed in Great Britain by
Thomas Nelson (Printers) Ltd, London and Edinburgh

PREFACE

TO THE ORIGINAL EDITION

THIS book is a continuation of *The Glory that was Greece,* written with the same purpose and from the same point of view.

The point of view is that of humanity and the progress of civilisation. The value of Rome's contribution to the lasting welfare of mankind is the test of what is to be emphasised or neglected. Hence the instructed reader will find a deliberate attempt to adjust the historical balance which has, I venture to think, been unfairly deflected by excessive deference to literary and scholastic traditions. The Roman histories of the nineteenth century were wont to stop short with the Republic, because "Classic Latin" ceased with Cicero and Ovid. They followed Livy and Tacitus in regarding the Republic as the hey-day of Roman greatness, and the Empire as merely a distressing sequel beginning and ending in tragedy. From the standpoint of civilisation this is an absurdity. The Republic was a mere preface. The Republic until its last century did nothing for the world, except to win battles whereby the road was opened for the subsequent advance of civilisation.* Even the stern tenacity of the Roman defence against Hannibal, admirable as it was, can only be called superior to the still more heroic defence of Jerusalem by the Jews, because the former was successful and the latter failed. From the Republican standpoint

---

* Probably few would now endorse this judgment of some fifty years ago; it is indeed not substantiated by what is said in the following pages about Rome's constructive achievements in government and administration, in avoiding civil strife at home for centuries, in establishing peace throughout Italy and what was at first an orderly system of government in the overseas provinces (in these spheres it was the last century of the Republic rather than the earlier ones that was the period of decline), in developing its system of law, and not least in its very considerable achievements in the field of literature and art, architecture and engineering. EDD.

v

Rome is immeasurably inferior to Athens. In short, what seemed important and glorious to Livy will not necessarily remain so after the lapse of nearly two thousand years. Rome is so vast a fact, and of consequences so far-reaching, that every generation may claim a share in interpreting her anew. There is the Rome of the ecclesiastic, of the diplomat, of the politician, of the soldier, of the economist. There is the Rome of the literary scholar, and the Rome of the archaeologist.

It is wonderful how this mighty and eternal city varies with her various historians. Dionysius of Halicarnassus, from whom we learn much of her early history, was seeking mainly to flatter the claims of the Romans to a heroic past. Polybius, the trained Greek politician of the second century B.C., was writing Roman history in order to prove to his fellow-Greeks his theory of the basis of political success. Livy was seeking a solace for the miseries of his own day in contemplating the virtues of an idealised past. Tacitus, during an interval of mitigated despotism, strove to exhibit the crimes and follies of autocracy. These were both rhetoricians, trained in the school of Greek democratic oratory. Edward Gibbon, too (I write as one who cannot change trains at Lausanne without emotion), saw the Empire from the standpoint of eighteenth-century liberalism and materialism. Theodor Mommsen made Rome the setting for his Bismarckian Caesarism, and finally M. Boissier has enlivened her by peopling her streets with Parisians. It is, in fact, difficult to depict so huge a landscape without taking and revealing an individual point of view. There is always something fresh to see even in the much-thumbed records of Rome.

Although a large part of this book is written directly from the original sources, and none of it without frequent reference to them, it is, in the main, frankly a derivative history intended for readers who are not specialists. Except Pelham's *Outlines,* which are almost exclusively political, there is no other book in English, so far as I am aware, which attempts to give a view of the whole course of ancient Roman History within the limits of a single volume, and yet the Empire without the Republic is almost as incomplete as the Republic without the Empire. As for the Empire, although nothing can supersede or attempt to replace *The Decline and Fall,* yet the scholar's outlook on the history of the Empire has been greatly changed since Gibbon's day by the discovery of

Pompeii and the study of inscriptions. Therefore while I fully admit my obligations to Gibbon and Mommsen (as well as to Dill, Pelham, Bury, Haverfield, Greenidge, Warde Fowler, Cruttwell, Sellar, Walters, Rice Holmes, and Mrs Strong, and to Ferrero, Pais, Boissier, Seeck, Bernheim, Mau, Becker, and Friedländer) this book professes to be something more than a compilation, because it has a point of view of its own.

The pictures are an integral part of my scheme. It is not possible with Rome, as it was with Greece, to let pictures and statues take the place of wars and treaties. Wars and treaties are an essential part of the Grandeur of Rome. They should have a larger place here, were they less well known, and were there less need to redress a balance. But the pictures are chosen so that the reader's eye may be able to gather its own impression of the Roman genius. When the Roman took pen in hand he was usually more than half a Greek, but sometimes in his handling of bricks and mortar he revealed himself. For this reason—and because I must confess not to be a convinced admirer of "Roman Art"—there is an attempt to make the illustrations convey an impression of grand building, vast, solid, and utilitarian, rather than of finished sculpture by Greek hands. Pictures can produce this impression far more powerfully than words. Standing in the Colosseum or before the solid masonry of the Porta Nigra at Trier, one has seemed to come far closer to the heart of the essential Roman than ever in reading Virgil or Horace. The best Roman portraits are strangely illuminating.

J. C. S.

PREFACE

TO THE THIRD EDITION

W H I L E this third reprint had been planned before the author's untimely death, he himself was not able to proceed far with the work of revision and the obvious duty of a reviser in such a position was to tamper as little as possible with the book. Some details have been corrected and a few paragraphs rewritten where the progress of research seemed to make change inevitable, but otherwise Mr Stobart's text stands. The illustrations have been revised, a number of new ones added and some of the older plates withdrawn; among them more than one old favourite which has long served to illuminate Roman history in this country, only to meet with condemnation at the hands of this specialist generation.

F. N. P.

PREFACE TO THE FOURTH EDITION

CONSIDERABLE changes have been made in the text of the Third Edition (1934), in which Mr. F. N. Pryce had only slightly modified Mr. Stobart's Second Edition (1920). On the historical side the time has come to redress the balance in favour of the Roman Republic; care has been taken to ensure that the Empire, for which Stobart was so enthusiastic, has not suffered in the process. The advance of knowledge during the last thirty or forty years has made alterations necessary in the account of early Rome and Italy. The pages on literature, notably those on drama and elegiac poetry, have also undergone substantial change. It is to be hoped that readers of the present edition will not miss Stobart's engaging flippancy on these aspects of the Roman heritage. The progress of photography has both compelled and enabled us to improve on many of the former illustrations.

1961

W.S.M.
H.H.S.

PUBLISHER'S NOTE

THE great majority of the photographs for the plates have been supplied through the kindness of Dr. E. Nash of the Fototeca Unione at Rome, to whom the editors are greatly indebted. Acknowledgement of other sources is made where appropriate throughout the List.

CONTENTS

xi

LIST OF ILLUSTRATIONS

Head of Augustus with Wreath of Oak-leaves *Frontispiece*

An idealised portrait of the emperor in middle life. He wears the *corona civica*. From a photograph by Bruckmann of the original in the Glyptothek, Munich.

Plate

1. Iron Age Hut

In 1948 the floors of three Iron Age huts of the eighth century B.C. were found on the Palatine hill. The position of the post-holes, together with the evidence provided by the Latin cinerary hut-urns (see p. 12), have made reconstruction possible. This model is in the Antiquarium on the Palatine, Rome.

2. The Capitoline Wolf

A large bronze from the Capitol, dating from *c*.500 B.C., probably Etruscan work and in the tradition of the artists of Veii. During the Renaissance the twin figures of Romulus and Remus were added. Palazzo dei Conservatori, Rome. *Mansell-Alinari*.

3. Etruscan Statues

(a) An Etruscan warrior. British Museum, London.
(b) The Apollo of Veii. An over-life size statue of painted terracotta, found in 1915 at Veii. It formed part of a group representing a struggle between Hercules and Apollo; the figures probably stood on the roof of a temple. It shows the influence of early East Greek (Ionian) art. The statues of the temple of Jupiter Optimus Maximus on the Capitol at Rome were the work of the same artist. Villa Giulia Museum, Rome.

4. Etruscan Tombs

Hundreds of tombs survive in the ancient necropolis of Caere (modern Cerveteri). The chamber tombs were cut in the rock and heaped over with earth. The larger tombs contained many burials.

5. Interior of an Etruscan Tomb

'Tomb of the Stuccos' at Caere, a somewhat late work (third century B.C.?). It resembles the inside of a house. The dead were laid in the niches along the walls. The surface of the walls and pillars are decorated with painted stucco reliefs which represent many objects of daily life. *Mansell-Alinari*.

Plate

ILLUSTRATIONS IN THE TEXT

INTRODUCTION

questa del Foro tuo solitudine
ogni rumore vince, ogni gloria,
e tutto che al mondo è civile,
grande, augusto, egli è romano ancora.

CARDUCCI

THE PERSPECTIVE OF ROMAN HISTORY

ATHENS and Rome stand side by side as the parents of
Western civilisation. The parental metaphor is almost irresistible.
Rome is so obviously masculine and robust, Greece endowed with
so much loveliness and charm. Rome subjugates by physical conquest and government. Greece yields so easily to the Roman might
and then in revenge so easily dominates Rome itself, with all that
Rome has conquered, by the mere attractiveness of superior
humanity. Nevertheless this metaphor of masculine and feminine
contains a serious fallacy. Greece, too, had had days of military
vigour. It was by superior courage and skill in fighting that Athens
and Sparta had beaten back the Persian invasions of the fifth century before Christ and thus saved Europe for occidentalism.
Again it was by military prowess that Alexander the Great carried
Greek civilisation to the borders of India, hellenising Asia Minor,
Syria, Persia, Egypt, Phoenicia, and even Palestine. This he did
just at the moment when Rome was winning her dominion over
Latium. Instead, then, of looking at Greece and Rome as two
coeval forces working side by side, we must regard them as predecessor and successor. Rome is scarcely revealed as a world-
power until she meets Greek civilisation in Campania near the
beginning of the third century before Christ. The physical decline
of Greece is scarcely apparent until Pyrrhus' phalanx returns
beaten in battle by the Roman legions at Beneventum. Moreover,
in addition to this chronological division of spheres there is also

1

a geographical division. Greece takes the East, Rome the West, and though by the time that Rome went forth to govern her Western provinces she was already pretty thoroughly permeated with Greek civilisation, yet the West remained throughout mediaeval history far more Latin than Greek. When Constantine divided the empire he was only expressing in outward form a natural division of culture.

The resemblances between Rome and Greece are very clearly marked. In many respects they are visibly of the same family, and though we no longer speak as loosely of "Aryan" and "Indo-European" as did the ethnologists and philologists of the nineteenth century, yet there remains an obvious kinship of language, customs, and even dress. Many of the most obvious similarities, such as those of religion and literature, are now seen to be the result of later borrowing, but there remains a distinct cousinship; both peninsulas may be regarded as exhibiting phases of a common Mediterranean culture, reposing possibly on a common aboriginal stock which has been variously influenced by intruding tribes and by geographical conditions.

But with all these resemblances, one of the most interesting features of ancient history lies in the psychological contrast between Greece and Rome, or rather between Athens and Rome. Athens is rich in ideas, full of the spirit of inquiry, and hence fertile in invention, fond of novelty, worshipping brilliance of mind and body. Rome is stolid and conservative, devoted to tradition and law. Gravity and a sense of duty are her supreme virtues. Here we have the two types that succeed and conquer, set side by side for comparison. To which is the victory in the end?

To the Englishman of to-day Rome is in some ways far more familiar than Greece. Apart from obvious resemblances in history and in character, Rome touches our own domestic history, and any man who has marked the stability of old Roman foundations or the straightness of old Roman roads has already grasped a fundamental truth about her. He is surely not far wrong in the general sense of power, energy and law, which he associates with the name of Rome. Thus there is not, as there was in the case of Greece, any radical misconception of the Roman character to be combated.

But there is, it appears, a widely prevalent false perspective in the common view of Roman history. The modern reader, especially if he be an Englishman, is liable to be a stern moralist in his judgment of other nations and ages. In addition to this he is a citizen of an empire still extremely self-conscious and somewhat bewildered at its own magnitude. He cannot help drawing analogies from Roman history and seeking in it "morals" for his own guidance. The Roman Empire bears such an obvious and unique resemblance to the British that the fate of the former must be of enormous interest to the latter. For this reason alone we are apt to regard the *fall* of Rome as the cardinal point of Roman history. To this must be added the influence of Gibbon's great work. By Gibbon we are led to contemplate above all things (with Silas Wegg) her Decline and Fall. Thus Rome has become for many people simply a colossal failure and a horrible warning. We behold her first as a Republic tottering to her inevitable ruin, and then as an Empire decaying from the start and continuing to fester for some five hundred years. This is one of the cases which prove that History is made not so much by heroes or natural forces as by historians. It is an accident of historiography that the Republic was not described by any great native historian until its close, when amid the horrors of civil war men set themselves to idealise the heroes of extreme antiquity and thus left a gloomy picture of unmitigated deterioration. As there was no great historian in sympathy with the imperial regime, the reputation of the early Empire was left mainly in the hands of Tacitus and Suetonius, the former of whom riddled it with epigrams while the latter befouled it with scandal. Nearly all Roman writers had a rhetorical training and a prejudice in favour of the past; many of them had also a satirical bent. Thus it is that Roman virtue has receded into an age which modern criticism declares to be mythological. It is a further accident that the genius of Rome's greatest modern historian was also strongly satirical. It was a natural affinity of temper that led Gibbon to continue the story of Tacitus and to dip his pen into the same bitter fluid.

Thus Rome has found few impartial historians and not many sympathetic ones. But is it possible to be sympathetic? While every man of imagination feels a thrill at the name of Greece, there are few who *love* ancient Rome. At the first mention of her name the average man's thought flies to the Colosseum and the Christian martyr "facing the lion's gory mane" to the music of Nero's fiddle. His second thought is to formulate his explanation of her decline and fall. The explanations are as various as political complexions. "Luxury", says the moralist; "Heathendom", says the Christian; "Christianity", replies Gibbon. The Protectionist can easily show that it was due to the importation of free corn, while the Free Trader draws attention to the enormous burdens that Roman trade had to bear. "Militarism", explains the peace-lover; "neglect of personal service", replies the conscriptionist. The Socialist, the Liberal, and the Conservative can all draw valuable conclusions from Roman history in support of their respective attitudes of mind. "If it had not been for demagogues like the Gracchi and Marius", says the Conservative, "Rome might have continued to exhibit the courage and patriotism which she displayed under senatorial guidance in the war against Hannibal, instead of rushing to her doom by way of sedition and disorder." With equal justice his political opponents point to the stupid bigotry with which that corrupt oligarchy, the senate, delayed necessary reforms. That, they say, was the cause of the downfall of Rome. That was the writing on the wall.

Whether it is or is not possible to love Ancient Rome, I would suggest that this attitude of treating her merely as a subject for autopsies and a source of gloomy vaticinations for the benefit of the British Commonwealth is a preposterous affront to history. The mere notion of an empire continuing to decline and fall for five centuries is ridiculous. It is to regard as a failure one of the greatest civilising forces in all the history of Europe, one of the most stable forms of government, one of the strongest military and political systems that the world has seen.

The destiny or function of Rome in world-history was nothing more or less than the making of Europe. The modern family of European nations are her sons and daughters, and some of her daughters have grown up and married foreign husbands and given birth to offspring. For this great purpose it was necessary that the city itself should pass through the phases of growth, maturity and decay. In political terms, it was part of the Roman destiny to translate the civilisation of the city-state into that of the nation or territorial state. Having evolved the Province it was necessary that the City should expire. Expansion on a colossal scale was part of the programme, absolute centralised control was another part. For this purpose the change from republic to autocracy as necessary.

Greece, as we have seen elsewhere,* by her system of small states enclosed and protected by city walls, had been able, long before the world at large was nearly ripe for it, to develop a civilised culture with habits of thought and speech that are now called European or Western. It was in a highly concentrated social life and under artificial conditions that Athens and other cities had laid the foundation of all our arts, sciences and philosophies. It was, however, as we saw, impossible for the civic democracy to expand naturally. Athens could hold a little empire for a few years by means of precarious sea-power. She could throw off a few daughter cities made in her own likeness. But for missionary work on a large scale the city-state was not adapted. Something much larger than a city and much more single-minded than a democracy was necessary for that purpose. The genius of Alexander the Great, an autocrat and a Macedonian, enabled him to do much towards propagating Hellenism in the eastern part of the Mediterranean littoral. But his early death prevented the fulfilment of his task and his Greek background led him to consider the planting of new Greek cities the chief means for fulfilling it.

Here then was the part which Rome had to play. She had to do for the West what Alexander had attempted for the East. In some respects her task was harder, for her work lay among war-like barbarians, but easier in that she had not to face the corrupting influence of a rival and more ancient civilisation.

Rome too began as a city-state, and it was while she was still in that condition that Greek civilisation came to her and took her by storm. It was the new wine that burst the old bottle when Rome failed to transform herself into a Greek democracy, and ultimately became a monarchy once more. It was not, therefore, a case of "decline and fall" when Rome ceased to be a republic; it was an oligarchy that had for a century deserved to be replaced by something better. If we can but turn our minds away from the gossip of the court and the spite of the discontented aristocracy to a just survey of that majestic and enduring system of provincial government, we shall be able to discern progress where some historians would have us lament decay.

It was progress again when Rome gradually ceased to be a city-state with a surrounding territory and became successively

* See *The Glory that was Greece*, pp. 7 ff.

the leader of an Italian confederacy, the capital of an empire and then one of half a dozen great centres of government. Finally it was progress when the artificial ramparts on the Rhine and the Danube broke down and new nations developed. By that time Rome had accomplished her work.

Some such convictions as these are, I think, inevitable to any one who views European history as a whole in the light of any theory of historical evolution. Rome has long been the playground of satirists and pessimists. Unfortunately at this date it is difficult to shake off their verdict and to read Roman history in the new light. To do so you cannot follow the literary authorities, for they were all on the side of deterioration. The idea of progress was unfamiliar to the ancient world, and the Romans were especially disposed to believe that their Golden Age was behind them. It becomes necessary therefore to extract truth from unwilling witnesses, always a precarious undertaking. Most Roman men of letters believed with Horace :

> damnosa quid non imminuit dies?
> ætas parentum peior auis tulit
> nos nequiores, mox daturos
> progeniem uitiosiorem.*

Unless we are prepared to accept the rank of *progenies uitiosissima* we are compelled to discount this tendency of thought and read our authorities between the lines. They were rhetoricians, mostly bent on praising the past at the expense of the present and the future; few of them were over-scrupulous in dealing with evidence. If, however, we turn to the inscriptions, we get a very different picture of the Roman Empire, a picture much brighter and, I think, in many respects more faithful to truth.

LATINISM

Hellenism we know and understand; the true classical scholar is a Hellenist by conviction. But Latinism seems to be less securely established and the devotees less self-confident. Except for the choicest Latin poetry of the Republican and Augustan Ages, what

* Is there anything that ruinous Time does not impair? Our parents, a generation worse than our grandparents, have produced in us, a race more veil, soon to give birth to offspring more wicked still. (*Odes*, III. vi. 45-8.)

that is Latin can compete in popularity with Greek literature?
Who reads Lucan out of school hours? Who would search Egypt
for Cicero's lost work *De Gloria?* Who would recognise a quota-
tion from Statius?

It has not always been so. Once they quoted Lucan and Seneca
across the floor of the House of Commons. The eighteenth century was far more in sympathy with Ancient Rome than we are.
In those days it would not have seemed absurd to argue the
superiority of Virgil over Homer. Down to that day Latin had
remained the alternative language for educated people, the
medium of international communication, even for diplomacy,
until French gradually took its place. Only if you specifically
sought to reach the vulgar did you write in English. Though Dr
Johnson could write a very pretty letter in French, he conversed
with Frenchmen in Latin; not that it made him more intelligible,
for, in fact, no foreigner could understand the English pronuncia-
tion of Latin; but he did not wish to appear at a disadvantage with
a mere Frenchman by adopting a foreign jargon. As for public
inscriptions, though half the literary men in London signed a
round-robin entreating the great autocrat to write Oliver Goldsmith's epitaph in English, Johnson "refused to disgrace the walls
of Westminster Abbey with an English inscription".

What is the cause of the eclipse which Latin studies are still
suffering? One cause, perhaps, is to be found in the misuse of the
languages by the pedagogues and philologists of the past in the
school and the examination-room. But another cause is discoveries
about Greek civilisation, which have confirmed the opinion that
Latin culture is in the main secondary and derivative. At the present moment we are passing through a stage of revolt against
classicism, convention, and artificiality. We know that Greek culture, truly discerned, is neither "classic" nor conventional nor
artificial, but Latinism is still apparently subject to all these terms.
The Latinity of Cicero, Virgil, Ovid, Horace, Lucan, and the
greater part of the giants, in fact all the Latin of our schools is—
what Greek is not—really and truly classical. They were not writing as they spoke and thought. They had studied the laws of
expression in the school of rhetoric, and on pain of being esteemed
barbarous they wrote under those laws. Style was their aim. The
Romans were grammarians by instinct and orators by education.
Thus Latin is fitted by nature for schoolroom use, and for all who

would learn and study words, which after all represent thoughts, Latin is the best training-ground. The language marches by rule. Rules govern the inflexions and the concords of the words. The periods are built up logically and beautifully in obedience to law. Latin, of all languages, is the most challenging—and rewarding—for the translator.

In the world of letters, as in that of politics, there are the virtues of order and the virtues of liberty. Our own eighteenth century was logical in mind because it had to clothe its thoughts in a language of precision. But even Pope and Addison fall short of the standards of Virgil and Cicero. *De gustibus non est disputandum* —let some prefer the plain roast and others the made dish. But it must be a very dull soul that is unmoved by the grandeur of Roman history, the triumphant march of the citizen legions, the dogged patriotism which resisted Hannibal to the death, and the pageantry and splendour of the Empire. One must be blind not to admire the massive strength of her ruined monuments, arches, bridges, roads, and aqueducts. And one must be deaf indeed not to enjoy the surges of Ciceronian oratory or the rolling music of the Virgilian hexameter. Greece may claim all the charm of the spring-time of civilisation, but Rome in all her works has a majesty which must command, if not love, wonder and respect. Mommsen justly remarks that "it is only a pitiful narrow-mindedness that will object to the Athenian that he did not know how to mould his State like the Fabii and Valerii, or to the Roman that he did not learn to carve like Phidias and to write like Aristophanes".

Under the flowing toga of Latinism the natural Roman is concealed from our view. It is possible that the progress of research and excavation may to an increasing extent rediscover him and distinguish him, as it has already done for his Hellenic brother, from the polished courtiers of the Augustan Age who have hitherto passed as typical products of Rome.

It is astonishing how little we really know of Rome and the Romans after all that has been said and written about them. The ordinary natural Roman is a comparative stranger to us. It is certain that he did not live in luxury like Maecenas, but how did he live and what sort of man was he? We can discern that his language was not in the least like that of Cicero. It is possible that he neither dreaded nor disliked emperors like Nero, as did Tacitus and Juvenal. As for his religion, much has already been done, and more still remains to be done, to show that he did not really worship the Hellenised Olympians who pass in literature for his gods. Recent scholarship has done something to reveal to us the presence of a real national art in Rome, or at any rate of an artistic development on Italian soil, which freed itself from Hellenic leading-strings and made visible steps of its own. We can also discern in the Roman temperament with its rigid adherence to legal precedent and to ancestral custom something very widely different from novelty-seeking Greece. Thus there is some hope that the real Roman will not always elude us. But for the present in the whole domain of art, religion, thought, and literature, Greek influence has almost obliterated the native strain. For the present, therefore, we must be content to regard Roman civilisation as mainly derivative, and our principal object will be to see how Rome fulfilled her task as the missionary of Greek thought. This object, together with the unsatisfactory nature of the records, must excuse the haste with which I have passed over the earlier stages of Roman republican history. It is obvious that the first three centuries of our era will be the important pa t of Roman history from this point of view. Also, if the progress ot civilisation be our main study, little in Roman history before the beginning of the second century B.C. can come directly under our attention. When the Romans first came into contact with the Greeks they were still backward, with little literature, art, industry or commerce. The earlier periods will only be introductory.

ITALY AND THE ROMAN

The pleasant land of Italy needs no description here. Our illustrations will recall its sunny hillsides, its deep shadows, its vineyards and olive-yards. But there are one or two features of its geography that have a bearing upon the history of Rome.

To begin with, the geographical unity of the Italian peninsula is more apparent than real. The curving formation of the Apennines really divides Italy into four parts—(1) the northern region, mainly consisting of the fertile plain of the Po valley, which throughout most of the Republican period was scarcely considered as part of Italy at all, and which was for some time inhabited by barbarian Gauls; (2) the long eastern strip of Adriatic coast, an exposed, waterless and harbourless region with a scanty population, which hardly comes into ancient history; (3) the southern region of Italy proper, hot, fertile, and rich in natural harbours, so that it very early attracted the notice of Greek mariners, and was planted with luxurious and populous cities long before Rome came into prominence; and (4) the central plain facing westward, in which the river Tiber and the city of Rome occupy a central position. The width of Italy is only about eighty miles, so that there is no room for any considerable rivers to develop, and in fact, there are only four rivers of any importance in a coast-line of more than 300 miles. The central western region can be called a plain in distinction from the Apennine highlands, but it is plentifully scattered with hills high enough to provide an impregnable citadel and to this day crowned with huddled villages.

Rome on her Seven Hills began her career by securing dominion over the Latin plain which surrounded her on all sides but the north. The Roman Campagna was then all populous farmland and not until the end of the Empire did it become the desolate and fever-stricken waste from which it has recently been reclaimed. The river Tiber provided possibilities of navigation, though these were limited by its silting mouth and rapid current; but Ostia was a good artificial harbour at its mouth, and the valley formed a land-route into the heart of the peninsula. We may conclude that Rome, set at a crossing of the river a day's march from the coast and thus protected from sea-pirates, was geographically placed in a favourable position for securing the control of Italy and of the Mediterranean, especially of the western part.

It is worth while also to notice the neighbours by whom she was surrounded when she first struggled forward into the light. Just across the Tiber to the north of her were the Etruscans, of whom we shall see more in the next chapter. Their pirate ships scoured the sea while their merchants did business with the Greeks of Sicily, Magna Graecia and Massilia. It was doubtless her position at the *tête de pont* across the Tiber that led to Rome's early prominence in war. To the south rich and flourishing Greek colonies fringed the coasts of Italy and Sicily as far north as Naples and Cumae. Across the water on the coast of Africa was the Phoenician city of Carthage, which for centuries strove to gain control of the island of Sicily. All these were seafaring commercial peoples, but it was not by sea that Rome met them; in fact, be-

tween Greeks on the south and Etruscans on the north the Latin
coast forms an area in which foreign colonisation is absent; either
this stretch possessed no attraction in the way of mineral or
pastoral wealth for the foreigner, or the Latins were strong enough
to keep him out. On the land side, behind Rome, among the
valleys and in the hill-towns on the spurs of the Apennines were a
whole series of sturdy highland clans who had the mountaineer's
delight in a foray and who were in constant turmoil. It was in the
unceasing bickerings with these Umbrians, Marsians, Pelignians,
Sabines and Samnites that the Roman sword was ever kept bright
in those early days.

As to the Romans themselves and their origin there is still much
uncertainty, despite increasing archaeological evidence. One
thing is clear enough, if we can place any reliance whatever upon
literary records—the national characteristics of the ancient
Roman were very unlike those of the modern Italian. The one
was bold, hardy, grave, orderly and inartistic : the other is sensitive, vivacious, artistic, turbulent and quick-witted. There is not
a feature in common between them and yet the modern Italian is
surely the normal South European type. As you go southwards
through France you find the people approaching these characteristics more and more. The Spaniard and the Greek share them.
The Ancient Roman of republican days, unless he is a literary
invention, is assuredly no southerner in temperament, though the
southern qualities undoubtedly begin to grow clear as Roman
history progresses. Here the archaeologist with his spade may help
us, for his discoveries suggest a possible explanation. There was
in Italy during the Neolithic and Bronze Ages a population of
which all we need say is that it seems to be of southern, Mediterranean origin and that it buried its dead; further, that in the
areas of Italy with which we are mainly concerned, Latium and
Etruria, these early inhabitants have left very scant traces, and it
is conjectured that volcanic activity led them largely to shun these
districts. In the course of the Bronze Age, during the second
millennium B.C., peoples of a different stock were invading Italy
from the North, coming probably from the Danube area. They
spoke Indo-European dialects, cremated their dead and were
mainly agriculturalists and stock-farmers; but they also developed
textile and ceramic industries and showed great skill in metal
working in bronze. One group of these newcomers, which has

been named by modern archaeologists the Terramaricoli, settled in the Po valley; they were once thought to have spread far to the south, perhaps even to the future site of Rome, but it is now believed that they did not expand beyond the Po valley and that their curious settlements with huts raised on wooden platforms on pile-foundations can have had no influence on the way the Romans later laid out their towns or constructed their camps. Other groups of Bronze Age peoples, however, probably did advance over the Apennines and penetrate farther south; at any rate, whatever its origin, central Italy enjoyed a so-called "Apennine" culture during the Bronze Age.

At the beginning of the Iron Age, sometime after 1000 B.C., we find northern and central Italy populated by another group of invaders from beyond the Alps, who probably came from Bohemia and Hungary. Their culture has been called "Villano-van" from a cemetery at Bologna where it was first discovered, but while one group spread out in North Italy around Bologna, others

Early Latin hut-urn

went southwards to Etruria and even to the site of Rome and the Alban Hills. The Villanovans also cremated their dead, preserving the ashes in urns covered with a pottery bowl or a metal helmet, while those in Latium used urns shaped like the huts of the living (see figure above). In particular they developed great skill in bronze and iron work, which they exported widely, so that eighth-century Bologna has been called "the Birmingham of early Italy".

Thus in prehistoric times Italy experienced the same fate as throughout the ages of history. The Alpine passes are easier to cross from north to south than in the reverse direction, and the smiling plains of North Italy have always possessed an irresistible attraction for the barbarian who looks down upon them from those barren snow-clad heights. Whether the invader be a "Villanovan" or Gaulish or Gothic or Austrian warrior, Italia must pay the price for her "fatal gift of beauty".

Although the origin of the Roman people still defies precise analysis, they were in part at any rate descendents of the Iron Age inhabitants of Italy who in their travels from Central Europe had for centuries battled their way over Alps and Apennines in search of permanent homes. In the process the sense of social solidarity, the military discipline, and the ritual conservatism which remained for centuries as the outstanding traits of the Roman people were doubtless developed.*

* A reference should perhaps be made to the theory adopted in the former editions of this book, that the distinction between the Patricians and Plebeians in Rome indicates some racial difference between the two Orders. This view is now generally rejected. In late times the Roman *plebs* notoriously came to include much alien blood, but most modern authorities are inclined to doubt whether this was originally the case; the Romans themselves recognised no racial distinction between patrician and plebeian, and in primitive communities difference of tribal rank may exist without implying extra-tribal origin.—F.N.P.

For a somewhat different interpretation of the movements of the various peoples in Italy during the Bronze Age and Iron Age see M. Pallottino *The Etruscans* (1955), chs. 1 and 2.—EDD.

I

THE BEGINNINGS OF ROME

arx æternæ dominationis.

TACITUS

T H A T Rome was not built in a day is the only thing we really know about the origin of Rome. There is, however, nothing to prevent us from guessing. The modern historian of the Economic School would picture to us a limited company of primeval men of business roaming about the world until they found a spot in the centre of the Mediterranean, a convenient depot alike for Spanish copper and Syrian frankincense, handy for commerce with the Etruscans of the north, the Sicilian Greeks of the south, and the Carthaginians of the African coast. They select a piece of rising ground on the banks of the river Tiber, about fifteen miles from its mouth, a spot safe and convenient for their cargo-boats, and there they build an Exchange, found a Chamber of Commerce (which they quaintly term *senatus*), and institute that form of public insurance which is known as "an army". Thus equipped they proceed by force or fraud to acquire a number of markets, to which in due course they give the name of "Empire".

This picture, being modern, is naturally impressionistic and rather vague in its details. From all accounts a good deal of engineering would be required to make the natural Tiber suitable for navigation on a large scale. Not only does its mouth silt up year by year, but just between the hills on the very floor of Rome every spring made pools and swamps. Nor is there any tide in the Mediterranean to help the rowers up to the city against the stream. The Etruscans, who diversified their commercial operations with systematic piracy, held almost the whole of this western coast in subjection. The Greeks of the south, who have plenty to say about Etruscan and Carthaginian seafarers, have forgotten

14

to mention their early. Roman customers. But perhaps that is because the primeval trader from Rome cannot have had anything much to sell, and certainly had no money at all to buy with. In founding his Bourse he seems to have forgotten to provide a Mint; at any rate, long after his neighbours had evolved a coinage of gold and silver, which in the case of the Sicilian Greeks attained a height of artistic excellence that has never been surpassed, Rome was still content with barter, and until comparatively late Republican times she had no other means of exchange than rude lumps of metal, which had to be weighed out at every transaction. And when in the end, sometime after 300 B.C.,* Rome began to mint coins, what she first produced was the heavy clumsy copper *as*, an example of which is illustrated on p. 31. I think we may confidently dismiss external trade from among the causes of the early rise of Rome. The coinage supports this view; in Latin the equivalent for "money" is a word denoting "cattle" (pecunia), which illustrates the early form of wealth. Whoever the early Romans were, they were mainly, as all their religion and traditions show, land-soldiers and farmers.† Excavations at the early levels in Rome have produced much material of the primitive Latin civilisation that has been described, but imported objects are not numerous. Plainly Rome in earliest times lay outside the main currents of trade.

Livy takes a more sensible view. He admits that the current accounts of the foundation of the city are involved in mystery and miracle, but he asserts with justice that if any city deserved a miraculous origin Rome did. Thereupon he proceeds to relate the pleasant tale of her foundation in the year 753 B.C. by Romulus and Remus.

It is not very profitable to search deeply for grains of truth in the sands of legend which cover the early traditions of Rome, but it is sometimes interesting to conjecture how and why the legends were invented. The story of Romulus and Remus, for example, was known in Rome at least as early as 268 B.C., when a wolf suckling two infants was depicted on the coinage. It is less certain whether the legend is also reflected in the famous bronze statue of the Capitoline wolf‡ because although the wolf itself is an ancient

* See pp. 31, 140.
† For the linguistic evidence see Palmer, *The Latin Language* (1954), pp. 69-72.—EDD.
‡ Plate 2.

work of art, the figures of the children have been added in modern times.

We do not know what the word Rome means : it may be Etruscan. The earliest settlement probably was a shepherds' village on the Palatine, one of the most isolated and defensible of the Seven Hills and not far from a ford across the Tiber. Traces of this settlement were found in 1948, and we can now see the floors of some of the huts dug out of the tufa rock, with the holes for the posts that supported the wattle-and-daub walls. These huts of this early Iron Age settlement continued to be inhabited for a long period (c. 800-550 B.C.) and they resembled in appearance the clay models in which the ashes of the dead were buried. The cemetery of this primitive community has been found at the foot of the hill in the marshy ground that afterwards became the Roman Forum. We also find that some of the other hills (e.g. the Quirinal) were soon occupied by settlers who buried their dead and were probably Sabines, tribes of Indo-European stock, who may have come from the mountainous country to the East (Picenum) and have been allied to the Illyrians across the Adriatic. Eventually the villages on the various hills amalgamated to form a single community. Legend preserves the memory of this coalition in the story of the Rape of the Sabines and in the Sabine name of the second king of Rome, Numa Pompilius.

The Seven Kings of Rome have been held by the over-sceptical to be mere names which have been fitted by rationalising antiquarians, presumably Greek, with inventions appropriate to them. Romulus is simply the patron hero of Rome called by her name. Numa, the second, whose name suggests *numen*, was the blameless Sabine who originated most of the old Roman cults. Tullus Hostilius and Ancus Martius were the *hostile* and *martial* inventors of military systems. Servius Tullius was a man of *servile* origin, and on this foundation Freeman built his belief that the Roman kingship was a career open to talent! It is now generally recognised, however, as unlikely that the actual names were merely inventions, even if some of the histories attached to them are unreliable. Romulus admittedly seems a figure of imagination, but the others may well be regarded as historical characters. That some sort of early kingship existed at Rome is certain; the whole fabric of the Roman constitution and its fundamental theory of *imperium* imply the existence of primeval royalty.

As for the two Tarquins, the latter of whom was turned by Greek historians into a typical Greek tyrant, their names are Etruscan; and hence it is suspected that towards the end of the regal period Rome passed under Etruscan domination. There is other evidence for this : reluctant admissions in history and literature; the fact that the ritual and ornaments of supreme authority at Rome seem to be of Etruscan origin; traces of building and artistic activity on a scale not equalled for centuries afterwards. We can trace a southward movement of the Etruscans towards Campania in the course of the seventh century, and it is most improbable that they did not make an effort to secure the passage across the Tiber at Rome, which lay directly in their route. Lastly, the horror with which the last Tarquin was always regarded is more reasonably explained if we regard him as a foreign despot who long troubled the city. Thus we conclude that towards the end of the sixth century Rome was ruled by Etruscan princes— it does not follow that Etruscans were ever present in the city in large numbers, in fact Etruscan remains are scanty—and that it was among the ports and cities which were embraced by the Etruscan empire.

The origin of these mysterious Etruscans has formed the theme of an internecine war of monographs. One theory popular in the nineteenth century, that they came to Italy from Central Europe over the Rhaetian Alps, is now generally abandoned. Opinion, however, still remains divided between two other views. Many hold, as they themselves seem to have thought, that they were the descendants of pirates and adventurers from Lydia or elsewhere in Asia Minor, who wandered overseas during the turmoil of the early Iron Age. Other writers, with perhaps less probability, consider them an aboriginal people of Italy who somehow managed to turn the tables on the Villanovan invaders. What is certain is that by the seventh century B.C. they were a rich and powerful aristocracy ruling in walled cities over the population between the Tiber and the Arno; later, they spread farther, northwards over the Apennines into the valley of the Po, southwards through Latium into Campania.*

* For these and other views of the origin and formation of the population of Etruria see M. Pallottino, *The Etruscans* (1955), ch. 2.—EDD.

Not much can be made of their language, which even in antiquity was said to resemble no other known speech.*

They seem originally to have had little art or culture of their
own; even writing they learned from the Greeks. At first they
imported and imitated Oriental wares; afterwards, as the Greeks
ousted the Phoenicians, they turned to Greek art, even employing
Greek craftsmen, who settled among them. What is called Etrus-

Etruscan fresco: Head of Hades

can art is to a considerable extent a copy of Greek art with modifications to suit local conditions. Thus, their sculpture was not

* The language, which is almost certainly not Indo-European, ceased
to be popularly spoken about the beginning of the Christian era; Roman
antiquarians, of whom the Emperor Claudius was one, preserved a knowledge of it up to the end of the Western Empire. At present we know the
meaning of a considerable number of words, and of some grammatical
terminations, but can go no farther.—F.N.P.

of marble, but mainly in bronze* or terracotta;† the coarse local stones were only used for carving coffins or tomb-ornaments. The coffins‡ were often ornamented with reclining figures, representing the dead feasting in paradise. Their temples were bright with gaily-painted slabs of terra-cotta; as bronze-workers their reputation stood high, even among the Greeks. Their pottery was at first developed from the native Villanovan ware—black smoked earthenware with patterns incised or in relief; but they soon began to imitate the painted vases of Greece. Although their artistic

Early Etruscan Pottery

efforts were mainly imitative, they are yet marked by an unmistakable individuality. It is as though the Greek sweetness had been soured in the alien atmosphere of Etruria. The ancient accounts depict the Etruscans as cruel, gluttonous and superstitious, much preoccupied with thoughts of the tomb and fears of

* Plate 3a.   † Plate 3b.
‡ Plate 6.

the Underworld. They buried the dead in large family tombs, often gaily frescoed with scenes of feasting and hunting, sometimes with pictures of Hell. Their funeral customs, however, show much variety; in some districts they used cremation.

The struggling communities of early Rome learned much from the Etruscans.* It was during this period of Etruscan power that Rome became a city, the various settlers amalgamating into a real unit; recent archaeological evidence suggests that this took place around 575 B.C. If the wall which king Servius Tullius traditionally built around the city should be dated later, at least the Etruscans strengthened the fortifications, drained the swamps by canals so that the Forum became habitable, and gave the city a symbol of unity by erecting on the Capitoline Hill a temple to Jupiter, Juno and Minerva. Besides building temples to house the gods, the Etruscans probably first introduced to the Romans the anthropomorphic conception of deities and developed the practice of augury. To the Etruscan kings Rome owed some of the insignia that their magistrates later used : the purple toga, ivory rod, curule chair, and the lictors' rods and axes (fasces). Further, the growth of town life led to increase in trade and industry, while Etruscan skill in metal and clay found its imitators among native craftsmen. In art Rome learned much : it was an Etruscan artist that made the painted terracotta ornaments for the new Capitoline temple and also the cult-statue of Jupiter himself. Thus remembering the artistic relations between Greece and Etruria we see that Rome was prepared for the reception of Greek culture in very early times. But while under her Etruscan rulers Rome developed into a city of some importance, with which in 509 B.C. the great trading city of Carthage deigned to make a treaty, and while she borrowed much, yet she remained essentially Latin in race, language and institutions.

Towards the end of the sixth century, however, the power of the Etruscans began to decline. Their advance into Campania was checked when they were defeated in battle by Aristodemus of Cumae (524 B.C.); their kings were ejected from Rome and they lost hold of all Latium; later, in 474, they were defeated in a naval battle off Cumae by Hiero, king of Syracuse, who from the spoils dedicated to Zeus at Olympia an Etruscan helmet, now in the

* This paragraph and much of the next ten pages have been redrafted or rewritten.—EDD.

British Museum. Thus all their southern dependencies were lost, and Campania was laid open to attack by the warlike Sabellian tribes of the southern Apennines. Finally, the Etruscan settlements north of the Apennines were later overrun and sacked by Gallic tribes to the north. Thus the wide-spread Etruscan Empire collapsed, the Etruscans were confined to the district known as Etruria, and an opportunity was given to the Romans to achieve later what the Etruscans had failed to accomplish, the political unification of Italy. Meantime, after expelling their Etruscan King Tarquinius Superbus in 510 B.C., the Romans replaced the monarchy with a Republic: the city was to be governed by a senate of nobles and by two consuls, a pair of equal colleagues. The more splendid days of the Etruscan regal period were over and Rome gradually lapsed into a more parochial state.

THE GROWING REPUBLIC

Much that is recorded about the foundation and early growth of Rome is clearly legendary, but nevertheless the record contains a nucleus of fact. The position is not much better for the first two centuries of the Republic. No contemporary records survive, and we derive most of our knowledge of the period from writers like Livy and Dionysius who lived centuries later in the reign of Augustus; much in their accounts and in those of their immediate predecessors in the first century B.C. is obviously of late concoction. The great families of 200 B.C. and onwards became rich and powerful; they had great historic names, and when there was a funeral in the family they sent out a long procession of waxen images to represent the noble ancestors of the deceased. At such times there would be funeral orations recounting the deeds of these heroic ancestors. Every family had its traditions, as glorious and sometimes as authentic as those of the descendants of Brian Boru. The series of heroic actions attributed to the Fabii and deeds of wicked pride ascribed to ancestral Claudii derive, at least in part, from such family traditions. Further, later writers might wish to find precedents in the past for some of the political actions of their own day, and not finding them they might invent them. Thus there is much antedating and reduplicating of later constitutional struggles in the accounts of the earlier ones, and these writers might also incorporate folk-tales into their reconstruction of Rome's early history. But there is another side to the picture. The skeleton on which Livy and his predecessors built up their accounts was a work in eighty books called the *Annales Maximi*, published by the Pontifex Maximus, Mucius Scaevola, about 125 B.C., which embodied the *fasti* of the Republic. These *fasti* were calendars kept by the priests, recording the official events of each year, both religious and secular, including the names of the magistrates. The basic authenticity of these records is not now doubted, but of course Scaevola's work involved much research and reconstruction, and he may not always have succeeded in discovering a great deal of sound detailed information about the fifth century; however, his account must have been essentially reliable from at least the beginning of the fourth century onwards. Thus at the heart of the later annalistic accounts, with all their exaggerations and inventions, there lies a reliable nucleus. It is, however, curious that the Romans waited so long before writing up their own history, and in fact, when they began to do so about 200 B.C., the earliest Roman historians were senators who wrote in Greek; the first to write in Latin was Cato the Censor.

By the end of the age of the kings, Rome had developed from the village on the Palatine to the city of the seven hills, protected, if not by a continuous wall, at least by an earth rampart and ditch to the north-east. Although not all the conquests attributed by tradition to the kings can be accepted, nevertheless they had advanced to the Tiber's mouth, and to the Alban Hills, where they defeated Alba Longa; in all, they may have gained some three hundred square miles of territory in northern Latium. But the subsequent period of the early Republic is marked by retrogression; few public works were constructed and Roman influence in Latium was shaken. Rome was essentially a pastoral and agricultural community, expressing wealth in terms of cattle, ploughing and reaping so much of the Campagna as their farmers could reach in a day or their armies protect. From the very earliest times the community consisted of a few great houses of patrician blood, an increasing number of plebeian families, numerous clients and some slaves. In every house the father was king absolute with power of life and death over his sons, daughters, and slaves. Daughters passed from the hand of the father to the hand of the husband, like any other property, by a form of sale. Out of remote

1. MODEL OF IRON AGE HUT (8th Century B.C.) on the Palatine Hill.

2. THE CAPITOLINE WOLF

3.

(a) *left* AN ETRUSCAN WARRIOR

(b) *right* THE APOLLO OF VEII
(second half of 6th Century B.C.)

4.
ETRUSCAN ROCK
TOMBS AT CAERE
(modern Cerveteri)

5.
'TOMB OF
THE STUCCOS'
AT CAERE,
somewhat later
(3rd Century
B.C.?).

6. ETRUSCAN SARCOPHAGUS. A man and woman reclining as if feasting, painted terra-cotta (second half of 6th Century B.C.)

7.

ETRUSCAN
PAINTING.

Fresco from the
Francois Tomb at
Vulci depicting
a scene from
the Trojan War.

8. HEAD OF MAENAD. About 500 B.C.

9. HEAD OF DEITY OF UNCERTAIN IDENTITY.
Early 5th Century B.C.

10. BRONZE STATUE OF AN ORATOR.
Etruscan work. 2nd Century B.C.

11. AIR VIEW OF PAESTUM.
A Greek Colony in Lucania (southern Italy).

12.
AIR VIEW OF
THE CENTRE OF
PAESTUM, showing
early temples and
Roman forum.

13.   TEMPLES AT PAESTUM.

14. (*Above*) DETAIL OF ALBA FUCENS, an ancient town
in central Italy.

15. (*Opposite*) 3rd CENTURY REMAINS AT COSA IN
ETRURIA.

16. SECTION OF THE VIA APPIA LEADING SOUTHWARDS FROM ROME, WITH ROMAN TOMBS.

antiquity, from a law of Servius Tullius,* comes a piece of genuine
Latin :

> si parentem puer uerberit ast olle plorassit, puer
> diuis parentum sacer esto

—"If a boy beats his father and the father complains, let the
boy be devoted to the gods of parents", i.e. slain as a sacrifice.
It was a commonwealth of such parents whose chiefs met to discuss policy in the Senate, and who themselves assembled in a body,
fully armed, as the *comitia*, to vote upon the Senate's decrees
conveyed by the consuls.

Grim and despotic in peace, these Roman aristocrats were fierce
and tenacious in war. As soon as she was free, Rome had to face
a war against the rest of the Latin cities, which refused to recognise
the claim of the new Republic to the hegemony in Latium which
her kings had enjoyed. Organised in a League these cities fought
against Rome at the battle of Lake Regillus, and thereafter a
treaty was concluded between Rome and thirty Latin cities as
two independent powers. By it not only was perpetual peace established between the two partners and arrangements made for
mutual aid in case of external attack, but Rome also shared with
each of the cities what was known as the "private rights" (*iura
privata*) of her own citizenship, i.e. the right to intermarry, hold
property, and trade with her on the same terms as her own citizens
enjoyed. Thus the Republic started its history with a typical act
of generosity in sharing its citizenship with others, which con-
trasts strongly with the exclusive attitude shown by many Greek
cities, as for instance Athens in the fifth century B.C. But Rome
and her new Latin allies were soon being hard pressed by the
Aequi and Volsci; these tribes, which lived in the hills to the east
and south, began to covet the fertile plain of Latium. Rome, however, showed now, as so often, a genius for statecraft and discovered the secret of *divide et impera* : she made an alliance with
another tribe, the Hernici, and thus drove a wedge between the
Aequi and Volsci. Rome also had to face attacks from the Sabines
in the north-east, while on her northern frontier lay hostile
Etruria. It was during these wars, which lasted intermittently
throughout the fifth century, that the early Romans learnt their

* In Festus, edn. Lindsay, p. 260.

trade as warriors, and if any one seeks to know the causes of Rome's victorious career, the answer is, I suppose, that she fought very bravely and obeyed her generals better than her enemies obeyed theirs. Discipline was her secret, and discipline was first learnt, no doubt, in the strict patriarchal system in her homes.

At the end of the fifth century Rome grappled in a mortal struggle with Veii, the southernmost city in Etruria, which fell after a long siege in 396; but no sooner was this danger surmounted than Rome had to meet a yet sterner trial. Some of the Celtic tribes that were swarming over the northern plain of Italy (see p. 9) decided to look for booty farther south. In 390 a group of them advanced on Rome, defeated the Roman army by the little stream of the Allia, eleven miles north of the city, and then sacked the city itself except the Capitol, which was traditionally saved because the cackling of the sacred geese gave the alarm against a surprise attack. Though in due season the Gauls returned northwards (they had come to plunder, not to settle), Rome had to face renewed attacks from her old enemies, the Aequi and Volsci, and not many summers passed without her army having to march out : for summer, when the corn could be left to do its own growing, was the season for battle. Rome also faced the hostility of some of the southern Etruscan cities, as Tarquinii and Caere, while the Latins became restless and were forced in 358 to accept a renewal of their old treaty with Rome on less favourable terms. Their discontent increased and finally blazed into open war : in 338 the forces of the Latin League were defeated after a short, sharp struggle. Rome dissolved the League and deprived the Latin cities of all joint political activity : each city was to be bound to Rome alone, and not to another Latin community. This destructive policy would by itself have led to future trouble; but Rome showed great political wisdom. She created a Confederacy and bound the conquered Latins to herself by ties of common interest within the framework of a common organisation. Thus Rome became the dominant power in central Italy, and even before the Latin War Carthage had thought fit in 348 to renew the treaty with Rome, which had been made some 150 years earlier. The terms show us that Rome's commercial interests were still very humble, but at the same time her claim to speak for the cities of the Latin coast was specifically recognized. In return for acknowledgment of her authority in central Italy Rome was quite prepared to see Carthage turn the western Mediterranean into a trade preserve.

We have seen elsewhere* that citizenship in a city-state implied membership of a corporate body, a close partnership in a company of unlimited liability with very definite privileges and responsibilities. Full citizenship at Rome meant a vote in electing the city magistrates and a vote in the *comitia,* which decided matters like peace and war. It was obvious that you had to be very jealous about extending these rights to outsiders. But Rome went part of the way, granted parts of the citizen rights, and thereby showed finer imperial statecraft than any Greek state had yet discovered. Her first offshoot was probably at Ostia, the town she planted at the mouth of her river only fifteen miles off, her first *Colonia.* These settlers remained citizens of Rome, and might vote in the elections if they thought it worth while, but were exempt from the duty of serving in the army, because their own town formed a standing garrison in the Roman service.

These Roman colonies were normally established on the coast and were not numerous. Roman citizens might also be granted allotments of public land annexed during the conquest of Italy : thus after the fall of Veii, part of its land was distributed to poor Romans, who settled there but retained their citizenship. Rome also on occasion granted full citizenship to a whole community and incorporated it into the Roman State, as e.g. Tusculum : such towns retained their local magistrates and were called *municipia* in imitation of the municipalities proper, mentioned below. With some of the peoples whom Rome conquered in Etruria and Campania she exchanged social rights (intermarriage, trade, etc.), whereby these local *municipia* retained full autonomy, except in foreign policy, and supplied troops to the Roman army. But gradually this status of *municeps* came to be regarded as an inferior form of citizenship, "citizenship without the vote", and Rome often gave it to conquered communities (e.g. the Sabines) not yet considered politically mature enough for the duties of full citizenship; it was thus a useful method by which Rome trained more backward tribes in political responsibility.

Where Rome did not extend her state by incorporating others in it with grants of citizenship, she made treaties of alliance with the peoples she encountered. These cities or tribes remained in-

* See *The Glory that was Greece,* p. 11.

dependent communities, their detailed conditions depending on
the terms of the treaty which they had made with Rome. The
most privileged received what were called "Latin rights" : they
comprised some of the old Latin cities and the Latin colonies. The
Latin colonies were more numerous than the Roman ones and
had been founded at various strategic points throughout Italy
during the wars of the early Republic; they were indeed one of
the chief factors to which Rome owed her success in these long
struggles. Romans could join them, but in doing so forfeited their
own Roman citizenship, because these Latin colonies were independent states with complete internal self-government. They were
bound not to each other but to Rome, with which they had the
"private rights", and if one of their citizens migrated to Rome he
could obtain Roman citizenship. All the allies had to supply troops
for the common army, providing roughly the same number as
did the Roman citizens themselves, but Rome very wisely imposed
no tribute or taxes on them; only citizens had to pay these. Thus
Rome built up a Confederacy, which ultimately embraced the
whole of Italy, and by this liberal granting of rights she showed
high statesmanship. Already she was beginning to display her
genius for empire-building : often relentless in conquering, she
was generous and broadminded in governing. Such was the wisdom of her council of rulers—the Senate.

The latter part of the fourth century shows the growing state
embarked upon a terrific struggle which lasted on and off from
summer to summer for nearly fifty years. Her principal foes were
the warlike Samnites of the central and southern Apennines. This
tremendous conflict is clearly a turning-point of Roman history.
At various stages nearly all the peoples of Italy rose and enrolled
themselves among the enemy, the Latins, the Etruscans, the
Umbrians, the Marsi, the Gauls (for they too were brought in
again by the Etruscans in their last efforts for freedom), and the
Samnites themselves, a race of born fighters under competent
generals. Once, in 321 B.C., both consuls and the Roman army
were entrapped at the Caudine Pass, but Rome never thought of
surrender. Doggedly her senate refused to know when it was
beaten and continued the struggle. Fortunately it was one purpose against many, and Rome beat her enemies in detail until she
was able to emerge victorious.

The history of that great conflict has come down to us in an incomplete state full of distortions and omissions, but it is clear that the Roman senate showed extraordinary resolution and tenacity, as it did in the next century against foreign enemies. Beaten to its knees again and again, it refused any terms of peace short of victory. It is to be noted that this was the war in which Rome learnt the new system of fighting whereby she was fated to conquer the world. Hitherto in Roman warfare a battle-array had meant a solid line in which the men stood shoulder to shoulder in several ranks, pressing on with spear and shield against a similar line of the enemy. It was largely a question of weight in the impact. You tried to make your line deep enough to prevent yielding and long enough to envelop the enemy's line to secure victory. But the Romans, either because they were often outnumbered on the field of battle, or, as some say, in fighting the Gallic warriors with their long swords, found it necessary to fight not shoulder to shoulder but in more open order—not in a solid phalanx but in open companies or "maniples". The rough glens and hills of Samnium also compelled the Romans to use less conventional methods of fighting. Thus the Roman soldier became self-reliant and learnt to fence skilfully with his favourite weapon, the sword, instead of merely pushing a long pike as his neighbours did. The maniple of 120 men was not only far more mobile than a solid phalanx, but it covered a length of ground equal to that of three times its own numbers. Formerly only the front rank—the *principes*—had required a full suit of armour and it was only the richest who could afford it. Now all three lines which made up the heavy infantry were armed much alike, and this reacted upon the social and political system of the city.

THE CONSTITUTION

Rome's domestic history during the two hundred years that followed the fall of the monarchy consists largely of the Struggle of the Orders, whereby the plebeians sought protection from, and then equality with, the patricians. Shortage of land increased the economic difficulties of the small farmers, many of whom because of the harsh laws of debt were falling into a state of virtual serfdom. At the same time the richer plebeians wanted political and social equality with the patricians, who monopolised the senate and the magistracies and controlled religion and law. Many of the details

of Livy's story of the struggle between the Orders, including elaborate reports of the speeches delivered, are clearly free compositions, influenced in part by the agrarian reforms and political
controversies of the later Republic. There is a great deal of confusion and contradiction in the accounts of the various legislative
measures by which the plebeians gradually won their battle. But
the method that they used, secession or striking, scarcely seems an
invention. To put it shortly, when they were refused the rights
for which they were agitating, they refused to join the citizen levy
and marched out under arms to the neighbouring Sacred Mount
(the Aventine). There they threatened to set up a new organisation of their own. Where the patricians had their two consuls, the
plebeians had their two tribunes. Where the older state had its
Senate and Assemblies meeting by groups called "curies" and
"centuries", the plebeians had their Council meeting in "tribes".
The tribunes, the new champions of the plebeians, were themselves protected not so much by law as by an oath : their persons
were declared sacred, and they gained the right to thrust their
persons between any plebeian and the consul's lictor who came to
arrest him, thus expressing the ultimate sovereignty of the Roman
People, to whom the right of appeal was allowed. We cannot
trace here, even in outline, the stages by which the plebeians
succeeded in winning complete political equality with the patricians and even secured by 287 B.C. that the resolutions (*plebiscita*)
of their own Council should be binding on the whole State, on
patricians and plebeians alike. But the history of the struggle is
one of the great triumphs of the Roman people. Whereas many
Greek states had failed to solve their internal differences and were
subject to intermittent outbreaks of party-strife, which often resulted in bloodshed and civil war, the Romans by a triumph of
commonsense and compromise managed things better and welded
the two classes into a unity without recourse to fighting.

But it must not be supposed that even now the Roman republic
was anything like a Greek democracy. The Roman *comitia* never
debated like the Athenian *ecclesia*. They assembled to listen to
such speeches as the magistrates or their invited friends might
choose to make upon topics which had previously been selected,
discussed and decreed by the senate; they were there to ratify the
senate's decisions with "Yes" or "No". Even then they did not
vote as individuals; each "century", each "cury", or each "tribe"

according to the form of meeting summoned, was a single voting unit. Everything in the system tended to put real power into the hands of the executive. When you get the executive able to control policy you may get efficiency, but if you want liberty you must adopt other means. The senate at Rome gradually came to consist entirely of retired magistrates, and so to exhibit knowledge, competence, experience, and bigoted self-confidence. Further, the Senate was drawn from a very limited number of families : these now included plebeians as well as patricians, but in practice the government remained in the hands of an oligarchy. Few men outside these "noble" patrician and plebeian families had much hope of reaching high office or influence in the state.

The republican constitution had invented two devices to save itself from tyranny, and, according to tradition, had invented them at the very beginning of the Republic. One was the collegial system by which every magistracy was held in commission by two or more colleagues. There were two consuls from the first, sharing between them most of the royal prerogatives, heads of the executive in peace and supreme generals in war, with power of life and death, or full *imperium,* at any rate on the field of battle. There was at first only one praetor, established in 366 B.C. for the administration of justice in Rome but he was technically subordinate to the consuls; he was given a colleague in 242. There were, it is said, at first two tribunes of the plebs, mainly charged with the protection and leadership of their own order; but as the city grew their numbers were increased to ten. So there were two aediles, who principally looked after affairs of police in the city. There were two censors, ranking highest of all in the hierarchy of office because their sphere was so largely connected with religion. Their duty was to number the people and to perform a solemn rite of purification. In numbering they also had to assess every man's property for the purpose of fixing his position in the army and in the state. All these magistrates had powers of jurisdiction in various spheres. All the priests, too, of whom there were many varieties, were formed into colleges, of which the two most important were the Pontiffs and the Augurs. We are too familiar with the working of "boards" and "commissions" to misunderstand the purpose of this system. Theory required unanimity in each board of magistrates; each member of it had power to veto action by the others. Another powerful weapon was the religious system whereby nothing could be attempted without favourable omens. You had only to announce unpropitious auspices to stop any official action.

One drawback to the principle of collegiality is that through disagreement between colleagues action may be stultified, and this may become particularly serious in time of war. So the Romans devised a safety-valve. All the existing magistrates could temporarily be overshadowed by the appointment of a dictator. He was given absolute power even within the city; but he held office only for six months, after which he had to retire. Thus the dictatorship was an emergency, not a regular office.

The other great check against official tyranny was the system of annual tenure. All magistrates, except the censors, who had a lengthy task before them and therefore held office for eighteen months, were annual. While this was some safeguard for liberty, it told heavily against efficiency, especially in the case of military leadership by the consuls. It also meant the gradual creation of a great number of office-holders, past and present. It was not quite so effective as the corresponding Athenian system of balloting for office in checking personal eminence, but it certainly succeeded in putting some nonentities and failures into high office—even the supreme command of the legions.

THE EARLY ROMAN

It is only very dimly that we can trace the outlines of public history as Rome grew to be a power in Italy. We can scarcely hope to trace the lineaments of the individual Roman even in outline. It is sometimes said that even if the earliest history of the city is obscure, we can draw valuable deductions as to the Roman character from the sort of actions regarded as praiseworthy in the earliest times. There is some truth in that view, though it might be objected that most of these stories took literary shape only in the second and first centuries B.C. It might be added that men often admire qualities just because they feel that they themselves cannot claim them. But, on the whole, I think we can get from even the period of legendary history some insight into Roman character. There is a remarkable difference between the Roman hero and the Greek. Greek mythology and anecdote are very largely concerned with stories of cleverness—how Heracles outwitted his foes, smart *équivoques* by the oracles, ingenious devices of Themistocles, wise sayings of Thales and Solon. It is mainly the intellectual virtues that are admired. But the Roman of these early days is not clever. Most of the old Roman stories are in praise of courage—for example, the contempt of pain shown by Scaevola, who held his right hand in the flames to demonstrate Roman fortitude; the courage of the maiden Cloelia, who swam the river, or of Horatius, who held the bridge against an army; the devotion to his country of Quintus Curtius, who leapt in full armour into the chasm which had opened in the Forum. Many stories celebrate the true Roman virtue of sternness and austere devotion to law, as when Roman fathers condemned their sons to death for breaking the law under most excusable circumstances. The love of liberty is extolled in Brutus, who helped to expel Tarquinius Superbus, the love of equality in Valerius and Cincinnatus, called from the plough to supreme command. Chastity in women is praised in the stories of Lucretia and Virginia. All these we may well set down as the virtues admired and, we hope, practised in early Rome; they form a consistent and quite distinctive picture.

But the early Roman had few accomplishments to embellish his virtues. What art and civilisation he had known during the Regal Period declined. It is likely enough that all the city's energies were occupied with the one business of fighting. Some hints of civilising reform hang about the name of Appius Claudius, who was censor in 312 B.C. The landless citizens in Rome were now drafted for

Roman *as*, about two-thirds of full size

the first time into the ancient tribes, which were voting and political units, and sons of freedmen were admitted to the Senate; but these measures were soon repealed. Appius Claudius also improved the water supply of the city by building the first of the Roman aqueducts. To this great censor also belongs the first of the famous Roman military roads, the Appian Way, which led southwards to the Greek cities of Campania. Even to-day the Via Appia, flanked with its ruined tombs—for the Romans often buried their dead along the highways—running like a dart across the Campagna, is one of the most striking spectacles that modern Rome has to offer.

Of anything that can be dignified with the name of literature we have scarcely a relic. What there is seems ludicrously rustic and uncouth. Consider, for an example, the ancient hymn of the exclusive priestly college known as *Fratres Aruales,* a tantalizing relic whose text and interpretation are alike uncertain.* It was sung by the brethren at the spring festival of Dea Dia, accompanied by a ritual dance (*tripodatio*):

ENOS LASES IVVATE (*ter*)
NEVE LVE RVE MARMAR SINS INCVRRERE IN PLEORIS (*ter*)
SATVR FV FERE MARS. LIMEN SALI. STA BERBER (*ter*)
SEMVNIS ALTERNEI ADVOCAPIT CONCTOS (*ter*)
ENOS MARMOR IVVATO (*ter*)
TRIVMPE (*quinquies*)

which is probably to be translated :

Come, aid us, Lares (*thrice*)
And, Mars, let not plague or ruin attack our people (*thrice*)
Be sated, fierce Mars. Leap on the boundary mark. Stand there
    (*thrice*)
Call in turn upon all the Semones (*thrice*)
Come, aid us, Mars (*thrice*)
Triumpe! (*five times*)

EARLY RELIGION

In our quest for the essential Roman we shall find nothing more illuminating than religion. With some people culture takes the place of religion, but it is far commoner to find religion taking

* C.I.L. VI. No. 2104. See L. R. Palmer, *The Latin Language* (1954), pp. 62-64.—EDD.

the place of culture: it did so with the Hebrews, and it formerly did so to a great extent among the English. The Romans were never a really religious people. Probably they lacked the imagination to be really devout. They had scarcely any native mythology. But they were ritualists and formalists to the heart's core. If the Arval Brethren had jumped only four times at the word "Triumpe", the whole value of the rite would have been lost: if no worse thing befell them they would have had to begin again from the beginning. Thus religion, always conservative, and therefore a rich hunting-ground for the antiquarian in search of prehistoric history, is almost our only source of information as to the mind of the early Roman. Of course, Roman religion is so deeply overlaid with Greek mythology that it takes some digging to discover the real gods of old Rome. But that has been done by the patience and insight of such scholars as Mr Warde Fowler and Sir J. G. Frazer, so that we now have a good deal of information about the original Roman religion, which reflects the life and habits of thought of an agricultural people.

Some of the old Roman festivals are worth a brief description, for they are the authentic history of the early Romans. For example, on the Ides of March the lower classes streamed out to the Campus Martius on the banks of the river and spent the day in rustic jollity with wine and song in honour of Anna Perenna, perhaps the goddess of the recurring year. On another day there was a ceremony like that of the Hebrew scapegoat. Two dates in the calendar are marked for the king to dissolve the *comitia*. The assembly had to be summoned by the blast of special trumpets of peculiar un-Italian shape (some say Etruscan), and the trumpets had to be purified by a special service on the previous day. Although the Romans abolished their political kingship, religion required the retention of the title for numerous ceremonial purposes. Then there were the Palilia, or Parilia, in honour of the old shepherd god or goddess Pales, when sheepfolds were garlanded with green, the sheep were purified at the dawn, and rustic sacrifices were paid to avert the wrath of the deity in case you had unwittingly disturbed one of the mysterious powers who dwell in the country—the nymphs and fauns of pool and spring and tree. There was a prayer to this effect of which Ovid* has given us the substance, and "this prayer", adds Mr Warde

* *Fasti* IV, 747-776.

Fowler, "must be said four times over, the shepherd looking to the east, and wetting his hands with the morning dew. The position, the holy water, and the prayer in its substance, though now addressed to the Virgin, have all descended to the Catholic shepherds of the Campagna". There were other primitive agricultural deities, such as Robigus or Robigo (the red rust on the corn), on whose festival sheep and dogs were sacrificed; Terminus (the boundary god), to whom you slaughtered a sucking-pig and a lamb on the boundary stone; or Ops Consiva, possibly the deity who protected your buried store of corn. Such names and their attributes indicate a certain poverty of religious imagination. There were more abstract, or, rather, less tangible powers, such as the Lares, either farm-land deities or spirits of dead ancestors, who figured as guardian angels of the home; the Penates, spirits who watched over the store-cupboard; the Genius and the Iuno, guardian angels of the individual man or women and of their procreative powers; the Manes, the kindly dead; or the Lemures, dangerous ghosts of the unburied. The house, like the fields, was full of unseen presences to be appeased with appropriate ritual, which had to be most punctiliously performed. Every year at the Lemuria the master of the house would rise at midnight and, with clean hands and bare feet, walk through the house, making a special sign with his fingers and thumbs to keep off the ghosts. He fills his mouth with black beans and spits them out as he goes, carefully keeping his eyes averted, and saying, "With these beans I redeem me and mine". Nine times he speaks these words without looking round, and the ghosts come behind him unseen to gather up the beans. Then the father washes himself again, and clashes the pots together to frighten the spirits away. When he has repeated the words "Depart, ye kindly spirits of our ancestors"* nine times, he looks round at last and the ceremony is complete.

The history of Rome, as Mr Warde Fowler discerned it in religion, begins with an extremely simple rustic worship of natural forms, meteoric stones, sacred trees and animals such as the wolf and woodpeckers associated with Mars; to this stage belong many of the curious spells and charms against ghosts. This sort of worship is not distinctively Roman, but common to the greater part

* Ovid, *Fasti* V, 443, where the Lemures are strangely addressed a Manes.—EDD.

of Central Europe. From these savage local cults we pass to the more centralised worship belonging to the household, and that household an agricultural one. The father is the priest, and his principal deity is Janus, the god of the doorway; his sons are the subordinate *flamines*; and his daughters have special charge of Vesta, who presides over the family hearth-fire. Their agricultural activities are reflected in the more orderly rural ceremonies in honour of Saturn, Ops, and Vesta. Thirdly, we have a series of cults which indicate the beginnings of a community with the king for chief priest, supported by State Vestals and *flamines*. In these three stages it is mainly an affair of formless powers or "numina", deities very scantily realised, with little or no personality, scarcely to be termed anthropomorphic at all. Instead of temples there were only altars, chapels and groves.

We can next trace a period of public worship when the deities were clearly anthropomorphic, with temples, priests, and probably images of their own. This tendency developed under Etruscan influence. The trinity Jupiter, Juno, and Minerva seems to be an Etruscan grouping; at any rate the building of great temples to three deities was an Etruscan habit. Now begins the pre-eminence of greater gods more or less personified and more closely resembling those of the Greeks—such as Mercury, Ceres and Diana. It is now that the important priestly colleges of pontifices and augurs are founded, largely replacing, as being more important politically, the old agricultural brotherhood of the Fratres Aruales and the Martial fraternity of the Salii.

Thus in religion as in art the Romans were prepared by their Etruscan connections for their subsequent capture by Greek civilisation. It was inevitable that a Greek should recognise Diana as Artemis, Minerva as Pallas, Mercury as Hermes, and Juno as Hera. It was equally inevitable that the Romans should be willing to clothe these bare and chilly abstractions with the charming fabric of Greek mythology. That process, and the simultaneous reception at Rome of Oriental cults, form still later stages in the progress of Rome's religious and literary development.

There is little to elevate or inspire in Roman religion. The only virtue belonging to it was reverence and the strict sense of duty which a Roman called *pietas*, explaining it as "justice towards the gods". "Religion" meant "binding obligation" to the Romans; its source was fear of the unseen, its issue was mainly punctilious formalism. No doubt the gods would punish disrespect to a parent or rebellion against the state, no doubt a fugitive or a slave had altars and sanctuaries where he might claim mercy; but there is little more than that to connect virtue with religion at Rome. On the other hand, we are not to suppose that when much later the eastern cults of Dionysus (Bacchus) or Cybele came to Rome, they came to corrupt a race of pious puritans. True Roman deities like Flora, Fortuna Virilis, and Anna Perenna had a native licentiousness of their own. The simple rustic is seldom a natural puritan, and we must beware of idealising our Early Roman as a Scottish Covenanter. Blood sacrifices were common, as at the Fordicidia, when a cow in calf was killed, and on very rare occasions there was even reversion to the primitive propitiatory sacrifice of human victims. The streak of cruelty in the early Romans increased under Etruscan influence and is seen later in the gladiatorial combats.

Mommsen has drawn our attention to the business-like relation between worshipper and god, for that is also typical of the old Roman character. "The gods", he says, "confronted man just as a creditor confronted a debtor. . . . Man even dealt in speculation with his god; a vow was in reality as in name a formal contract between the god and the man by which the latter promised to the former for a certain service to be rendered a certain equivalent return". Nay, he might venture to defraud his god. "They present to the lord of the sky heads of onions or poppies, that he might launch his lightnings at these rather than at the heads of men. In payment of the offering annually demanded by father Tiber, thirty puppets plaited of rushes were annually thrown into the stream". It may be true, as Mr Warde Fowler argues, that the bargain sometimes took the form of a lively sense of favours to come, but a *votum* was essentially a business transaction.

The deity was very dimly visualised : the cult was everything, the god nothing. The true Latin gods did not marry or beget children—did not, at least, till the Greek theologians came over and married them all suitably and provided them with families. Before history began the Romans had forgotten the little they had ever known about their most ancient deities. The rite, perhaps the altar, was preserved, but no one remembered the object of it. This is a typical Roman prayer as we have it in old Cato :—*

* *De Agri Cultura* 139.

"The proper action in thinning out a grove according to Roman custom is as follows. Sacrifice a pig as a peace-offering and utter the following words : God or goddess, whichever thou art, to whom this place is sacred, as it is thy right to receive a pig as a peace-offering for the thinning of that sacred grove and for these acts, whether done by myself or by someone at my bidding, so that it may be rightly done, to that end, in sacrificing this pig to thee as a peace-offering, I beseech thee with good prayers (—'humbly beseech thee') to be favourable and propitious to me and my house, to my household and my children; to these ends be thou worshipped with the sacrifice of this pig as a peace-offering." To misplace a word in this formula would have been fatal. The vagueness of the address is typical : the wood is sacred, no doubt to some invisible *numen*; the woodman must guard himself against addressing the wrong power. Much of the Roman worship is thus offered "to the Unknown God".

*Finally, a guild of priests called the Fetiales must be mentioned. They were established by one of the early kings to perform a ritual for which he had been responsible; the formal declaration of war and the swearing of treaties. When complaints of any act of aggression by their neighbours reached the Senate, the fetial board investigated the matter. From our knowledge of the procedure and formulae that were used we see that the normal international status between Rome and her neighbours was peace, not war, and that Roman custom did not acknowledge aggression or territorial covetousness as legitimate causes for war. It is well to bear this in mind when we are considering the centuries of Rome's wars in Italy. The Romans did not always remain faithful to the spirit of this religious sanction, but at least it suggests that they were not more aggressive than their neighbours. Indeed, since the Romans and their Latin allies held the more fertile plains, it is likely that the poorer hillsmen often tried to seize the better land. Thus, although the early Roman fought fiercely and doggedly when he felt that he was in the right, he hardly deserves to be called "that old unquestioned pirate of the land". Rather, the fetial procedure suggests that he recognised the value of peace and had an inherent desire for correct relations with his neighbours.

* Paragraph added by EDD.

LAW

It was that quality of precision and formalism that made Rome the lawgiver of Europe. Roman law was originally a series of formulae, and like all ancient law a part of religion. First the king and then the priests were the only people who knew these formulae. Thus the king was the sole judge both in private and in public right; he might summon a council of advisers or he might delegate his powers to an inferior officer, such as the prefect of the city or the "trackers of murder". Both these rights, that of choosing a *consilium* and that of delegating authority, remained inherent in the Roman magistracy. In all cases, private or public, the king or the magistrate who replaced him had to pronounce the *ius* first: that is, to state the proper formula for the case in question; then he would send the case for trial of fact, or *iudicium*, before judge or jury. The formula would run "if it appears that A.B. has been guilty of ... condemn him to ...; if not, acquit him". *Ius*, human right, was inseperably connected with *fas*, divine right: no layman could properly interpret either. For a long time it was necessary for one of the priests to be present in court to see that the proper formularies of action were observed with strict verbal accuracy. This was, of course, an enormously powerful weapon in the hands of the patricians, since they alone were members of the priesthoods.

During the struggle between the orders the plebeians demanded that the laws should be written and made known to all. Tradition records that after commissioners had been sent to Greece to study foreign legal systems, it was decided in 451 B.C. to establish Decemvirs, who issued a code. A similar commission was appointed for the next year, but these decemvirs, who included Appius Claudius, began to usurp their position and to govern oppressively until after acts of violence they were compelled by a secession of the plebs to abdicate. Many of the details of this account are highly suspicious, but there is no good reason to doubt that the famous Twelve Tables of law were published at this time. Though not directly modelled on Solon's code at Athens, they do show traces of Greek influence. Thus the plebeians won a great victory, but the set forms of words in which pleadings were to be conducted (*actiones*) still remained the secret of the patrician pontiffs for another 150 years, until they were published by Cn. Flavius, an aedile and magistrate's clerk, either with the help of, or against the wishes of, another Appius Claudius, the famous censor of 312 B.C.

The whole fabric of Roman law rested upon the foundation of the Twelve Tables, which embraced both private and public life. They regulated and defined the rights and duties attaching to the family and to private property, and also dealt with offences against the community. The fragments that have come down to us are a medley, reflecting both survivals of a primitive society and more advanced measures. Fines had to be paid in metal by weight. Joint creditors had the right to carve up the *partes* (his body or his property?) of a debtor. An attempt was made to strengthen the caste system, since plebeians were forbidden to intermarry with patricians. But the Twelve Tables also carried something of a charter of liberties for the citizens in that capital punishment could not be inflicted without right of appeal to the assembly, and no law could be proposed against an individual. The language of this famous code is of a rugged simplicity and directness that is truly Roman. On the whole Roman law is merciful, considering its strict character: though much of Roman pleading, as we have it in the mouth of Cicero, is full of appeals to sentiment, Roman law itself allows no appeal to anything so vague as abstract justice. The written letter stands, and there can be no pleading without a legal formula.

The character of the ancient Roman is best described by his favourite virtue of *grauitas*. In that word is implied serious purpose, dignified reserve, fidelity to one's promise, and a sense of duty. Levity is its opposite, and among the things repugnant to true Roman gravity were art, music, and literature. It is on the battlefield, in the senate-house, and in the law-courts that the old Roman is most truly at home.

II

CONQUEST

quæ neque Dardaniis campis potuere perire
nec quom capta capi, nec quom combusta cremari,
augusto augurio postquam incluta condita Roma est.
                                                    ENNIUS

THE great Samnite wars, which had lasted on and off from 343 to 290 B.C., had been the school of Roman valour. In her citizen legions Rome had evolved a fighting machine unequalled, probably, until the Musketeers of Louis XIV and Marlborough. Also she was learning politics and the art of government. She was now mistress over the greater part of Italy; all, in fact, except the Gallic plain in the north and the Greek cities in the south. The Pyrrhic War which followed after a short breathing-space forms the transition between domestic expansion and foreign conquest. Our business here is not with wars and battles for their own sake, but it will be important to observe in what manner Rome was launched on her career of empire-making. Seeley has shown how the British Empire grew up in a haphazard manner, without wise policies to direct its growth, with continual neglect of opportunities, and often in contemptuous ignorance of the work that private citizens were undertaking for its honour and advancement. We shall see that it was very much the same with the Roman Empire. One responsibility leads to another, one conquest leads to many entanglements: if the coast is to be held the hinterland must be conquered. Thus power follows capacity, and the doctrine which seems so unjust, "Unto everyone that hath shall be given, but from him that hath not shall be taken away even that which he hath", is fulfilled in all the dealings between Providence and imperial peoples. By coming into contact with the Greeks of the south Rome was brought definitely to deal with a superior but declining civilisation. The career of Agathocles, the brigand tyrant of Sicily, had lately shown how easy a thing it was to make empires among the opulent and luxurious cities of the Calabrian and Bruttian shores.

One summer's day in 282 B.C. the people of Tarentum were seated in their open-air theatre, watching the performance of a tragedy. They looked out above the stage over the blue waters of the Gulf of Taranto, and there they saw a small detachment of the Roman fleet sailing into their harbour. The ships were on a voyage entirely peaceful, but there was an old treaty forbidding the Romans to pass the Lacinian Promontory, and these bar-barians had lately been interfering in the affairs of their Greek neighbours, always in favour of oligarchy against democracy. The mob was seized with a sudden access of fury; they rushed down to the harbour, butchered or enslaved the sailors, and put the admiral to death. The Roman senate met this atrocious insult with calm, even with generosity. But the Tarentine mob would have no peace. Looking abroad for a champion they invited the Prince of Epirus to their aid. Pyrrhus was a young man of charm, ability, and ambition almost equal to that of Alexander the Great, whose career he longed to emulate in the West. He was called the first general of his day, and he brought with him 20,000 infantry-men of the phalanx, 2000 archers, 500 slingers, and 3000 cavalry. Moreover he had twenty Indian war-elephants. The boastful Greeks had offered to provide 350,000 infantry, but when it came to the point they were reluctant to submit to military discipline. However, Pyrrhus was victorious in the first battle near Heraclea, although his casualties amounted to 4000 men as against Roman losses of 7000. The victory was won, it is said, by the final charge of the elephants. The simple Romans had never seen an elephant before; they called them "snake-hands" and "Lucanian cows", and their horses were even more alarmed than they.

After this victory Pyrrhus marched northwards against Rome, hoping that Rome's allies would rally to his standard. But Capua, Naples and other cities barred their gates against him, the Latins showed no signs of disaffection, Roman forces hung on his heels, and so when forty miles from Rome he was forced to abandon the attempt and returned to Tarentum for the winter. He then sent to Rome with overtures of peace a smooth-tongued courtier named Cineas, who was much impressed with the incorruptibility of the political chiefs and their wives. It was he who described the senate as a "council of kings", so grave and majestic were their bearing and discourse. Nevertheless the Roman senate would have made terms if it had not been for the great censor Appius Claudius, now blind and infirm, who laid down the celebrated doctrine that Rome never listened to terms while there were foreign troops on Italian soil. Fresh conscripts eagerly enrolled themselves to make a new army.

After another ineffectual "Pyrrhic" victory near Asculum, where the losses on each side corresponded closely to those at Heraclea, Pyrrhus proceeded to the island of Sicily, where he drove the Carthaginians from point to point until they were confined to their great stronghold of Lilybaeum in the west. But all the time his position was precarious. The coalition on which he depended was composed of faithless and useless allies. While his stiff Epirot phalanx was depleted at every victory, fresh levies of citizens seemed to spring from the soil to replace the Roman losses. So at length, after he had returned to Italy and had been defeated by the Romans in battle, probably near Beneventum (275 B.C.) he decided to return home to Greece. Thus Pyrrhus leaves to history the reputation not of a conqueror but of an adventurer. The Romans had faced and overthrown the Greek phalanx at its best, and were now masters of Italy from Pisa to Reggio, with Sicily obviously inviting their next advance. That Rome was now formally accepted among the great powers of the Mediterranean world is shown by an embassy from Ptolemy II of Egypt offering friendship.

Rome had a breathing-space of eleven years before the first of her two great conflicts with the Carthaginians. Carthage, a colony of the Phoenicians of Tyre, had grown rich and prosperous on the fertile soil of what is now Tunisia. Her government was controlled by an oligarchy which was primarily devoted to trade. She had reduced the native Berber population to subjection and had turned the Western Mediterranean into a Carthaginian preserve, controlling southern Spain, Sardinia and western Sicily. War was not her main business, but when she sought fresh markets she was apt to fight with horrible ferocity, sacrificing her prisoners in hundreds to hideous gods when she was victorious, and impaling her generals when she was not. As a military power she varied greatly : the small Greek states of Sicily had been maintaining a fairly equal struggle against her for centuries. But she used armies composed of mercenaries, and thus everything depended on the general. Had it not been for the inexperience of the Romans at sea and the extraordinary genius of the Barcid family, Carthage would never have come as near victory as she did. We have no history of the struggle from the Punic side, and Carthage herself must remain somewhat of a mystery even when illuminated by the brilliant imagination of the author of *Salammbô*.

For entering upon this war, which Rome did ostensibly in response to an appeal from a parcel of ruffianly outlaws for whom she must have had no sympathy whatever, we can for once discover no motive but desire of conquest. Messina, the home of the said ruffians, was for her merely the *tête de pont* which led from Bruttium into Sicily. The conquest of that rich Greek island was plainly the objective, but she plunged into war without foreseeing the immensity of her undertaking.* The chief interest of the First Punic War, which lasted from 264 to 241, lies in the creation of a Roman navy which occurred in the course of it. Although we may agree with Mommsen that "it is a childish view to believe that the Romans then for the first time dipped their oars in water", yet tradition says that the Romans constructed a fleet in a great hurry, taking for model a stranded Carthaginian galley. It was at any rate her first war-fleet worth mentioning. The tradition is proved by the lack of seamanship displayed by the Romans; for every storm cost her enormous losses by shipwreck. The device by which she overcame the Punic ships—a sort of grappling gangway on pulleys affixed to her masts, so that her soldiers could fight the enemy as if on shore—was a successful but essentially a land-lubberly invention. Her annual consuls, transformed for the occasion into annual admirals, had not even as much opportunity as Colonel Blake to learn their trade. The ships were rowed and manned chiefly by her allies, but the real business of fighting was done by the 120 legionaries on each vessel, who came into action

---

* The basic cause of the war is more likely to have been defensive imperialism on the part of Rome, commercial imperialism on the part of Carthage: both sides rushed in to sieze the key position of Messina. Rome, who at the time of the Pyrrhic war had allied herself with the many Greek cities of S. Italy, now had to think of their commercial interests. It was not till after some four years of warfare that Rome realized that peace could be obtained only by driving the Carthaginians out of the whole island, and this involved the creation of a large navy.—EDD.

when the enemy was grappled and the gangway fast in his deck. Though by a magnificent achievement, launching fleet after fleet, the Roman "land-lubbers" succeeded in defeating in a series of naval engagements the Carthaginians who had ruled the western waves for centuries, the war dragged on for nearly a generation until at length the Carthaginians made peace, and Rome gained Sicily.

The peace was clearly nothing more than a respite : the command of the Western Mediterranean was not yet settled. Rome spent the interval in fresh wars. First she seized the opportunity, when Carthage was weakened by a dangerous rebellion of her mercenary troops, to annex the islands of Sardinia and Corsica, alleging with more ingenuity than geographical exactitude that these were among the islands between Sicily and Africa which Carthage had agreed to surrender. Then she intervened in Illyria in order to clear the Adriatic of piracy, and so acquired influence in that quarter. Soon afterwards the Gauls of the northern plain began under pressure from their kinsmen across the Alps to threaten invasion, but the Romans marched out to meet them, defeated them at Telamon in Etruria, less than a hundred miles north of Rome, and thus rounded off Roman control over the peninsula. The affair of Sardinia undoubtedly looks like conscious empire-building, but against both the Illyrians and the Gauls it is clear that Rome was only thinking of self-defence.

In the second Punic War, which lasted from 218 to the end of the century, Rome was not the aggressor. At Carthage by this time the rebellion of the mercenaries had been put down with a heavy hand. It seems that Carthage had internal dissensions, the democrats being for war, and the aristocracy of rich merchants for peace. The democracy was led by the celebrated Barca family, which had long supplied the state with famous generals and now occupied a position of unrivalled eminence. Constitutionally a Carthaginian could rise no further than to be one of the two *shophets* who corresponded to the Roman consuls, but actually the Barcas were more like a family of dictators. From the first Hamilcar Barca foresaw that Rome was still the enemy, and he is said to have made his little son Hannibal swear an oath at the altar that he would prosecute that enmity to the death. But first it was necessary to acquire resources and an army for the purpose. This he resolved to do, as Julius Caesar did after him, by foreign conquest. He thereupon led his army into Spain, to which Carthage had some ancient claims, and there began to build up a province and a native army under his absolute control. Though Gades (Cadiz) was already a Carthaginian market and there were a few Greek colonies on the north-east coast, and the ships of Tarshish* were known even to King Solomon, this is the first real appearance of Spain in history. There was metal to be had from the mines, gold, copper, and silver, and there were hardy tribesmen in the hills who only needed training to become excellent soldiers. So Carthage began to acquire a western substitute for her lost province of Sicily. Hamilcar died; his son-in-law, Hasdrubal, was assassinated; and then the army chose for its leader Hamilcar's son Hannibal, then a young man of twenty-six.

This man, though his history, as known to us, mainly was written by his enemies, stands out as one of the greatest leaders in history. In strategy he was supreme; in statesmanship he had the gift which Marlborough shared of being able by his personal influence to hold unwilling allies together even in adverse circumstances. He was a cultivated man who spoke and wrote Greek and Latin. He is charged by the jealousy of the Romans with cruelty and perfidy, but in fact history scarcely substantiates these charges: on the contrary his actions are often magnanimous and honourable. His brilliance as a general largely sprang from his power of entering into the mind of his enemy. This was the man who inherited his father's deep-laid plans of vengeance and set out, his heart burning with hatred of Rome, to fulfil them.

We cannot dwell upon his wonderful march over the Alps and his brilliant series of victories on the soil of Italy. Hannibal's whole plan of campaign was, briefly, to invade Italy by land with a compact striking force and raise the supposedly unwilling subjects of Rome against her. But it contained three serious miscalculations which brought it eventually to ruin. First, the southern Gauls, on whom Hannibal relied for his communications and his base, proved fickle and untrustworthy allies; secondly, he underesti-

---

* Tartessus, probably to be identified with Tarshish, lay near the mouth of the Guadalquivir not far from Cadiz, but its exact site has not been found. It was destroyed by the Carthaginians sometime about 500 B.C.
F.N.P.

mated the cost in men of crossing the Alps; and thirdly, he found that Rome's mild imperial system had not produced unwilling subjects such as Carthage possessed in Africa. Moreover, while the Romans showed a tenacity and power of recuperation unsurpassed in history, Carthage was prevented by Roman sea-power from getting many reinforcements through to him. The firmness and courage of the Roman senate and people were amazing. Beaten again and again in the field at the Ticinus, the Trebia, Lake Trasimene, and Cannae, Rome never lost hope. At the crisis of the war she had twenty-five legions in the field, beside naval and garrison forces—nearly 200,000 citizens under arms, without counting the contingents of her allies. In the year 212 she had one army in Spain menacing Hannibal's base; another in North Italy watching that the Gauls sent him no help; two legions in front of the city of Rome; six grimly besieging Capua, which had deserted to Hannibal after the disaster at Cannae; four more in South Italy, keeping in touch with Hannibal himself; another four in Sicily, where Hannibal had found friends in Syracuse; troops in Sardinia and even in Greece, where Philip, King of Macedonia, had joined the Punic cause after Cannae, watching every avenue through which reinforcements might come to him. If they could not beat Hannibal in the field, at least they could wear him down. When the consul Varro returned in defeat and disgrace from the awful disaster at Cannae (216 B.C.), the senate thanked him for not having committed suicide—-"for not having despaired of the salvation of his country".

No doubt Rome owed something, but not as much as her poets and orators pretended, to the cautious tactics of Quintus Fabius. At any rate, he gave her time to grow used to the presence of the invader and to recover from the shock of the great disasters with which the war opened. The Romans had never before been called upon to face a consummate strategist. Pyrrhus had been, within the limitations of Greek warfare, a clever tactician. But Hannibal was more even than a strategist; he was a psychologist, who knew when the opposing general was rash and when he was wary, he had spies everywhere and could supplement their intelligence by disguising himself to do his own scouting. Scouting was an art that the Romans had yet to learn by bitter experience. At the Trasimene Lake they blundered straight into a natural death-trap. But the Romans were good learners, and, as usually happens,

the amateur patriot army steadily improved during the war while
the hired professionals steadily deteriorated. The actual tactics by
which Hannibal won several of his battles were simple enough.
It was the policy of a long weak centre into which the Roman
legions buried themselves deep while the two strong wings of the
enemy closed round on their flanks and rear. In his Numidian
horsemen Hannibal had the finest light cavalry yet known to European warfare.

For a time all went brilliantly for the invader. Italians, Greeks,
and Gauls joined his victorious standard. Rome was on the brink
of despair. The very gods began to tremble; their statues sweated
blood, and cows in Apulia uttered prophetic warnings with human
voices; the most horrible of omens portended destruction. But the
city and the senate never lost heart, and gradually as the years
passed by Hannibal began to see that his cause was lost. The Latin
allies stood firm for Rome. The Romans were able to recover and
hold Sicily and even despatched a brilliant young general named
Scipio to reconquer Spain. Thus the longed-for reinforcements
were cut off. The shortsighted aristocrats of Carthage were jealous
of their great soldier, and when at last a reinforcing Punic army
from Spain managed to slip through into Italy, Nero caught it at
the River Metaurus in north-east Italy before the junction was
effected. The first news of that battle came to Hannibal at Lari-
num, far away to the south, when the Romans tossed over the
rampart into his camp the head of the defeated general, his own
brother Hasdrubal. Horace has sung of this tragic episode in his
noblest manner :

> quid debeas, o Roma, Neronibus
> testis Metaurum flumen et Hasdrubal
>   deuictus et pulcher fugatis
>   ille dies Latio tenebris.

>   .   .   .   .   .

> dixitque tandem perfidus Hannibal :
> "cerui, luporum præda rapacium,
>   sectamur ultro quos opimus
>   fallere et effugere est triumphus.

>   .   .   .   .   .

Carthagini iam non ego nuntios
mittam superbos. occidit, occidit
spes omnis et fortuna nostri
nominis Hasdrubale interempto".*

This was in 207 : in 206 Scipio won a decisive victory in Spain, and in 204 he made a counter-invasion upon the coast of Carthage. It was only "a forlorn hope of volunteers and disrated companies", but it caused the recall of Hannibal and gained valuable African allies for Rome. The last scene of the duel was the victory of Zama in 202, in which Scipio won his title of Africanus and became the hero and saviour of Rome. Carthage ceded Spain and the Spanish islands, lost her whole war-fleet, and agreed to pay a large indemnity. But her end was not yet. For another fifty years, during which she made a remarkably quick economic recovery, she was permitted to exist on sufferance.

Now, frightful as had been the losses of Rome in this seventeen-years' conflict, and great as was her exhaustion, she proceeded in the very year following the peace with Carthage to enter upon a fresh series of campaigns. The Gauls of the north made a desperate revolt, sacked Placentia (Piacenza) and invested Cremona, but the Romans quickly brought them under control. The Gauls could not, of course, receive any of the rights of citizenship as yet, but they received back their independence and were left free of tribute to act as a bulwark against their northern cousins. There was incessant fighting in Spain also. In Sardinia there were perpetual slave-drives, until the market was glutted with slaves, and the phrase was begotten "as cheap as a Sardinian". How could the senate at such a moment declare a fresh war with the greatest of European powers? Was it under pressure of that greedy commercial party at Rome of which we are beginning to hear? The suggestion is absurd. There were hard knocks and little money to be got from Macedon; and it is difficult to conceive how any powerful commercial interests could have arisen at Rome during

* What thou owest to the stock of Nero, O Rome, let Metaurus' flood bear witness, and vanquished Hasdrubal, and that fair dawn that drove the darkness from Latium . . . And at length spake treacherous Hannibal: "We are but deer, the prey of ravening wolves, and yet we are pursuing those whom to elude and escape is a rare triumph . . . No more shall I send proud reports to Carthage: perished, perished is all our hope and all the fortune of our race, now that Hasdrubal is dead".
(*Odes*, IV. iv. 37-40, 49-52, 69-72).

the seventeen years of the Hannibalic War. If ever there was a nation whose early history declined the economic interpretation, it was the Romans. Even when the Romans had conquered Macedon they temporarily shut down the famous gold mines. Nor, I think, was it any large-minded *Welt-politik* that led Rome into the Second Macedonian War. Doubtless Philip, who was attacking some Greek cities in the East, was a dangerous and uncomfortable neighbour, and no doubt it was true that Philip of Macedon and Antiochus of Syria had formed a compact to divide up the realms of the boy-king of Egypt. But the war might have been postponed for years by negotiation, since Philip probably did not want to fight Rome. The Romans may have wished to punish him for having sided with Hannibal in the recent war and at the same time to take preventive action against future trouble in the East,* but to imagine the Romans of 200 B.C. as calculating their actions on the basis of commercial interest must be unhistorical.

In their attack on Philip the Romans were on the side of the most respectable elements in Hellenistic politics: Rhodes, the commercial republic; Pergamum, the kingdom of the cultivated Attalus; Athens, the ancient home of art and learning; Egypt, the centre of commerce and literature. Elsewhere† I have described how the simple Romans comported themselves in this land of higher civilisation. They trod almost reverently into the circle of Greek culture; they were flattered when the Athenians initiated them into the Eleusinian Mysteries, or when the Achaean League permitted them to take part in the Isthmian games. And when they had beaten Philip—not without difficulty, nor without indispensable aid from the Aetolian cavalry—at Cynoscephalae (197 B.C.), they made no attempt at annexation. Leaving Philip crippled, they were content. Flamininus, their philhellenic general, was proud to proclaim the liberty of Greece before he retired. He and many of his officers carried away with them an ineffaceable

---

* The most plausible explanation of the Macedonian War is that the Roman senate, ignorant of Greek affairs, allowed itself to be bluffed or dragged into hostilities by its noisy Greek friends and allies. They had everything to gain by enlisting Rome on their side; the alliance between Philip and Antiochus certainly meant danger for them, and there was no one at Rome who could contradict them if they represented that it was directed against Rome. It is expressly recorded that the Roman people were opposed to the war and were only with difficulty persuaded to take up arms.—F.N.P.

† See *The Glory that was Greece*, p. 290.

impression. They were returning to the more backward civilisation of central Italy from a land rich in ancient temples of incredible splendour, crowded with works of art. They had seen the
tragedies in the theatres, the runners in the games. They had
heard the philosophers disputing in the colonnades, the orators
haranguing in the market-place. A world glowing with life un-
dreamt-of, where there were other things to live for than battle,
had suddenly flashed upon their eyes.

The next great war was against Philip's accomplice, Antiochus
of Syria. This war was as inevitable as the last. Antiochus, puffed
up with the pretensions of an Oriental King of Kings, was eager
to match his strength against the *parvenu* Romans. Rome seemed,
and perhaps was, reluctant to undertake the apparently enormous
task at this moment. One strong cause for war was that Antiochus
had given a home to Hannibal, Rome's hunted and dreaded foe.
If the great King had but had the sense to give Hannibal power
over his great host it might yet have gone hard with the Romans.
When Antiochus invaded Greeece at the invitation of the Aeto-
lians, the Romans acted. They sent an army across the Adriatic
and drove him out, and then they crossed to Asia Minor where
they again defeated him at the battle of Magnesia (190). But even
with the wealth of Syria spread out at her feet, Rome annexed
nothing; not out of any spirit of self-denial, for she exacted a very
large indemnity, but because she was not prepared to undertake
the responsibility of governing regions so vast and so much more
civilised than herself.

Actually, of course, the effect of these wars was to give Rome
complete command of the Mediterranean coastlands. Though she
did not annex, she exercised predominance; that is, she controlled,
or attempted to control, foreign policy. Rome became the patron;
Macedonia, Syria, Egypt, Pergamum, Rhodes, Bithynia, Athens,
the two leagues and all the ancient states of Greece were her
dependents. The position of policeman and nurse of the Aegean
world had been thrust upon Rome because she was strong and
just. Even that was a terrific and bewildering responsibility. Every
day fresh embassies came to Rome to complain of neighbours and
solicit assistance—clever Greeks who would talk your head off
with sophistries, and rich Asiatics who would try to corrupt you
with bribes and blandishments. In the West there were provinces,
in the East allies; it was difficult to know which gave most trouble.

So we come to the next stage, when the Romans began to annex and subjugate. It was the only way. In Macedonia, after Philip had been conquered and pardoned, the conduct of his successor Perseus finally provoked Roman military intervention (171 B.C.). After Perseus had been crushed and his kingdom dismembered, a pretender Andriscus arose and headed a revolt, joined by the Greeks. Obviously there was nothing for it but to round off the business by sending a permanent army under a permanent general to Macedonia, and to call it his "province". Not even yet did the Romans dream of making cities like Athens her subjects. They felt, however, that these free cities needed a sharp lesson; and Corinth, as an almost impregnable fortress, which had been a centre of Achaean obstruction to Rome, was selected for punishment and destroyed in 146 B.C.

In the same year came the destruction of Carthage. During the last fifty years there had been incessant trouble there. Rome had left Carthage prostrate before her dangerous African enemies, and refused all her appeals to be allowed to defend herself. All the time Carthage was undoubtedly recovering financially from her defeat, in spite of the large annual tribute imposed upon her. This sight moved the fears and jealousy of the Romans. Intelligent people like Scipio Nasica might mock at their fears. It was the Old Roman party, with their spokesman Cato and his endless refrain of *delenda est Carthago,* that constantly kept their nerves on edge, until at last in sheer panic they obeyed. A long feud between Carthage and a neighbouring Berber chief Masinissa came to a head in 154. Goaded beyond endurance by his constant encroachments on her western frontiers, Carthage broke her treaty with Rome by going to war with Masinissa and was beaten. Then Rome declared war upon her—the Third Punic War. Two consuls landed with a large army and Carthage offered submission. The consuls demanded complete disarmament. Carthage submitted. Then the consuls demanded that the existing city should be destroyed and the inhabitants settled ten miles inland. That meant not only the destruction of their homes and hearths and temples, but the end of the commerce by which they lived. This preposterous demand shows that Cato's policy had triumphed. Carthage could not submit to it, and there followed one of those frightful sieges in which the Semitic peoples show their amazing tenacity. Three years it lasted, by favour of the incompetence of the Roman generals; until at last a Scipio came to turn the tide once more. Carthage was destroyed utterly with fire and sword, her very site laid bare, and the soil sown with salt, in token that man should dwell there no more.

The destruction of these two cities, Corinth and Carthage, together with other facts such as the unreasonable irritation which Rome displayed against her Greek allies, Rhodes and Pergamum, have been taken by some modern historians to indicate, once more, a policy of commercial jealousy instigating the destruction of rival markets. In the one case, however, it has been shown that Corinth was no longer a great centre of Greek commerce when she was destroyed, and in the case of Carthage it was the party of Cato, who was much more of a farmer than a company-promoter, that urged destruction. A man of business might indeed be foolish enough to want to close the principal markets which bought and sold with him—there may be such business men today —but he would scarcely be so mad as to have a fine commercial centre with its docks and quays utterly destroyed and cursed for ever. Similarly, when Macedon was conquered, her rich gold mines were shut down by order of the senate. The truth is that Rome was tired and exhausted with her colossal wars, irritable and nervous beyond expression with the gigantic task of government which she had found thrust upon her. Surrounded with false friends and secret enemies, she was losing the noble *sang-froid* she had displayed in times of real crisis. Corinth was destroyed as a warning to the Greeks, Carthage as an expiation for the *lemures* of the unburied Roman dead.

THE PROVINCES

In considering ancient imperial and provincial systems it is necessary for the modern to divest himself of all the geographical notions which spring from the study of maps. The ancients probably had only the most vague notions of territory. Natural frontiers such as mountains, rivers, and coasts were of course familiar to them, from the strategic point of view. Within those were cities great and small, which in the case of civilised people formed the units of life and government. In the case of barbarians there were tribes and nations, seldom sufficiently settled to produce any notion of geographical area. Thus, when Rome conquered Sicily, she was acquiring not so much one geographical unit, an island, as a collection of states of various types and constitutions. Similarly, in the case of Spain, she said and thought that she acquired Spain, although a considerable part of the Iberian peninsula remained unconquered for another century and a half. To remember the limitations of ancient geographical knowledge is essential to the understanding of the Roman provincial system. *Prouincia* means in the first instance a sphere of official duty; a man's *prouincia* might be the feeding of the sacred geese or it might be the control of an army. It was not for a long time that the word came to connote a territorial area. When it did so, the day of the city-state was coming to an end.

The earliest Roman provinces were *Sicily,* acquired by conquest in the First Punic War, 241 B.C., then *Corsica and Sardinia,* annexed in the diplomatic intrigues which followed. Spain, or rather *"the Spains",* Further and Hither, were the fruit of the Second Punic War (206). After the Third Punic War (146) the territory of Carthage became a province under the name of *Africa.* In the same year the Macedonian War gave Rome the province of *Macedonia.* To complete the list so far as the Roman Republic is concerned : Attalus III of Pergamum bequeathed his kingdom to Rome in 133, and this became the province of *Asia.* In 120 the conquest of Southern Gaul gave Rome *Gallia Narbonensis.* In 102 the prevalence of piracy on the southern coasts of Asia Minor impelled the Romans to make *Cilicia* a province. The king of *Bithynia* in 74 imitated Attalus in bequeathing his kingdom to Rome. *Cyrene* also was bequeathed to Rome and later united in one province with *Crete* in 68. In 64 Pompey the Great deposed the King of *Syria* and annexed his kingdom. About the same time, on the death of Mithridates, western *Pontus* was added to Bithynia as a united province. In 51 Julius Caesar completed the conquest of Gaul and added it as *Gallia Comata* to the old province of Narbonensian Gaul. Finally in 31 Octavianus conquered *Egypt.*

It was not the Roman way to think a situation out with the logic and directness of a Greek or a Frenchman. More like the Englishman, he took things as they came and made the best of them with as little derangement as possible to his pre-existing system and preconceived ideas. The Roman Empire was not governed on a system as it was not acquired by a policy. When Sicily came into Roman hands, it came piecemeal in the course of the war. Various cities accepted Roman "alliance" on various terms. Rome had never been able to grant full citizenship to Greek states, because their inhabitants, speaking a foreign language, could not give the equivalent in military service. If Sicily had been Italian, it would no doubt have entered the Roman alliance as a collection of *municipia*; as it was, the sixty-five or so separate Sicilian states continued to enjoy for the most part their previous constitutions under various agreements with Rome. Some were "free", some were "free and confederate"; similarly of kings who yielded to Rome, some were styled "allies", some "allies and friends". The cities would have their charters and the kings would have their personal treaties with Rome which lapsed with the death of each. But in a region conquered in war most of the tribes or states were simply "stipendiary", that is, tribute-paying. The *stipendium* paid was originally, and in theory, an indemnity or a contribution for the maintenance of a military force by people who were unqualified to give personal service. This, together with the general principles of administration, was generally settled by a commission of ten members of the senate, who went out to organise a newly acquired territory and drew up the charter for the province (*lex prouinciae*). This *stipendium* was by no means extortionate. In Macedonia, for example, the people only paid to Rome half as much as they had previously paid to their kings. The amount once fixed could often be paid not only in money but in kind (corn, metallic ore, etc.); in one or two provinces, such as Sicily and Sardinia, it was not a fixed annual payment but a tithe of the value of the harvest in corn, oil, etc. The Romans did not, however, evolve a theory of state ownership of provincial land leased back for a consideration to the original proprietors: rather, the provincial revenue was regarded as a tax paid by the governed to the state. As a matter of fact, few of the provinces were remunerative to the Roman state. Spain, where warfare was incessant, was certainly a heavy loss. Macedonia was no source of profit. Sicily, largely owing to the Roman Peace, became the granary of the capital, but Asia alone was a source of great wealth to the treasury. There were, of course, harbour dues for the provinces as for Italy herself.

On the whole, it is fair to say that local autonomy was generally preserved. Either through policy or, more probably, because the Romans habitually took things as they found them, the previous laws and constitutions of conquered units, whether cities or tribes, remained in force. In Syracuse, for example, the taxation-system of King Hiero remained, and it was much better for the Sicilians to pay their taxes to Rome than to be subject to the personal extortions of a tyrant like Agathocles. In law-suits between citizens of one Sicilian state the trial was to be held in that state by a native judge and according to the native laws—possibly with a right of appeal to the Roman governor. In suits between Romans and Sicilians the judge was to be a native of the defendant's state. So far the Roman sway is one of the mildest and most benevolent systems of government ever imposed by an empire upon conquered subjects. Athens, it will be remembered, had grown rich and beautiful by misapplying the contributions of allies, which she had converted into the tribute of subjects. Sparta had put garrisons into every conquered city. So had Carthage.

But in every conquered territory it was necessary to have an armed force, large or small according to circumstances, and for the soldiers a general. As all the Roman magistrates were military in the first instance, but also judicial and executive—as, in fact, the nature of Roman ideas of *imperium* implied an unlimited competence in every department of rule, the provincial general was also, necessarily, a provincial judge and administrator free from all control during his year of office. No doubt the Romans, if they had possessed the wisdom and retrospective foresight so lavishly displayed by their modern critics, would, in sending officers to distant parts, have revised their notions of *imperium* and defined the spheres of duty which they entrusted to their generals. If they had studied political science they might have learnt that it is wise to separate the legal functions from the administrative, and both from the military. Or, if they had made historical researches, they might have discovered that the Persian administrative system of three independent functionaries in each satrapy was the best that had yet been discovered. But they did none of these things: they simply blundered on in the old Roman way, *more maiorum*. They did not foresee the demoralising effect of absolute power in an alien and subject land. They did not foresee the necessity for central control in a Roman Colonial Office; there was no Latin equivalent for the Franco-Grecian term "bureaucracy". Thus they were compelled to trust to the honour and sense of justice that were, when this colossal experiment began, still

G.W.R.—6

believed to exist in the heart of a Roman officer and gentleman, unaware that corruption was beginning even then to taint the whole body of their aristocracy.

They might, one would think, have realised the superhuman temptations in the path of a Roman governor. He went out, with a company of his own friends, chiefly ambitious young men, for a staff, with a senatorial legate chosen by himself, and a quaestor as his subordinate to keep accounts, if he could : for there was no competitive examination in book-keeping. The governor went for a year only among a people whose traditions, laws, and even language, were alien to him. He left an austere and uncultivated republic to act as monarch among sophisticated Greeks or fawning Asiatics. No power on earth could even criticise him while he held the *imperium* : afterwards he might be impeached, it is true, but before a court of his own peers. He had just held a civic magistracy, and these were often won by means of lavish bribes and public entertainments. Opportunities to recoup himself were irresistible.

True to the *mos maiorum,* the Romans invented no new magistracy for the provinces. Already as early as the Samnite Wars they had found it necessary sometimes to modify the annual system by proroguing a magistrate's term of office in order that he might finish a campaign. If he were praetor or consul, he continued for another year as propraetor or proconsul. When Sicily was conquered the Romans added another praetor to the two functionaries already existing, another for Sardinia, and then two more for Spain; but after that the new provinces were entrusted to propraetors and proconsuls, or, in case of a war, to the consuls themselves during the latter part of their year of office. The senate decided what the magisterial provinces should be and which of them should be consular; then generally the qualified balloted for them.

The same want of elasticity in the Roman system spoilt their good intentions in the matter of finance. As we have seen, the State imposed no crushing burdens upon its vassals. Had the *stipendium* been honestly collected by official emissaries under proper control, the provincials would have had little cause for complaint. But the Romans here again provided no new functionaries for the new duty. In some cases they allowed the subject communities to collect their own taxes and pay their quota to the governor's quaestor, but when the communities employed *publicani* as agents peculation might occur. Where this was impossible, the senate farmed out the collection of taxes under contract to certain individuals who bought them at auction. The *publicani* quickly grew into a regular institution, grouping themselves into capitalist syndicates which combined tax-farming with money-lending. Banks were established in every provincial centre. This capitalist class soon established itself as a political body at Rome, where it exerted a powerful and sinister influence over public policy. Just below the senatorial order were the *equites*. Of old they had been real cavalry, for it was only the rich who could afford to maintain a horse and the necessary equipment; later it became mainly a titular distinction, implying a certain income. It was here that the bankers of Rome and the financial interests were grouped in a single powerful class. In 123 B.C. these "knights" actually secured control of the jury court that had been established in 149 B.C. to try charges of exhortion (see p. 80). Then the lot of the provincials was wretched indeed : to pay their greedy and extortionate tax-gatherers they had often to borrow from the same individuals in their capacity of usurers, and then, if they ventured to journey to Rome with a complaint, they would meet the same evil class in the very judges who heard their complaints. This was how "publican and sinner" came to be an appropriate conjunction.

The corruption, as we shall see later, began to be serious with the acquisition of Asia. At first the incompetence due to the inexperience of the governors and their staffs was the chief failing of the system. But when Asia with its stored-up capital, its possibilities of exploitation, and its extreme helplessness fell to Rome, traders and money-lenders swarmed down upon it, so that there were 80,000 Italians there when Mithridates ordered his famous massacre (88 B.C.). Thus money poured into the capital, and there was an unseemly scramble for wealth. But for the present we are only concerned with the system of provincial government as it was in the beginning. I think we may conclude that it started with the best intentions, but with two inherent defects, both due to the conservatism of the Roman character. Their constitution was municipal and their outlook parochial. Their empire-building was precisely of the narrow-minded, well-intentioned character that one would expect if the Marylebone Borough Council suddenly found itself presented with Ireland, France, and half Spain, and asked to govern them.

THE IMPERIAL CITY

A poor man cannot become a millionaire without at least altering his way of living, and a little backward provincial town cannot find itself the mistress of a great empire without undergoing very profound modifications. In 211 B.C. Rome was struggling for her life with a foreign enemy raging at her gates. Some sixty years later she was mistress in the Mediterranean, and responsible for a vast empire.

One of the effects of the change was a prodigious influx of wealth into the city. Vast sums flowed into the coffers of a state which had till recently conducted its business with lumps of copper. It has been calculated that between 200 and 157 B.C. war indemnities brought in over 150 million *denarii* and booty over 100 million, and this at a time when the annual wage of a labourer may have been about 300 *denarii*. Vast tracts of public land were gained, and there was a steady influx of tributary corn and money : public mines, such as those in Spain, must be added. There never had been regular direct taxation in the city : a Roman paid his dues in the form of personal service, and a *tributum* only as a temporary war contribution. But in 167 B.C. all taxation ceased at Rome except an indirect tariff on salt and the customs at the ports. Henceforth Rome was living on her empire and growing fat upon it. It is true that expenditure was also increasing. In the earliest days there had been little public finance. A war was conducted by an army of citizens, who marched out for a few days' campaigning in the neighbourhood, wearing their own armour and carrying a commissariat provided by their wives. The only public expense was the religious duty of providing beasts for sacrifice, and even that was largely defrayed by fines paid to the treasury. But now expeditions cost money, armies soldiering for months or years in distant lands had to be fed and maintained, ships had to be built, equipment and machines provided. Nevertheless, with wise financial administration the treasury probably had a decent surplus. Book-keeping was one of the points in which the old Roman paterfamilias especially took pride, and although the public treasury of Rome, which had the temple of Saturn for its bank, was managed by the quaestors, the general budgeting was in the hands of the censors. But the slow development of a complex financial system shows how far wrong are those historians who make Roman greatness dependent upon economic advantages. Any maladministration of finance was not due to dishonesty at first : Polybius, the Greek historian, who was brought up in the heart of Greek politics under Aratus, the cunning chief of the Achaean League, and came to Rome in the second century as a hostage, was genuinely astonished at Roman honesty.

During Rome's early days little public money was spent upon public works. To begin with, there was no desire for fine architecture at Rome, nor indeed for art of any sort. The private houses were mainly built of unbaked bricks or tiles, often with thatched or shingled roofs : the interiors retained the bare simplicity of a country farm-house. And then Roman religion, which, as we have seen, was always somewhat cold towards the high Olympian gods, offering its real devotion to obscurer rustic powers, made little claim for temples and stately shrines. Large temples had been built under the Etruscan domination in the sixth century B.C. and immediately afterwards some Greek gods, as Castor and Pollux and Apollo, were introduced and were housed in new temples. But in the fifth and fourth centuries there was little public building in the city : the Romans were too busy fighting and building roads and colonies in Italy. Most of what was built between the Tarquins and Hannibal was of wood or brick or rubble with small architectural pretensions. It is not until the end of the third century that architecture reappears in Rome in the form of imitations of the temples, basilicas, and colonnades the Romans had seen and admired in such Greek cities as Tarentum or Syracuse. In fact with the influx of wealth from the foreign wars, a new era of building commenced. Of the new temples, some were built in the old Tuscan style, which Cato and the old-fashioned preferred, others in the new Hellenistic manner, with walls of tufa covered with bright stucco, like contemporary buildings at Pompeii. Roman nobles began to imitate the atrium houses of Pompeii, while tenement houses were erected for poorer citizens.

What the *nouveaux riches* of the second century B.C. found to spend their money on it is hard to say. In 218 B.C. the people passed the Lex Claudia, a resolution forbidding senators to engage in foreign commerce. It is very unlikely that the senate would have allowed that if they had already been deeply involved in business. But this enactment checked the only fruitful use of wealth : it turned, and was possibly intended to turn, the money of the great houses into land speculation. This was followed by disastrous results. The Punic Wars had thrown thousands of acres

Map of Italy, showing ground over 1,000 feet high

out of cultivation. That land which had belonged to rebels passed to the Roman state as public land and the scramble for it was the cause of momentous political conflicts in the succeeding generation. But rich senators acquired enormous estates which many of them began to regard as objects of economic speculation; personal interest often decreased and many became absentee land-owners and lived in Rome. In fact, the common notion of Italy at this time as a vast smiling cornfield, dotted with little farm-houses and country cottages full of stalwart husbandmen, needs modification. The Italian farmer lived—like the mediaeval Euro-pean farmer—mostly in townships which he called "cities", and it was only the plain-land in the vicinity of a town which was regularly ploughed and sown. A glance at the map will show how little of Central Italy is suited for cereal cultivation. But, if the records are true, 400 Italian townships had been destroyed in the great wars and that meant, perhaps, 400,000 acres out of cultiva-tion. And what had become of their inhabitants? Thousands, of course, had left their bones on Roman battlefields, but thousands more, when their term of service was done, went to swell the pro-letariat of Rome. There they herded in ill-built, ill-drained quarters on the low ground of the city. Physically and morally they declined. Since no great industrial or commercial developments were set on foot to absorb their labour, they gradually formed an idle urban proletariat and an unemployment problem of increas-ing intensity arose.

As we have seen in the case of Greece, ancient city-states under-took duties which the modern community has regarded, up to recent times at least, as private and not public. The city-state regarded it as part of its business to see that its shareholders did not starve, therefore the supply of corn and the price of it was a matter of state supervision. From the early Republic there had been officers whose duties came to include oversight of the city's corn-supply. Now corn was beginning to arrive in the form of tribute from Sicily and Africa. Soon we shall have the agrarian laws and all the disorder that resulted from them. But it is impor-tant to observe that the depopulation of the Italian countryside resulted from war and politics as well as from economic causes. Of course economic causes kept it depopulated. Nature never intended Central Italy for a wheat-growing land; the vine, the olive and the fig, are its best products. Now that the seas were open for free imports, it no longer paid to plough and sow the stony upland farms.

Thus much land passed out of cultivation. As in England, graz-ing was found to be cheaper, easier, and more profitable than agriculture. Oxen were used for ploughing or reserved for sacrifice. The Italians, like the Greeks, seldom ate meat and then little but smoked bacon, but, as Romans wore the woollen toga, sheep-farming was profitable. In summer the sheep grazed on the Sabine hills, in winter on the Latin plain among the stubble of the corn-fields or beneath the olive-trees. Wild slave-shepherds tended them.

Slavery was the canker at the root of ancient civilisation. It assumed more awful proportions at Rome than in Greece owing to the hard materialism of the Roman character. Of course it had existed from the earliest times as the common lot of the prisoner of war, but probably such prisoners were not numerous in the small-scale wars of the early Republic. It is difficult to assess their lot : no doubt there was often merciless exploitation, but often too no doubt the slave was treated as a servant of the family and he would work in the fields alongside his master who would generally belong to the same or a similar race. But as time passed, conditions probably deteriorated. It was cheaper to buy slaves than to let them breed, cheaper to sell them for what they would fetch when they grew old than to keep them. You could dodge the gods, who enjoined holidays even for slaves, by giving your slaves work in-doors on feast-days—such are some of the maxims of the venerable Cato, who is the type of the old Roman squire. With overseas wars, slaves were becoming more numerous and cheaper than ever. You might have to pay as much as £1000 for a pretty boy or girl, but a wild Sardinian or Gaul or Spaniard cost very little.*

* It is not practicable to attempt to estimate the value of Roman money in terms of modern currency. Even apart from the fluctuating value of the latter in relation to prices, there are too many difficulties: e.g. the variation of purchasing power in different places and at different times. Thus the old equivalence of a *denarius* with 10d. is not very helpful now. When this book was first published (1912), it might be said that gold in Cicero's day had roughly three times the purchasing power that it had in 1912: but even that would be misleading, since some goods and services were much dearer, others much cheaper. Thus it will be better to quote sums of money in the original form. In Cato's time, for instance, a luxury slave might cost 24,000 *denarii*, an average able-bodied slave about 500. At this time a bushel of wheat cost about 3 *denarii*, meat about ½ *denarius* a pound, and a plough-ox 60-80 *denarii*. Wages were low: a slave could be hired out at ½ *denarius* a day, while free labour received only a little more, perhaps one *denarius*. If a labourer could just support himself on some 300 *denarii* a year, at the other end of the social scale was a man like Scipio Africanus, whose estate at death may have fallen not far short of a million *denarii*. But even this was modest compared with later days, since Crassus, the triumvir, it is said, had at one time real estate worth 50,000,000 *denarii*.—EDD.

Hence began the really pernicious system of specialised slavery. Each slave was trained simply for one special task—cook, barber, footman, bearer, lackey, or schoolmaster. The shepherds and gladiators might retain their manhood, as indeed they did, and showed it in frightful revolts during the last century of the Republic. But the domestic slaves of the capital had no hope but to cringe and wheedle their way into favour by flattering and corrupting their masters. One alleviation of the slave's lot there was : it was easier for a slave to earn his freedom at Rome than in Greece.* Worse than domestic slavery was the plantation system, which during all this period was growing in the country. At its worst it meant huge slave-barracks, in which the slaves lived in dungeons underground and worked by day in gangs, chained night and day. It was a profitable system of agriculture and it rapidly ousted free labour. In the city too, in the merchant ships, and in the mines, a cruel and vicious system of servitude was destroying free industry. The eighteenth-century view of an idealised Roman republic of citizens, free, equal, and fraternal, which inspired the Convention and coloured the periods of Mirabeau, is a historic fraud.

Equality beyond the name was certainly unknown at Rome. All government was in the hands of a close circle of aristocrats whose stronghold was in the senate. By virtue of the client system the great houses of the Claudii, the Cornelii, the Fabii, the Livii, the Aemilii, the Valerii, and a dozen others kept the high offices of state exclusively in their hands. By this time the censors drew up the senate-lists chiefly from the ranks of ex-magistrates, and the magistracies became a graduated course. It required extraordinary pushfulness or wealth or patronage for a new man to insinuate himself into the charmed circle. The old patriciate had gone, politically at least, and only survived for religious purposes, but Rome still remained a thrall to aristocracy of a far more dangerous type, an aristocracy of office. One of the troubles of Rome lay in the fact that this aristocracy was daily becoming more ambitious and self-seeking.

A great deal of nonsense has been talked about the luxury of

* Philip of Macedon, writing to the inhabitants of a city in Thessaly at the end of the third century, drew attention to the liberal policy of the Romans in granting full citizenship, including the right to hold office, to liberated slaves. For a translation of this letter see N. Lewis and M. Reinhold, *Roman Civilization* I, p. 386.

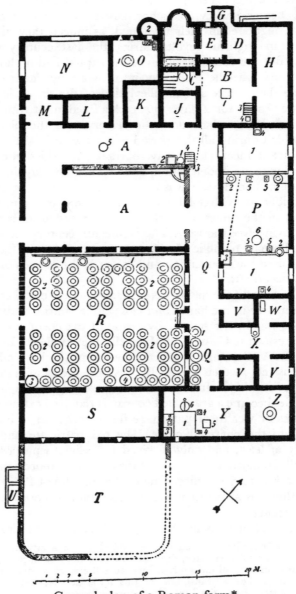

Ground-plan of a Roman farm*

the Romans as one of the causes of their decline. Even Mommsen relates with shocked emotion that they imported anchovies from the Black Sea and wine from Greece. Two hot meals a day they had and "frivolous articles" including bronze-mounted couches. There were professional cooks, and actually bakers' shops began to appear about 171 B.C. It is true that all this luxury would pale into insignificance before the modern worker's breakfast-table with bacon from Canada, tea from Ceylon or coffee from Brazil, sugar from Jamaica, eggs from Denmark, and marmalade from South Africa. Cato would have swooned at the sight of our picture-frames coated with real gold, for he taxed table-ware worth more than 1,000 *denarii*. The truth is that Rome, having grown rich, was just beginning to grow civilised. It is the everlasting misfortune of Rome that events occurred in that order.

In conquering Macedon Rome had become acquainted with civilisation. At that date civilisation meant Hellenism slightly tinctured with Orientalism, a culture which, though still alive and still original and creative, was certainly past its prime. The Hellenistic period of Greek art has been unjustly depreciated in comparison with the more youthful and virile age of Pericles. But it could still boast of great scholars, scientists, and philosophers, both at Alexandria and Athens. Theocritus, Bion, and Moschus form a group of charming and original poets, and an art that could produce the Aphrodite of Melos cannot with justice be termed decadent. Politically, morally, and physically Greece was no doubt long past the vigour of her youth, but intellectually she was still well qualified to play the part of schoolmistress to the lusty young barbarian of the West. We have seen that in early times Rome had come under Etruscan influences at a period when close cultural relations existed between Etruria and Greece.

---

* *A* is a courtyard with a gateway and a colonnade on two sides; 1 and 5 are cisterns, 2 a water-basin, 3 a leaden water-butt, 4 steps up to 3. *B* is the kitchen; 1 is the hearth, 2 a water-butt, 3 stairs to upper storey. *C, D, E, F, G* are a suite of rooms fitted as a bath. *H* is a stable. *J, K, L, M* are various living-rooms, *N* the dining-room, *O* a bakehouse. *P* is the room of wine-presses, one (1) on each side, between them various receptacles (2-5) for holding wine. *Q* is a corridor on one side of which is *R*, an open court containing rows of wine-holders, and on the other side *V, W, X*, small living-rooms. *S* may be a barn; *T* is the threshing-floor, *U* a water-tank. *Y* and *Z* contain the olive-press and oil-stores. This establishment is of the first century of our era and doubtless contains many luxuries which would not be found in farms of Republican times.

There had been a steady influx of Greek art and artists into Italy for some generations, so tradition relates and modern research agrees. Greeks may well have worked in Rome in the service of its Etruscan masters. Then came perhaps two centuries of relapse in the cultural sense while Rome was busy with warfare and conquest. In 300 B.C. she was almost entirely destitute of accomplishments, and even, if we may except law, politics, and military skill, of civilisation. The war with Pyrrhus and the conquest of Tarentum and then of Sicily brought in Greek slaves and semi-Greek South-Italian citizens who were bound to have some influence. Then came direct dealings with Greece in the three Macedonian wars, and every Roman who had fought under Flamininus or Paullus returned to Rome, if not an apostle of culture, at any rate a man who had seen civilisation with his own eyes and could no longer regard old Roman ways as wholly sufficient for man's happiness. How long could eyes that had seen the Zeus of Pheidias at Olympia glowing with ivory and gold remain content with the old vermilion Jove in his native temple?

Nevertheless it was very slowly that culture filtered in. All through the third century and for the first half of the second Rome was still incessantly occupied with war. Her tastes were brutalised and demoralised by it. When drama painfully began, the dramatists sadly lamented that their audiences would desert the theatre for the sight of a rope-dancer or a beast-baiting or, better still, a pair of gladiators. From the first it was vain to attempt the creation of a national drama for a people whose craving was for the sight of blood. Gladiatorial combats are said to have been of Etruscan origin. They first appeared at Rome in the early part of the third century in connection with funeral displays. From every African expedition wild beasts were brought home to be slaughtered in the Roman amphitheatres. These bloody shows indicate the real tastes of the Romans from comparatively early times. They are no spurious growth of the so-called "degenerate Empire.' On one occasion, in 167 B.C., when the music of some Greek flute-players failed to please a Roman audience, the presiding magistrate ordered the unlucky artists to fight one another, and the hoots of the crowd were instantly transformed to rapturous applause. The scene is described by Polybius (XXX, 22).

The arts were held in contempt and entrusted to slaves or the poorest kind of citizens.* Thus Hellenic civilisation was transported to Rome under a double disadvantage. Not only was Greek civilisation itself already past its prime, but it was interpreted largely by slaves. Every Roman of position had Greeks among his retinue—not, of course, the citizens of famous cities like Athens or Alexandria, which were still free, but nondescript, low-caste wretches from the great market at Delos or from the southern towns of Italy—for clerks, accountants, scribes, jesters, procurers, physicians, pedagogues, flute-players, philosophers, cooks, concubines, and schoolmasters. We may be sure that it was not the most favourable type of Hellenism that would creep into Rome by such channels as these. But it was precisely in this manner that Roman literature began. After the surrender of Tarentum in 272 B.C. a boy named Andronicus was brought to Rome as a slave and served as tutor in the house of a certain Lucius Livius. Later he received his liberty, and as Livius Andronicus set up a school. To supply his pupils with a text-book, he undertook the translation of Homer's *Odyssey* into the native Italian measure of Saturnian verse. Naturally this pioneer work was indifferently performed, but it remained a primer of education down to the school days of Horace.† Emboldened by this success he proceeded to supply the Roman stage with translations of Greek plays.

Such was the beginning; the sequel showed slow and painful development. Naevius, a junior contemporary of Livius, translated Greek comedies and tragedies, and also wrote plays on Roman themes. He attempted the old Greek custom of political allusions, but speedily found that there was less liberty of speech in Rome than had prevailed in the palmy days of Athenian

---

* What actual output of art there was in Rome at this period is not clear. The famous Ficorini cista, one of the finest of a series of bronze caskets generally assigned to Praeneste (Palestrina), a few miles to the south-east, bears an inscription to the effect that it was made at Rome, and it is not clear whether we are to regard this as an exceptional case or not. The Brutus of the Conservatori and the Priestess of the British Museum, London are examples of a number of sculptures in bronze which must have been made, if not in Rome itself, at any rate in its vicinity. North of Rome various Etruscan cities were enjoying a renaissance of activity after the desolation caused by the Gaulish invasions of the fourth century. The statue of the Arringatore (Plate 10) bears an Etruscan inscription, but its style is purely Italic.—F.N.P.

† Horace, *Epist.* II. i. 69-75.

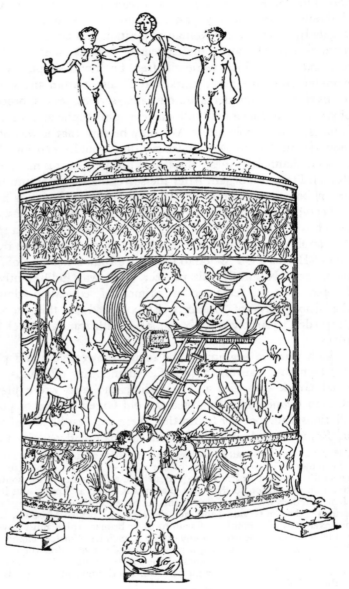

The Ficorini cista

comedy. An allusion to the Metellus family brought the famous
and thoroughly old Roman poetical retort:

dabunt malum Metelli Næuio poetæ,

which was fulfilled by the imprisonment of the dramatist. Thus
the beginnings of literature at Rome were by no means easy. The
dramatists were hampered by severe police restrictions as well as
by the cultural limitations of their public. It is interesting to note
that both these poets also attempted the epic style. Livius Andronicus was actually commissioned by the priests to celebrate the
victory of the Metaurus in verse, and Naevius wrote an account
in Saturnian verse of the First Punic War.

For comedy the Romans appear to have had some natural
taste. It seems that a rude and barbaric form of dramatic dialogue
mixed with buffoonery was native to Italy in the Fescennine Songs,
which are said to have been of Etruscan invention. So the Romans
at their festivals were content to listen to comedies if the humour
was obvious enough, if there was plenty of horseplay. The setting
was primitive. Instead of the magnificent marble theatres of
Greece, wooden booths were temporarily erected in the amphitheatre, and the audience did not usually listen with rapt attention to the efforts of the actors who tried to amuse them. Sometimes the chorus would be sung by trained musicians, while the
actors on the stage illustrated the words by pantomimic gestures.
It was all in marked contrast to what we hear of the beginnings
of Drama in Greece. There it had been a national service of worship to the gods. Here it was a trivial amusement in the hands of
slaves and foreigners.

Of the three great comic dramatists, Plautus, though a genuine
Italian of Umbria, had been reduced by poverty to the position
of a labourer; Caecilius was an Insubrian Gaul from the neighbourhood of Milan, who had been brought to Rome as a slave
and then set free; Terence was a Carthaginian by birth, belonging as a slave to the senator Terentius Lucanus, and subsequently
being liberated became a friend of the younger Scipio. Ennius, the
"father" of epic verse and tragedy, was a Greek-speaking Calabrian by birth, who became a friend of the elder Scipio and other
prominent men. Pacuvius, the best of the early tragedians, was a
native of Brundisium; he was a nephew of Ennius. The activity

of these writers belongs mainly to the first half of the second century. Not one of them was a Roman by origin, and we cannot postulate a distinctively Roman character for their work. The comic dramatists were engaged in translating the work of the Greek writers of New Comedy,* notably Menander and Philemon. From the artistic point of view the work was often carelessly done. There was little pretence of Romanising the characters or the scenes; generally they were Greek, with stray allusions to Roman life introduced for comic effect. The source from which they drew was by now a stereotyped comedy of manners with stock characters—the heavy father, either an undignified debauchee or a stingy curmudgeon; the old woman, generally a procuress; the gay and profligate young hero; the fair heroine, generally a *meretrix;* and a background of parasites, bullies, panders, slave-dealers, and scoundrelly slaves, who came in for recurrent beatings to the great entertainment of the audience. The situations are also "taken from stock", facial resemblances, disguised strangers, mistaken identities, veiled women and so forth. The "love interest", such as it is, almost invariably centres round a young man's passion for a courtesan. The atmosphere is often brutal and immoral. There is often a serious lack of dramatic imagination in the stage management. Yet the comedies of Plautus and Terence have played a larger part in monasteries and schoolrooms than any other literature in the world, and through Shakespeare and Molière have had a decisive influence in the history of the drama.

We do not possess enough of the original Greek sources to say with certainty how much of their own the Roman dramatists contributed. Even if we were better supplied with such information, it would still be unrealistic to judge Roman Comedy by Greek standards. It is equally unrealistic to judge it by Victorian standards of moral or aesthetic propriety. In any case there are great differences in morality and refinement within the Plautine *corpus,* to say nothing of the difference in these respects between Plautus and Terence. What Professor Beare calls the "genial cynicism" of Plautus is accompanied by considerable generosity of spirit and by genuine enthusiasm for the virtues that he valued most, loyalty, for example, and tenacity, and patience. His obscenity is Aristophanic in everything but its comparative rarity. Although his plots are derivative and his characters conventional,

* See *The Glory that was Greece,* p. 281.

17.
THE ROMAN FORUM,
view looking south-east towards the Arch of Titus, and
monuments of various ages;
the Palatine Hill rises on the
right.

18. **ROMAN FORUM WITH REMAINS OF BASILICA JULIA.** In background remains of temples and Arch of Titus. The rising ground is the Palatine Hill.

19. DORIC TEMPLE AT CORI.
Early 1st Century B.C.

20. TEMPLE OF FORTUNA AT PRAENESTE. (Palestrina 1st Century B.C.)

21. ORESTES AND ELECTRA.

Greco-Roman Sculpture of the 1st Century B.C.

22. BRONZE BOXER. 1st Century B.C.

23. JULIUS CAESAR.

24.   MARBLE BUST OF POMPEY.

25. CICERO, an early Imperial copy of an earlier work.

26. MARCUS JUNIUS BRUTUS.

27. STATUE OF AUGUSTUS, possibly contemporary.

28. BRONZE HEAD OF AUGUSTUS, probably contemporary.

29. HEAD OF LIVIA, WIFE OF AUGUSTUS.
Probably slightly later than Augustus' lifetime.

30.   HEAD OF OCTAVIA, sister of Augustus.

31. BUST OF AGRIPPA, general and minister of Augustus.

32. FORUM OF AUGUSTUS with Temple of Mars Ultor,
(Mars the Avenger) dedicated by Augustus.

his scenes rollick along with unflagging verve and his characters live because of the endlessly varied details of humorous portrayal. His genius is perhaps most evident in the language, which is Elizabethan in its comic exuberance, and in his skill, amazing in a pioneer, at adapting a large variety of Greek metres to dramatic use in his native language. While full justice has been done by critics to the leisurely progress towards perfection of the Latin epic and elegiac metres, Plautus' immediate and brilliant success with the many scenic metres has not been equally appreciated, or at least emphasized. His metrical adroitness and his irrepressible and ever varying liveliness of language combine to produce a medium of comic expression worthy of more suitable material than the extraneous subject-matter derived from the Greek New Comedy. Professor P. J. Enk rightly directs our attention to the fine *poetic* quality of such a passage as *Mercator* 830-41.

With the aesthetically dyspeptic Terence goes down better than his rude and hearty predecessor. Shockable readers are much more at ease in his company. His verbal polish and the urbane restraint that pervades his plays are in striking contrast to Plautus' linguistic adventurousness and broad humour. It is doubtful whether his world is, under the surface, morally much sounder than that of Plautus, but this friend of Scipio and his associates is more observant of the proprieties. Both his language and his use of metre are tame beside those of Plautus, but he is a much more careful writer, a model, indeed, of pure Latinity. He is also contemplative, unlike Plautus, and profoundly interested in subtleties of characterisation and in the problems of *la condition humaine*. As Julius Caesar said, his chief fault is his lack of the *uis comica* in which Menander excelled. Menander's recently discovered *Dyscolus* does not greatly support this judgment. If Comedy never established itself permanently in Rome, it was not the fault, as far as we can judge, of its pioneers. The unfamiliar background of the *fabula palliata* militated against its success with Roman audiences, and rival attractions of a grosser kind from the beginning competed successfully with literary drama. We are fortunate to have in these so different comic dramatists considerable evidence for the character of the spoken Latin of the age, evidence of which the development of the "literary dialect" under hellenizing and rhetorical influences largely deprives us for subsequent periods.

Ennius in his tragedies translated and adapted Greek models, notably Euripides. He was employed by the elder Scipio Africanus to educate and broaden Roman taste. He had learnt of the Greek philosophers to disbelieve in the gods, or rather he had learnt the Euhemerist doctrine that the gods of Olympus are but the memories of long dead human heroes, or that they sit, as Epicurus also taught,

> On the hills . . . together careless of mankind.

> ego deum genus esse semper dixi et dicam cælitum,
> sed eos non curare opinor quid agat humanum genus;
> nam si curent, bene bonis sit, male malis, quod nunc abest.*

He had, however, also imbibed ideas of a very different character from such teachers of Magna Graecia as Pythagoras and Empedocles. At the age of fifty Ennius set himself to relate the whole of Roman history in eighteen books of epic verse. Adopting the Homeric hexameter, he shaped that magnificent instrument for the hand of Virgil and most of the Roman poets, and it has been maintained that he vitally affected the literary language of Rome by preserving terminal inflexions that were dropping out of current speech. The fragments of Ennius that have survived, though often rough and sometimes ungainly, yet possess a massive dignity of their own, and often a most solemn majesty of cadence, as in the lines with which I have headed this chapter.

For some time now Roman religion had been losing its native character and becoming cosmopolitan and denationalised. As we have seen, its genuinely native elements were mainly rural, and now the Roman was a townsman with a townsman's light scepticism and craving for novelty and sensation. As early as 204 B.C., that is, in the throes of the Great Punic War, the worship of Cybele—the Great Mother of Phrygian ritual—had been introduced along with its begging eunuch priests. Apollo with appropriate athletic games had arrived earlier. New gods multiplied, old gods became hellenised, Roman priesthoods became either mere political posts, obtained after 104 B.C. by popular election like any other public office, or select dining-clubs of the aristo-

---

* I have always said and always shall say that divinities exist, but I think they take no care for the fate of human-kind; for, if they cared, the good would prosper and the evil perish, and that does not happen. (*Telamo*).

cracy. As the gods multiplied, faith declined. In 186 B.C. the Senate discovered a whole system of secret nocturnal orgies which, under the name of Bacchic mysteries, had spread with extraordinary rapidity throughout Italy. The Senate did not persecute the religious cult as such, but determined to stamp out the attendant public disorder and crime.

Morality, public and private, deteriorated equally. We have sufficient stories of bribery by candidates for office—not to mention the systematic corruption of the electorate by shows—to suggest that standards of political morality declined. As for private virtue, it may be that the world of pimps and prostitutes that flits across the Plautine stage is borrowed from Athens, but it was certainly familiar at Rome and rapidly domesticated itself. Slavery had always existed there, and immorality is inseparable from slavery. During the second century, with an increasing number of retired soldiers gathered promiscuously and without employment in the capital, immorality was multiplied in every class. As early as 243 B.C. there had been complaint of the unwillingness of Roman men of good family to face the responsibilities of marriage. Already, as in the case of C. Calpurnius Piso, consul in 180 B.C., alleged to have been murdered by his wife, there had been horrible domestic tragedies in great houses. Divorce, said to be unknown before the war with Hannibal, was growing common. As usual, the Pharisees of the day strove to combat immorality with prudishness. Cato the Censor punished a Roman senator for kissing his wife in the presence of their daughter.

Now, let it be remembered that this very age of which we are speaking, the age of conquest in the Punic and Greek wars, is the heroic age of Roman history, the age to which poets and historians of the Empire looked back as golden. Thus we see that all the vicious features of Roman society, the cruelty, the idleness, the debauchery, the political corruption, the lack of artistic taste, the immorality and crime in the noble houses, the injustice and oppression of the poor and helpless, are no products of the Empire, but deeply engrained in the Roman character and entwined about the roots of her history. No doubt, before Rome began to be a city and long before she began to have a history, there were simple laborious rustics on the Latin plains, who possessed, for want of opportunity, the virtuous abstinences of the poor. But it is manifestly false to ascribe degeneration either to the fall of the Republican system of government or to the introduction of Greek civilisation. If one cause more than another is to be assigned for the rapid growth of evil tendencies it is the exhaustion consequent upon incessant warfare and the brutality engendered by continual life in camp. The only thing that could mitigate the latter was surely education and culture. Instead, then, of Greek civilisation being the cause of degeneracy at Rome we may more truthfully assert that it came to save her from ruin at a time when she was threatened with internal decay. Had it come earlier or been accepted more willingly it might have done more to brighten the darker pages of Roman history.*

* This picture of Roman society is exaggerated, especially if it is applied to the period before 200 B.C. Public and private morality began to decline in the second century: we have the contemporary testimony of Polybius. But Polybius knew the Roman nobility intimately and his pages also remind us of the cultural and intellectual interests and the moral integrity of many of the Roman nobles.—EDD.

III

THE LAST CENTURY OF THE REPUBLIC

urbem uenalem et mature perituram si emptorem inuenerit.
Jugurtha in SALLUST

MANY of the disquieting symptoms which we have just noted as afflicting Roman society in the second century B.C. might have been allayed, and the causes might even have been removed, by a wise and foreseeing government. In dealing with the allies and subjects who formed the vast and growing empire the senate had to choose one of two courses—either centralisation or devolution of power, either a just and firm system of control or a liberal grant of autonomous rights. But the senate had little policy. It left things to shape themselves. Again, the agrarian difficulty of a deserted countryside and an idle, disorderly city proletariat could have been solved if it had been taken early, before the habit of city-life grew upon the discharged warriors. Here again the senate did nothing till it was too late. Then, having acquired an overseas empire all around the Mediterranean, the senate, if it had not been blind, should have seen that it was necessary to maintain a strong navy and police the seas in the interests of commerce. But again the government neglected its duty. For these and many other sins of negligence there was a heavy reckoning to be paid. It required no oracle to foretell disaster.

While the mass of the senate may have been indifferent, two small parties in the state had policies of their own. There was Cato (it is difficult to find a party for him to lead), who believed that by repeating the magic words *mos maiorum* he could put the clock back to the days of Cincinnatus, if not of Numa, mistaking symptoms for diseases and hoping, like many another revivalist, to

75

make people virtuous by making them uncomfortable, a task doomed to failure from the start.

Over against these were set a party who may almost be termed liberals, in that they were prepared to go forward hopefully in company with the spirit of their age. Their foremost representatives were the Scipios, who acted as patrons to some of the literary figures we have just described, and were themselves eager to accept the new culture. Unfortunately there was very little foresight or political courage among them, and, above all, there was an aristocratic pride which would have rendered them impossible as leaders even if they had had any idea of a destination. As a family the Scipios were by no means uniformly competent, and many of them subsisted on the glamour of the name, which itself had been very largely due to the opportunity and ability of Scipio Africanus the Elder and the Younger.

The special feature which distinguishes the age we have now to consider—that is, roughly, the hundred years from 146 B.C. onwards—is that the historian's attention now begins to be focussed on a series of personal biographies. It gradually becomes clear that some individual must dominate this imperial city, and the only question left is who it shall be. In the true polity of the city-state the influence of personality is reduced to a minimum, and various devices, such as the lot at Athens or the double and annual consulship at Rome, are employed to prevent that individual predominance which so easily turns to despotism. It is not so much through envy as through an instinct of self-preservation that republics are notoriously ungrateful to their great men. But personal eminence, if it is dangerous to the liberty of a republic, is almost essential to the government of a great empire and the control of huge armies. The incompetence of the annual generals, now that warfare was on a large scale and conducted far from the overseeing eye of the administration, became more noticeable. Already in the Third Macedonian War it had been disgracefully apparent. Now the long campaigns against Viriathus in Spain and Jugurtha in Africa reveal pitiful ineptitude, coupled with shameless dishonesty, in the republican generals of the aristocracy. Roman armies are no longer invincible in the field; they are not even disciplined.

THE GRACCHI

But first we have to recall an attempt at reform of the economic distresses of the imperial city. It is not so much the actual schemes of the brothers Gracchus which interest us as the manner in which reform was proposed and defeated. The Gracchi themselves belonged by numerous ties to the liberal aristocracy. Their famous mother, Cornelia—one of the many Roman women who by their influence help to make Roman history so different from Greek— was the daughter of Scipio Africanus. Tiberius, the elder brother, was married to a Claudia; among his friends were Scaevola and Crassus. Thus on all sides he belonged to the circle of progressive nobles. His education had been such as one would expect from such surroundings. As their father, Ti. Sempronius Gracchus, had died at an early age, it was Cornelia's task to make her two "jewels" worthy of her glorious name. Accordingly she employed the most eminent Greek teachers as their tutors. The boys were trained in Greek oratory and history, and from Greek political science they learned to divide constitutions up into monarchies, aristocracies and democracies, and to believe that in the latter all power belongs to the people. At the same time their military training was not neglected; in horsemanship and feats of arms they outshone all their comrades. Their prospects were in every way brilliant and hopeful. While still a youth of about sixteen, Tiberius was elected augur. The proud aristocrat, Appius Claudius, as it is related by Plutarch, offered him the hand of his daughter, and, having secured his consent, rushed home. As soon as his wife heard mention of a betrothal she exclaimed: "Why in such a hurry unless you have got Tiberius Gracchus for our daughter?" It is the misfortune of rhetorical history that all its good characters appear to be prigs and all its bad ones scoundrels; but it appears that, if Tiberius had been content with the easy road to fame which stretched before him in youth, he might without trouble have had the world at his feet. He accompanied his brother-in-law, the younger Africanus, in the last expedition against Carthage. In camp he was the most distinguished of the young officers and the first to scale the walls of the city. He served his quaestorship in Spain, and there showed all the diplomatic skill of the Cornelian family. He saved an army of 20,000 men from destruction at Numantia. The Spaniards loved him no less for his descent from the great Africanus than for his uprightness. Thus at the age of thirty-one he had his future assured. A brilliant orator with distinguished public service behind him, he was obviously destined for the consulship, and then for a province, for wealth, fame and honour.

Call him a doctrinaire, if you will, for not being content with that prospect. In passing through, on his way to Spain, he had seen the pleasant lands of Tuscany lying forlorn and desolate, chained gangs of foreign slaves working in the fields or tending the flocks of absentee Roman landlords, while the sturdy peasants who should have been in their place were loafing in the streets of Rome. The public land, conquered in war, had sometimes been simply embezzled by Roman politicians; sometimes granted to veteran soldiers only to fall into the hands of speculators. The old Licinian land-law, which had limited the amount of public land which might be held by one proprietor, was openly flouted, and leases were treated as freeholds.

Seeing these things, the young man was filled with a passion for reform, and deliberately devoted his life to that task. The modern historians who call him demagogue do not deny the awful mischief which he set himself to repair. It is hard to know what he should have done to please them. The senate, by now an entrenched stronghold of property dishonestly acquired and privilege dishonestly maintained, could obviously never be converted. Filled with Greek ideas, Tiberius determined to appeal to the people, to the *demos*. That of course was a mistake. There was no such thing as a *demos* at Rome, and there never had been. The relation between Senate and Comitia was not in the least the same as that between Council and Assembly in Greece. At Rome the Senate deliberated and the Comitia ratified; at Athens the Council prepared business for the Assembly to discuss and decide. It is not that the letter of the constitution really matters—when people are hungry it does not—but that there was lacking at Rome the very elements of democracy, an articulate commons, an organised will of the people. Failing that, any attempt to pose as champion of the people must be a fraud, conscious or unconscious. But it is grossly unfair to Gracchus to suppose that it was conscious. He thought that a tribune of the plebs might fairly claim to be a champion of the people, unaware that the plebs was now an anachronism, and the tribunate merely a clumsy brake on the wheels of the state. In 133 B.C. Tiberius was one of the ten tribunes, and he immediately prepared to introduce the millennium by legislative process.

He proposed to enforce the old Licinian law by which no individual citizen could claim a large holding of public land. At the same time he proposed to make his measure retrospective, so as to evict thousands of noble land-grabbers. The land thus escheated to the state he proposed to lease on nominal terms as small holdings to the poorer citizens of Rome. The distribution was to be carried out by a commission of three. Unwisely he made this commission a family party consisting of himself, his father-in-law, and his young brother. Property was immediately up in arms against him. The liberal senators discovered, as even liberals are apt to do, that one's own property has a sanctity far superior to other people's. Accordingly, they took the Roman constitutional method of putting up another tribune to veto the proposals of Tiberius. Thereupon Tiberius, with his fantastic notions of the people and the people's rights, declared that a tribune who opposed the people was no tribune, and so had his opponent deposed. The senate's answer was the only constitutional answer left to them, a threat of prosecution when the tribunate should be over. That, of course, made it necessary for Tiberius to perpetuate his office. He gathered a band of followers sworn to protect his life, proposed a string of attractive measures to secure popular support, and stood for a second term of office. The senate obstructed the elections. Thus the state was at a deadlock; there were no more resources for such a situation within constitutional limits, so some senators simply girt up their togas and, led by a Scipio, marched down into the forum to settle the question of reform in a practical manner. Tiberius Gracchus was murdered and his followers left for judicial assassination.

Ten years later Gaius Gracchus, with a similar programme and the added motive of piety to his brother's memory, took up the campaign afresh. The senate, indeed, having slain the author of reform, had been forced to allow the reforms themselves at any rate to start. Some lands had been redistributed, and when Scipio Africanus the Younger had a decree passed to modify the work of the land commission in so far as it affected the interests of the Italian allies, he died suddenly, not without suspicion of foul play;

but the redistribution went on, and it is clear that by this time the agrarian agitation was being largely appeased. Gaius was elected to the tribunate of 123; he was rather more practical, and therefore far more dangerous than his brother in the eyes of the stubborn and selfish nobility, and his proposals embraced a wider scope. Coupled with the land-agitation there was now a loud demand for granting Roman citizenship to the Latins and other Italian allies.

The platform upon which Gaius Gracchus stood was a radical one. Henceforth every poor citizen was to be supplied with corn at a reasonable price; the proposal was a guarantee against profiteering, not a dole. The land commission was to be fully restored. The senate was to be enlarged so that the preponderance of the old nobility might be neutralised. New colonies were to be founded, including one at Carthage—a most salutary measure. Easier terms of military service were to be granted. By these measures, some of them wise and just, some of them mere vote-catching devices, Gaius won the support of the people. Then he turned to the second estate—the capitalist Equites. To buy their favour he took up their demand that the taxes of "Asia", as the Romans called their new province bequeathed to them in 133 B.C. by King Attalus III, should be put up for auction npt locally but in Rome. It seemed to the Romans that since the Asiatics were bound to be plundered in any case, as indeed the unfortunate inhabitants of Asia Minor always have been plundered, the proceeds might as well flow straight into the pockets of Roman capitalists. To this he added the proposition that the jury-lists should henceforth be drawn from the Equestrian order and the senators excluded. It was probably more iniquitous that money-lenders and governors should be tried by a jury of money-lenders exclusively than that they should come before a jury of governors past and future. Neither would seem to us or to the provincials an ideal arrangement.

Some of this policy, we have to admit, was pure demagogy, but for that the conservative nobles, who cared little for the welfare of the state and were impervious to anything but force, are directly responsible. Gracchus drove his measures through the *comitia,* and secured his re-election for the next year. Feeling that his policy had secured him a large and faithful party of supporters, he now prepared to introduce a measure which he knew to be necessary for the salvation of his country, but which he must equally well have known to be unpopular at Rome, namely, the grant of citizen rights to the Italians. By this we see that Gaius Gracchus, if he sometimes stooped to the arts of the demagogue, was also capable of real statesmanship. The progressive grant of burgess rights as soon as subject peoples were sufficiently Romanised to be fit for them was the old Roman policy, which had made the city great in the past, and kept her safe in the shock of invasion. But the Romans had now become jealous and exclusive. The proposal was detested in Rome and was vetoed by another tribune. The situation in Rome quickly deteriorated : some disturbances followed and when the Gracchans occupied the Aventine Hill the Senate passed the *Senatus consultum ultimum,* in effect a declaration of martial law. The consul Opimius then crushed the Gracchans by force : Gaius lost his life and some 3000 of his followers were killed either in the fighting or after a perfunctory trial.

In all this it is evident that the Roman political system had completely broken down. The constitution had always been ill-defined. There is no doubt that sovereignty legally belonged to the people, and that senatorial government was a usurpation, as the Gracchi called it. By calling the citizen body of Rome a mob or a rabble you do not alter the rights of the case. It was largely the fault of the Government that they had been allowed to become so selfish, so disorderly, and so corrupt. The extraordinary machinery of the tribunate—ten officials, each with an absolute veto upon all government—had made it impossible to find any constitutional method of reform. The policy of Gaius Gracchus was the only possible one if Rome was to be saved, and as a matter of plain fact it was the policy which after a century of unceasing bloodshed Rome eventually adopted. It was to be a disguised monarchy, like that of Pericles at Athens, working on the basis of the tribunician powers. The old ascendancy of the senate could not stand a challenge; not only did it rest upon no legal title, but it had lost whatever claim to respect it ever possessed on the score of patriotism or statesmanship. For the agrarian problem it had no policy but to hold fast to its ill-gotten lands; to the demands of the Italian allies it had nothing but a miserly "no". It watched with indifference the ruin of Italy, the degeneracy of Rome, and the oppression of the provincial world. The policy of the Gracchi may have included dreams and nightmares, but it did look forward and hold out hopes. The Gracchi had now laid the foundation of a popular movement, and it is Rome's misfortune that this foundation was built of such rotten materials. The people had been bought by bribes, but it had failed to exhibit a spark of disinterested statesmanship. If ever a state needed a master that state was Rome. Henceforth until a master came the condition of Rome and Italy and the provinces was simply deplorable. Force was beginning to replace consent as the ultimate factor in politics.

MARIUS

The next conspicuous attempt at reform comes from a genuine son of the people, one of the very few countrymen who at this time succeeded in reaching highest office in Rome. In the wretchedly mismanaged Jugurthan war Gaius Marius shouldered his way to the front by sheer courage and capacity for war through a crowd of incompetent aristocrats, who almost openly trafficked with the foreign enemy of Rome. The course of this business requires a brief sketch if we are to understand the condition of Roman government at this period.

The king of the client state of Numidia dying in 118 B.C. divided his realm between two legitimate sons and an adopted one, his nephew Jugurtha. The latter straightway murdered one of his brothers and attacked the other, who fled to the Roman province and appealed to the senate for protection. Jugurtha, already knowing the ropes of senatorial policy, sent envoys with well-filled purses and easily convinced the senate of his innocence and good intentions. The senate decided to send out a commission to divide the kingdom equitably between Jugurtha and his brother. The result of its labours was that Adherbal received the urban part and the capital (Cirta), Jugurtha got the militarily important part of the country, and the commission returned home rich and happy. Jugurtha had now only to obtain the capital, but, as Adherbal refused to fight and kept appealing to Rome, there was nothing for Jugurtha to do but besiege Cirta. More Roman envoys came to him from the senate in the course of the siege, but he easily assured them of his pacific intentions. As soon as he had taken the city, he put his rival to death with torture and massacred the entire male population, including a great number of Italian merchants (112 B.C.).

The senate did not feel that this course of action was entirely meritorious, but it required the stimulus of a democratic agitation and another troublesome tribune to induce them to declare war. The senate sent out two of its best men in Bestia and Scaurus; the latter especially was generally reputed to be a veritable Aristides, for he had ventured to protest against the former iniquities. When the Roman army arrived, Jugurtha knew better ways than fighting. He submitted at discretion, surrendered the Roman deserters, whom of course he did not want to keep, and a few elephants, which he soon afterwards repurchased privately. In return he was permitted to retain his kingdom. Once more there were outcries at Rome, voiced by the same democratic tribune Memmius, who insisted that Jugurtha should be summoned to Rome under a pledge of safe conduct to answer for his sins. Meekly, but with bulging money-bags, Jugurtha arrived. As soon as Memmius began to cross-examine him another tribune interposed his veto. During his visit Jugurtha was able to purchase strong support in the senate; he also had time to procure the assassination of an obnoxious fellow-countryman in the city itself. This outrage, combined with the ambition of the new consul, Spurius Albinus, led to the renewal of war, Jugurtha himself being allowed to go home and prepare for it. As he departed he uttered the famous words, "Ah, Rome! Venal city! She will soon fall if she finds a purchaser".

When Albinus led out the second army, he failed to get to grips with the enemy. His brother, who conceived the spirited project of seizing the king's treasury for himself, instead of waiting for the more tedious and uncertain profits of bribery, led the Roman army into an ambush. It surrendered readily. It was forced to go under the yoke and evacuate all Numidia.

This was a little too much. Another tribune—in all this period we observe the tribunes acting as the heads of popular opposition quite in the Gracchan manner—proposed a special inquiry to investigate the matter, and bring the offenders to justice. Three of the worst—Spurius Albinus, Bestia, and L. Opimius, the destroyer of C. Gracchus—were banished, but the incorruptible Scaurus escaped condemnation by sitting on the bench. The treaty of peace was cancelled.

In the third campaign the senate really tried to do its best. Q. Metellus, the new general, belonged to the party of liberal nobles who were in favour of moderate reform. He raised fresh troops and had competent soldiers on his staff, including Gaius Marius and Rutilius Rufus. Arrived in Africa, Metellus had first to reduce the Roman army to order, and then, having failed to get his enemy assassinated, marched out to fight him. Jugurtha was beaten in battle (for the Roman army could still fight under decent leadership), and henceforth was driven to guerrilla warfare, in which he displayed such remarkable skill that the war soon came to a standstill.

At this point Marius, who had achieved popularity and renown through his valour, conceived the hope of winning the consulship. Success would be an unusual achievement for one who was not a noble by birth. Marius came from the hill-town of Arpinum and his sterling independent qualities had advanced him as far as the praetorship, but the consulship was normally barred to those who were not members of a noble's family. When he asked his consul for permission to go to Rome for the purpose, Metellus insultingly suggested that Marius had better wait until his general's son was old enough to stand for the consulship, in order that he might have a Metellus for a colleague. Marius, however, ultimately gained his way, went to Rome and by popular appeal won the consulship for 107 B.C. Moreover, a special decree of the people entrusted him with command of the army in Africa.

Marius undoubtedly displayed vigour and competence and gradually wore down Jugurtha's strength, but it was very largely the luck and diplomacy of his quaestor, L. Cornelius Sulla, that procured the seizure and surrender of the Numidian king. Marius, however, reaped the glory. Jugurtha graced his triumph (104 B.C.), and soon afterwards perished in a Roman dungeon.

Simultaneously with the Jugurthan war the Romans were called upon to face a far more serious affair, one of those great folk-wanderings from the north which occur periodically in the course of Mediterranean history. The Cimbri and Teutons, who may have numbered ancestors of our own among them, came down from the shores of the Baltic, travelling with their households in a train of waggons which took six days in defiling past the onlooker. These barbarians were terrible to the Romans, with their strange aspect, their long iron swords and savage war-cries, their fair hair and giant stature. But of course they were savages compared to the Romans, and they should never have inflicted more than one defeat on intelligent generals of disciplined armies. As it was, they faced undisciplined legions and incompetent consuls. First they defeated Carbo in the Tyrol; then passing north of the Alps, they entered Gaul, picking up recruits and allies on the way. In 109 B.C., turning south, they beat the consul Silanus in the Rhone valley. Then, united with the Helvetians, they inflicted a frightful disaster on Longinus; the surviving Romans were forced to surrender and pass under the yoke. In 105 a worse thing happened : the great defeat of Arausio (Orange) seemed more grievous even than Cannae in the extent of its losses; 80,000 fighting men are said to have perished. There was a panic in Italy, which seemed helplessly exposed to the fury of the northmen, but fortunately the aimless barbarians wandered off into the west and spent their strength on the warlike Spanish tribes.

As before, popular indignation at Rome, diverted from the real cause of the mischief, the rotten system of cliques which governed them, wasted its fury on individuals. Senators were mobbed and stoned. A proconsul was actually deposed from office. There was only one man deemed capable of dealing with the peril—Marius, the man of the people, the triumphant conqueror of Jugurtha. So, despite laws forbidding re-election, Marius became consul for a second time in 104 and again each year until 100. This was symptomatic of a changed Rome. It was, however, necessary. Amateur generals had had a long trial. From 104 to 100 Marius was continuously chief magistrate of the state as well as generalissimo of its armies. He did his work. First he had to get his army in hand, and accustom them to the sight of the terrible barbarians. Then he dealt two smashing blows at the Teutons near Aquae Sextiae (Aix-en-Provence) and on the Cimbri at the Raudine Plain in the Po valley. It was the misfortune of the Roman system of *imperium* that no general could attain to eminence in war without at the same time acquiring political importance. Hence Marius in 100 B.C. found himself absolutely first in the Roman state without education or even commonsense in politics. He presents a pathetic figure in the turbulent world of Roman statecraft, a war-scarred veteran, the indubitable saviour of Rome, called upon to play the part of a statesman, and yet a mere puppet in the hands of unscrupulous intriguers. First he fell into the hands of two shameless demagogues, Saturninus and Glaucia. Marius became consul for the sixth time, and a new reform programme

was drawn up, including an agrarian law to divide land conquered from the Cimbri into small holdings for the Marian
veterans. New colonies also were to be founded in Africa, Corsica,
Sicily and Macedonia, and the Italian allies were to have a share
in them. Further, there was to be a still further cheapening of
corn. Of course, there was violent opposition. The senate tried all
its old stratagems, tribunician veto, portents, and lastly bludgeons.
To meet the latter, Marius whistled his veteran soldiers to his
side, and the "Appuleian Laws" were carried, with the addition
of a very obnoxious clause that each senator was to take an oath
of allegiance to the new legislation within five days on pain of
forfeiting his seat. Q. Metellus alone had the courage to prefer
exile.

Then, it seems, the senate found it necessary to beguile the great
general over to the side of aristocracy. Marius was a child in their
hands. He boggled at taking the oath to Saturninus' legislation,
and added the remarkable proviso, "So far as it is valid". Saturninus and Glaucia in their turn tried violence, a former tribune
was assassinated, and Marius led the forces of the senate against
them. After a battle in the forum, the demagogues were slain.
Once more reaction had triumphed. For the time being Marius
was politically defunct.

But one side of his work was lasting and fraught with momentous
consequences for the Roman state. It was Marius, the first professional general, who laid the foundation of the professional army.
We noticed that Greece, even before the end of the fifth century,
had already begun to use paid and trained soldiers, partly owing
to the unwillingness of her comfortable or busy citizens to engage
in annual campaigns, but still more because it was found that the
more highly trained and better disciplined mercenaries were far
more efficient at their business. So for many centuries Rome had
now been the only power in the Mediterranean world to rely upon
a citizen militia. That citizen militia had indeed conquered the
world; but certainly in dealing with the trained troops of Pyrrhus
and Hannibal, the Roman forces had always begun with disaster
and slowly been schooled to their trade by defeat. So it was now
in the Jugurthan and Cimbric wars: the generals had to train
their armies in the face of the enemy, and while that is no doubt
the best training-ground it is terribly dangerous and expensive. It
implies, too, an almost inexhaustible stock of recruits to fall back

upon. With the decline of Italian agriculture and the growth of city life the stock of recruits was no longer inexhaustible. Moreover the art of war was becoming more intricate. Rome found it necessary to appoint a genuine soldier for her general against Jugurtha in view of the disastrous failures of aristocratic amateurs. In the same way Marius found it necessary to overhaul the Roman fighting machine, and by the end of his five years of successive consulship he had organised a semi-professional army. The principal change instituted by Marius seemed at first a small one and required no legislative sanction. Hitherto the army had consisted theoretically only of the propertied classes, the infantry of those who could afford a suit of arms, and the cavalry of the richest citizens who could maintain one of the state horses. The minimum property for a Roman soldier is said to have been 1100 *denarii*. The poorest had originally formed a light-armed support, the three middle classes were the line, and the richest the cavalry. But the three classes of the line had by now come to be drawn up not according to property but according to length of service in three lines, the youngest in front, the middle-aged in support, and the older men in reserve. But social changes were changing the army. As wealth increased and the gulf between rich and poor grew wider, the comfortable burgesses were no longer obedient or willing soldiers. Bad discipline—a monstrous violation of the old Roman spirit—had begun to appear in the ranks as early as the Macedonian wars. In the Jugurthan wars it was deplorably rife. The equestrian class, as the richest, was also the most mutinous: as early as the third century the knights had refused to work in the field alongside of the legionaries. By 140 B.C. they had ceased to act as a military force and become merely a grade of honour, or rather of income, in the state, though the younger knights continued to form a corps of noble guards to the general. As for the army as a whole, the theory down to the time of Marius was still that of the annual spring campaign; each consul levied his own army for a specific purpose. This levy had become more and more difficult. The simple innovation which Marius introduced was that in the process of holding his levy he began by asking for volunteers and enrolling those first, without inquiring whether they possessed the old property qualification. There was generally a distinct promise of rewards and booty. Thus, instead of the moneyed classes, Marius filled his ranks with the poorest and hardiest inhabitants of Rome and Italy. The auxiliary ranks were now supplied by foreign experts—cavalry from the Numidian deserts, slingers from the Balearic Islands or the Ligurian hills, and presently archers from Crete. Having thus professionalised his army Marius proceeded to abolish all distinctions in the ranks. All the men of the line now had a uniform equipment supplied by the state, and instead of a bewildering variety of insignia all the legionaries now fought under that emblem destined to be carried in victory to the four corners of Europe—the silver eagle. The eagle was the standard of the legion and it was regarded as sacred. In camp it rested in a special shrine and terrible was the disgrace attaching to its loss in battle. Now a legion became a fixed unit of 6000 men; for while the maniple, or double-company of two centuries, each of 100 men, still remained, the maniples were grouped into cohorts or battalions, which now became the regular tactical unit, and ten cohorts formed the legion. Moreover, while it was not until Augustus that the legions were formally established as permanent standing units, yet in the almost continuous wars of the last century of the Republic a state of permanency was practically if not legally attained. The mere fact that the army now contained less of the respectable citizen element anxious to be demobilised and to return to family and business, and more of those who saw in military service their one chance of livelihood or fortune, made it now easy to hold formations together from year to year, and thus regimental tradition and *esprit de corps* were fostered.

Beside the body-armour consisting of helmet, cuirass, and cylindrical shield, the uniform equipment of the legionary included the pilum,* a heavy javelin seven feet long for throwing at close quarters, composed of a long iron point in a wooden shaft; it is interesting to note that Marius invented an improved form, in which the point was fastened to the shaft by two rivets, one of iron on one side, on the other one of wood; this broke on impact, leaving the point swinging loose so that an enemy could not pick it out and hurl it back. Julius Cæsar improved further on this by making all the point except the head of soft iron, which would bend. It is recorded that in his Gaulish battles the enemy were compelled to cast away their shields because they could not detach

* The origin of the pilum is doubtful; most probably it was borrowed ırom the Samnites.

the pila lodged in them. There was also a broad-bladed sword which had been copied from the Spanish swordsmen in the Second Punic War. The latter was a very handy little weapon only about twenty-four inches long including the hilt, with two edges as well as a point, though the thrust was always advocated in preference to the cut. Marius now introduced a new drill which included lessons in fencing given in the first instance by masters from the gladiatorial schools. It must be repeated that the Roman maniple, unlike the close Greek phalanx, stood in open order with a six-foot square of space for each man so that there was room for individual prowess in swordsmanship. Lastly, Marius still further professionalised his army by introducing a system of bounties on discharge which made the army a really attractive career for poor citizens. He promised them each a farm at the end of the war and his example was followed by other generals. In fact a veteran soldier came to expect a handsome pension on retirement.

It is surely unnecessary to emphasise the meaning of all this. An army was now a trained corps against which no levy of recruits could stand for an instant. Hitherto it had been the chief guarantee against usurpation by a general that new armies could be summoned from the soil at any time. Now there was a weapon in the hands of a successful general against which the feeble safeguards of the republican constitution were powerless. As with the first trained army in English history, the general of such a force became master of the destinies of the state so long as the allegiance of the soldiers was personal rather than patriotic. The Roman soldier's allegiance had always been personal and now it became more so. Hence that day in 100 B.C. when the Appuleian code was carried under threat of the legions of Marius was of evil omen for the constitution. Less than twenty years were to elapse before a Roman army entered Rome in triumph to support the political enactments of Sulla. It was in reality henceforward one long state of civil war, open or concealed, between rival generals, until at last a permanent military monarchy was established. It only required a bold free spirit like that of Julius Cæsar to discern the real facts of the case. Marius, as we have already seen, had not sufficient intellect to play a political part with success; Sulla attained what was really a monarchical position but retired when he had won it. Pompeius never had the courage to face the situation. Cæsar had, but he was sacrificed to the republican tradition.

Finally the diplomatic Augustus realised the long inevitable fact.

Henceforth, then, it is merely a question of who shall be Emperor of Rome. The causes of the end of Rome's incoherent constitutional system, called by us a Republic, are already clear. There are the constitutional causes—above all the inelasticity of the Roman system, which made legitimate reform impossible, provided little machinery to express the will of the people, and rendered it inevitable that rioting should accompany every change. It was a constitution essentially municipal and the tribunate was the centre of mischief. Then there are the economic causes, now working more banefully than ever, and causing the decay of the agricultural population, the rise of a dangerous uneducated city proletariat, and the corruption of the governing aristocracy. There was the political fact that the government of a vast ill-organised empire destroyed the republican spirit and further increased corruption, while it denationalised the Roman temper. Further, there is the fact that Rome failed to create an adequate civil service to administer her empire. Lastly, there is the military cause, namely, the professionalisation of the army, putting excessive power into the hands of the general and replacing patriotism by *esprit de corps*. A provincial governor who enjoyed the personal loyalty of his troops might be driven by ambition to challenge the central government.

It strikes the onlooker that not one of these evils, nor even the accumulation of them, need have been fatal to the republican system if there had been a genuine spirit of patriotic enthusiasm determined to overcome them. For instance, if the great men of Rome had been loyal and patriotic, there is no reason why the excessive power of the generals should have led to high treason. And again, though the provincial system was misbegotten, it might have been corrected and reformed. But it was the spirit that failed. Was not that just because Roman power had outstripped Roman civilisation? For the upper-class Roman, faith was dead or dying, and there were no high interests of the mind to replace it. The last agony of the Republic in the period we are now considering is painful enough; but some may regard it as the period in which a new and much more hopeful order of things was gradually evolved.

SULLA

On the political eclipse of Marius there arose Sulla. Sulla was the aristocrat of talent, almost of genius, who tried to save the state by reaction. He tried, vainly and foolishly enough, to bolster up the rickety structure of senatorial ascendancy, but had not the patience or the wisdom to attempt even that with sufficient thoroughness. L. Cornelius Sulla was of the class of men to which Alcibiades and Alexander belong, but an inferior specimen of the class. Though of noble birth, he had risen from poverty and obscurity by his own talents. He was clever—and he did the most foolish acts in history. He was handsome—and his face in later life is described as "a mulberry speckled with meal". He was brave and successful in war; half lion and half fox, they said, and the fox was the more dangerous of the two. He secured the affections of his soldiers by giving them free licence to plunder or to murder unpopular officers. He was a rake and a gambler, reckless of bloodshed as he was careless of praise or blame, and he had that fatal belief in a star which has led better men than he to follow will-o'-the-wisps. He might have stood where Cæsar stands. He would have made a bad emperor, and whatever it was that made him decline to be one, it was not patriotism. He was as cultured as Nero, and showed it by sacking Athens, plundering Delphi, and looting a famous library. Like Nero, but unlike the majority of his fellow-countrymen, he had a sense of humour.

After the shelving of Marius and the destruction of his democratic associates the governing clique pursued its old course of headlong folly. For one thing the aristocrats soon fell out with the capitalists, which is always an unwise thing for aristocrats to do. The equestrian jury-courts established by Gracchus acted with brutal simplicity on behalf of their tax-gathering and tax-farming brothers against whatever honest governors proceeded from the senate. Men were condemned for honest administration in those days. For another thing the bitter cry of the Italian "allies" who fought alongside the Romans, and in return received increasingly harsh treatment, was persistently and contemptuously ignored. In 95 a consular law expelled them from the city so that they could not by their presence exercise any influence on the government. But presently there came forward a new reformer in M. Livius Drusus. This remarkable man might be described

as a third Gracchus, only that he saw the futility of the so-called
democracy of Rome, and adopted other means to attain his ends.
On the one hand he was a champion of the senate against the
knights, and on the other hand he was resolved to give their rights
to the Italians, who were forming a widespread secret organisation.
He then proposed four measures: the inevitable vote-catching
corn law and land-distributing measures, the jury-courts to be
restored to the senate, the senate for that purpose to be enlarged
by the inclusion of three hundred knights, and, lastly, citizenship
for the allies. The first three were carried, not without violence,
but the fourth was his stumbling-block. The Italians were by now
so clamorous that civil war was inevitable if it were refused, and
no man denied the justice of their claim. But neither justice nor
expediency had any power to move the deadweight of senatorial
conservatism. Drusus was murdered and his laws repealed. That
was the signal for the long and terrible Social War which completed the ruin of Italy and caused grave alarm for the very existence of Rome herself. In the course of this grim struggle in which
she ultimately got the upper hand, Rome conceded in fact the
prize for which the Italians were fighting. By laws passed in 90
and 89 some states received the franchise as a reward for fidelity
and others as a bait for submission. Thus at long last the whole
population of Italy became Roman citizens, but to secure this
belated concession the face of Italy had been covered with mourn-
ing. Even so the governing clique succeeded in nullifying the
political value of the concession for a few years by confining the
Italians to a few of the tribes, so that their votes were almost
useless.

The pressure of this war and of the great Mithridatic war
which began simultaneously in Asia led to a serious economic
crisis at Rome. Debt and usury were the symptoms, and in 89,
when a praetor named Asellio tried to meet it by reviving the old
laws against usury he was murdered in his priestly robes at sacrifice. Now we begin to hear the ominous cry of "Nouae tabulae"—
the clean slate for debtors. A popular orator named Sulpicius
Rufus, whose programme included the removal of all bankrupts
from the senate, and the distribution of the new citizens and freedmen through all the thirty-five tribes, is alleged to have protected
his valuable person with a bodyguard of 3000 hired roughs and
600 young knights. Then, since Sulla with his army threatened

opposition, he passed a decree giving the command of the great army destined to fight Mithridates to the old Marius. During the Social War both these generals had held command with some success, but on the whole the reputation of Marius had declined while that of Sulla had increased. Without hesitation Sulla now marched his army into Rome, and won a battle in the streets of the city. Sulpicius was of course executed, his head was nailed to the rostra, but Marius escaped under circumstances of romantic adventure. Sulla was thus in the year 88 completely master of Rome.

At this moment his real ambition was for more fighting. Mithridates, King of Pontus, was then in full career of rebellion against the Roman dominion in Asia, where 80,000 Roman and Italian traders and money-lenders were murdered in a sudden conspiracy. Sulla saw in Mithridates a worthy foeman, and much preferred glory on the fields of Asia to Roman politics; and besides, his army was clamouring for plunder. So he hastily flung out a series of constitutional reforms designed to restore the senate to its ancient predominance, and then set out for the East, heedless or ignorant of the fact that he had not really changed anything. On the contrary he had left in sole charge at Rome the new consul, Cinna, the most dangerous of all the demagogues. Sulla can hardly have fancied that an oath to obey his constitution would restrain such a man at such a time.

Consequently, as soon as his back was turned, a fresh revolution broke out. Cinna also brought an army to Rome and invited Marius to return. Then the old general, furious with all his disappointments, began a fearful debauch of bloodshed. Every distinguished senator left in Rome, including statesmen like L. Caesar, soldiers like Catulus, orators like Antonius and Crassus, were butchered by his slaves and their heads displayed in the forum. In 86 Marius gained the goal of his ambition, that seventh consulship which had been promised him long ago by a prophetess. In the same year he died. Now for three years Cinna ruled as virtual monarch at Rome. Each year he assumed the consulship and nominated his colleagues at his own choice. The laws of Sulla were repealed and bankrupts relieved by a bill which reduced all debts by 75 per cent., a measure which is truly typical of Roman democracy. More commendable was an act which completed the enfranchisement of the Italians by distributing them equally

among the "tribes" into which the Roman electorate was divided
for voting purposes, so that all free Italians were now equal members of the Roman state. Meanwhile, of course, the reckoning was
in preparation across the seas. Sulla was winning glorious victories
in Greece and Asia, and at length in 84 drove Mithridates to
surrender temporarily. Cinna, who does not seem to have understood that a Roman army belonged not to the republic but to its
general, audaciously set out to fight Sulla, but was murdered by
his troops.

Sulla, having offered terms which the government very foolishly
declined, came home in 83 after five years' absence bearing not
peace but a sword. He had five veteran legions of his own, the
exiled aristocrats joined him, and among them a young man
called Pompeius raised three legions in Picenum. The lead of the
popular party had now fallen into the hands of a young Marius,
and he, lacking troops to oppose the returning veterans, decided to
join the Samnite rebels who remained unconquered from the
Social War. Before leaving the city young Marius and his associates ordered a final and still more bloody massacre of the surviving aristocrats; practically all the men of distinction left in the
city suffered death. There was bitter fighting up and down Italy
all through the year 82, terminating in a pitched battle at the
Colline Gate of Rome, in which after a desperate struggle the
Sullans were victorious. The young Marius committed suicide.
Thus Sulla was once more master of Rome. His 4000 Samnite
prisoners were slaughtered in the Circus. Of his political opponents
at Rome, 80 senators, 1600 equites, and over 2000 private citizens
were proscribed, and their heads nailed up in the forum. Sertorius, an old officer of Marius who had withdrawn to Spain,
maintained a gallant struggle there for some years by the aid of a
native Spanish army trained on the Roman model, but although
he defeated Sulla's colleague Metellus and then fought successfully against Pompey, at last he fell by treachery.

For two years Sulla was monarch at Rome. For the purpose he
invented a sort of revival of the obsolete dictatorship, without
limit of time. If we care for the term, Sulla was at that time as
much "Emperor" as Augustus was fifty years later. He enacted
a whole constitution of his own—which it is scarcely necessary
to recount since scarcely anything of it survived—all designed
to put the senate on its throne again—and then simply abdicated

and retired into private life. I think he was bored with Rome and politics. It is generally admitted that he had a sense of humour. It may have been a very foolish thing to do. But Sulla's star was with him and he died in his bed. His dying moments were comforted by the apparition of his deceased wife (he had had five) and son, who invited him to join them in the land of peace and bliss beyond the grave.

Sulla was hardly dead before another consul, Lepidus, marched against Rome with his army and suffered defeat outside the city. But these were mere episodes. Before many years had passed, the streets of the sacred city were in an intermittent state of war: every serious politician had to organise his gang of roughs, and when later the very senate-house was burnt down in one such riot it only seemed an excessive display of political zeal. Of constitutional government there was little pretence. The seas were swarming with pirates, no longer isolated rovers who preyed upon commerce, but an organised pirate-state with headquarters in Cilicia, and a great fleet consisting of all the broken men and desperate outlaws of the unhappy Mediterranean world. They sailed the high seas in fleets under admirals who voyaged in state like princes. For their homes they had impregnable citadels among the creeks of the Cilician and Dalmatian coasts where they stored their families and their plunder. They were not afraid to march inland to sack a city or loot a rich temple. Commerce at sea was ruined; even the food-supply of the capital was occasionally threatened. On land and even in Italy things were not much better. We hear of risings among the slaves of Italy, not for the first time. Under the plantation system, the inaccessible Apennine highlands were swarming with desperate runaways who constantly committed minor acts of brigandage. In 73 they found a leader in Spartacus, the gladiator who was said to be of royal descent in Thrace. Starting as a mere handful the band swelled in the course of a few months to 40,000. Roman armies one after another and ten in all marched against them in vain. Two consuls were defeated, many legionary eagles were captured, Italy was at their mercy. Respectable towns like Thurii and Nola were seized, their prisoners were crucified like slaves or forced with grim irony to fight one another to the death like gladiators. Thus the most frightful form of civil war was devastating Italy. It was necessary to raise an army of eight legions to crush the slaves, and the command was entrusted to Marcus Crassus, who even then had to decimate a legion before he could get his cowardly troops to stand and fight. After several stubborn battles, and aided by the want of discipline which was even more conspicuous among the slaves than among the Romans, Crassus accomplished his task. Six thousand crucified slaves who lined the road from Capua to Rome testified to the restoration of order.

Abroad matters were little better. War against Mithridates, which had provided so many Roman triumphs and had so often been proclaimed at an end, broke out again, and its duration was due rather to the ineptitude of the government than to the prowess of the unmilitary Asiatics. In Spain it took ten years to defeat Sertorius with his native troops, and even then the result was only accomplished by assassination. If a Hannibal had entered Italy in these later days the state could not have survived. But there was only one military power of any consequence left in the world in those days, the Parthians. Here there were half-hellenised despots ruling over tribes of warriors only lately descended from the steppes of Central Asia and from the Armenian highlands, and still nursing a fierce mountain spirit though they occupied the rich plains of Mesopotamia. Crassus, the victor over the slaves, many years later was sent to fight them with a great army but the millionaire displayed wretched ignorance of strategy and especially of the perils of Eastern warfare. He blundered on into the wilderness and tried to meet the terrible mounted bowmen and mail-clad lancers of the East with his legions in a hollow square. The result was the great disaster of Carrhæ in 53, a defeat which amid all the shameful ignominies of this period rankled continually owing to the loss of the eagles and the tragic fate of the leader. Marcus Crassus himself was an almost wholly repulsive character, who had amassed a fortune, colossal even in those days of millionaires, by the most discreditable method. The foundations of his millions had been laid by speculating in the property of the victims of Sulla's proscriptions. He had been a slave-trainer on a large scale and at one time he had organised a private fire-brigade which he used for acquiring house-property cheaply in the midst of city fires. By lending money to the young spendthrifts of the aristocracy he obtained great influence at Rome, and indeed figures in the wretched politics of his day as a statesman on an equality with really great men like Cæsar and Pompeius. But he had no policy and was only of importance through his wealth and influence.

POMPEIUS AND CÆSAR

So we come to the final phase of the Republic—the great struggle between the giants Cæsar and Pompeius, with figures like Cicero, Cato, and Clodius in the background. I do not propose to linger over this period, because on the one hand it is so thoroughly well known as the period of fullest evidence in all Roman history, and therefore would require a volume for adequate treatment, and on the other hand because it has been such a battle-ground for partisan historians of all times that it is difficult in such a summary as this to do justice without detailed argument.

Gnaeus Pompeius Magnus* had first come into prominence as a supporter of Sulla. Son of the consul of 89 B.C., he was a born soldier. That is really the secret of his career. Like Marius he was a general and no statesman, but he was a very great general, and one of the few honest men, one might almost say one of the few gentlemen, of his period. The tragedy of his life was to be born in such a period. He had disdained the minor offices of state, and relying on his military renown and the army which he brought back from Spain but in defiance of the law, he stood for the consulship of 70 B.C. As the official aristocracy objected, he went over to the popular party and allied himself with Crassus. These two, elected under threat of Pompeius' army, straightway repealed most of the Sullan constitution and restored the balance of power to the knights and the assembly. At the end of the year Pompeius retired into private life. This was characteristic of him; he was capable of grandiose schemes but he lived in fear of public opinion, and he was really moved when orators spoke of illegality. Meanwhile there was a loud demand for some comprehensive scheme of attack upon the pirates. No ordinary consular command would do. Accordingly a Gabinian Law of 67 gave to Pompeius a command of unprecedented magnitude. Millions of money were voted to him, he was to be supreme over all the seas for three years, with a staff of twenty-four legates, and his authority was equal to that of all the provincial governors in this area for fifty miles

* Plate 24.

inland. The price of corn fell at once, on the mere announcement of his appointment. Then he began a systematic drive of the seas, and in about three months had cleared them. Thousands of pirates were caught and many of them were set up by Pompius as honest traders or peasants in Cilicia and elsewhere. All this made Pompeius the most powerful and potentially the most dangerous man in Rome.

Next the tribune Manilius, in whose support that rising *nouus homo* the friend of our youth, Marcus Tullius Cicero, pronounced an oration, proposed for Pompeius another huge commission against Mithridates, the irrepressible rebel of Asia. Pompeius succeeded, following up the work of his predecessors from Sulla to Lucullus, and the wicked old king was driven to suicide. Then Pompeius proceeded to organise the East like an Alexander, but always in perfect loyalty to Rome. He reorganised the eastern provinces, adding Syria to their number, established relations with many of the native rulers, who became client-kings of Rome, and founded many new cities with Greek institutions. Thus the Hellenistic East, which Mithridates had tried to lead in war against Rome, now became contented with the new regime.

While Pompeius was absent, the popular party, which mostly consisted of hired ruffians in the pay of discontented nobles, ruled the streets of the city. Among the young nobles who took this side was one more dissolute and more foppish than the rest, a notorious adulterer and spend-thrift, Gaius Julius Cæsar (born *c.* 100 B.C.) Though of the highest birth—the goddess Venus by her union with the father of Aeneas was counted among his ancestors—he was also by lineage associated with the popular party. His aunt was the wife of Marius, and his wife was a daughter of Cinna. When Julia the widow of Marius died in 68 B.C. young Cæsar in the funeral oration had stressed his connection with Marius as well as the glorious origins of the Julian *gens*. This, as was intended, set all the gossips talking, and his amazing extravagance kept him well in the public eye. In 63 B.C. he became *pontifex maximus*. On one occasion he exhibited three hundred gladiators in silver armour, although he was known to be penniless. Probably Crassus was his financier all along.

At this time there was another of the frequently recurring financial crises at Rome. Everybody was deeply in debt, and loud rose the cry for the clean slate, as part of the popular programme —the only intelligible part. This was the cause of the famous conspiracy of Catiline, who, if Cicero may be trusted, proposed to seize and burn Rome by the aid of the discontented veterans whom Sulla had set up as colonists in Etruria. Both Cæsar and Crassus were alleged by their enemies to have favoured the plot, but it is exceedingly difficult to see what a large owner of Roman house property had to gain by it. Cicero was consul for the year 63, and, though it is the fashion just now to sneer at Cicero, he seems to have displayed courage and promptitude in dealing with the conspirators. Unfortunately his execution of the Catilinarians was technically illegal. Cicero himself, as a *parvenu*, was naturally a supporter of the aristocrats, and his policy, though futile, was intelligible. Briefly, it was to unite the senate with the capitalist class (the *equites*) in what he called the "union of the orders" against the elements of disorder. Pompeius came home from the East to find the conspiracy crushed. He and his legions were not wanted. With incredible folly and ingratitude the senate refused even to grant the lands he had promised to his veterans.

Cæsar had gone as praetor to Spain, and there began to win military renown—much to the surprise of his friends—and money. He wanted the consulship for the next year, and therefore required the support of Pompeius, who had now been driven away from the aristocratic party to which he belonged by sympathy. Crassus came in as Cæsar's creditor and as the necessary millionaire. These three men therefore decided to co-operate and make an informal alliance, the so-called First Triumvirate of 60 B.C. As a result of this political backing Cæsar won the consulship for 59. By this time he had conceived high, possibly the highest, ambitions. Marius and Sulla, not to mention Alexander and Aeneas, had always been much in his mind. For the present his object was to acquire a lasting office and secure the allegiance of a trained army. Cæsar's colleague in the consulship was a certain Bibulus, who tried to stop the dangerous proceedings of his colleague by seeing bad omens in the heavens every day, but no one, least of all Cæsar, took any notice of him. The only serious opposition came from Cato the Younger, who represented the genuine and respectable aristocracy. This Cato was a queer anachronism at Rome, an honest man. He was also, if biography may be trusted, a bigot and a priggish eccentric. He was the sort of man to go about Africa without a hat, or to sit on the judicial bench without shoes, because such was the *mos maiorum*. He tried to revive the ways which had been styled old-fashioned in his great-grandfather. Nevertheless he was upright and brave, a good soldier, and a man with a clear though impossible policy. Once again it is the fault of rhetorical history that all the good men of Rome appear as prigs and eccentrics. This man most courageously opposed his veto to the proceedings of Cæsar, though he was hustled and beaten by the democratic hirelings, then organised under that most notorious scoundrel Clodius. But the result was that, though Cæsar's laws might pass, they could afterwards be declared illegal, and Cæsar would be liable to prosecution as soon as he became a private citizen. However, he had no immediate intention of becoming a private citizen. He secured the province of Gaul for five years with four legions.

Now Gaul was not reckoned an important province. It was only the peaceful plain of Upper Italy to which the senate had added Narbonensian Gaul, a southern strip of France, chiefly considered as a step on the road to Spain. Four legions was a small consular army for those days; no one supposed that he would have much fighting. But either Cæsar had received secret intelligence or else he had very good luck. At the outset he was called to deal with a great immigration of the barbarian Helvetii, who were migrating out of Switzerland into Gaul and threatening the province.

The conservatives at Rome maintained that Cæsar's conquests in Gaul were the result of wanton aggression—cheap victories over inoffensive savages, wholly unjustifiable and unauthorised. At this point it is scarcely possible to avoid entering upon the much-debated question of Cæsar's real character. For orthodox Romans Cæsar was the founder of the Empire, a person not only of divine descent, but himself divine. All emperors took his name, until that surname of Cæsar, once a mere nickname, came, in half the languages of Europe, to be synonymous with "Emperor". For the Middle Ages he stood with Constantine, who christianised the Empire, and Charlemagne, who revived it, as the founder of that divinely instituted polity which shared with the Church God's viceregency on earth. In the eyes of Dante, Cæsar stood very near to Christ, for the poet peoples the frozen heart of his Inferno with three tormented figures who writhe in the very jaws of

Cocytus. Along with Judas Iscariot are the two murderers of Julius Cæsar. Though the Renaissance stripped him of much of his legendary greatness, Cæsar remained for the men of Shakespeare's day the embodiment of imperial pride. Shakespeare himself was too great an artist to make any of his characters more or less than human, but it is evidently Brutus who has the sympathies of the dramatist. In the French Revolution, again, Brutus and Cassius were heroes and glorious tyrannicides. The reaction against early nineteenth-century liberalism brought Cæsar once more into honour, and Mommsen, the prophet of Cæsarism, makes him the hero of his great history. To Mommsen Cæsar was almost divine, the clear-sighted and magnanimous "saviour" who alone saw the true path out of the disorders of his city. From this view again reaction was bound to follow. To later critics the greatness of Cæsar, as delineated by Mommsen, appears abhorrent, and Ferrero depicted his most famous fellow-countryman as an unscrupulous demagogue who blundered into renown through treachery and bloodshed.

The historical principle by which this result is attained is rather typical of certain modern critical methods. Since the account of the Gallic Wars was written chiefly by Cæsar himself, and Cæsar is by hypothesis a scoundrel, the history of these wars must be found by reading between the lines of Cæsar's account, putting the most unfavourable construction upon everything and preferring any evidence to his, even if it be that of two centuries later. If any gaps or inconsistencies are noticed they must be treated as concealing defeats or acts of treachery. Written in this spirit, the story of the Gallic Wars is a very black one for Cæsar and Rome. Yet unbiased readers must generally admit that Cæsar was a very careful and on the whole an honest historian. The accusation that he was capable of relentless cruelty springs from his own admissions. It was in the Roman character to despise life, and when Cæsar thought that a rebellious tribe needed a lesson, he did not hesitate to massacre defenceless women and children or to lay waste miles of territory with fire and sword. But, on the other hand, his preference was for clemency and justice.

Without making him a demigod, we ought to be able to see his greatness. As a young man his ardour of soul, working in a debased society without ideals, made him simply more extravagant and more foppish than the spendthrifts and rakes who surrounded him. Doubtless the scandalous Suetonius has embellished the story of his early follies. Many of his youthful escapades were, one suspects, carefully designed to bring him into notice. It is probable that from a very early age he was ambitious, and his family connections clearly marked out his career as a popular leader. He had the failure of Sulla before his eyes. The greatness of his character lay chiefly in an instinctive hatred for muddle and pretence. He could not fail to see the hopeless confusion into which the Roman state had fallen. From the first, I think, he was aiming at power for himself in order to put things straight. Whether self or country came first in his calculations, it is hard, perhaps impossible to decide; but the historian is not necessarily a cynic when he demands strong proof of altruism in the world of politics. To obtain power the popular side was the only possible one, for the nobles stood for the predominance only of their class. Crassus was necessary to Cæsar as his banker and creditor until he had acquired a fortune for himself by conquest. Pompeius was the foremost soldier of the day, and it is probable that Cæsar deliberately sought to climb over the shoulders of Pompeius into monarchy. He saw—he could not help seeing, for it was written plainly in the history of the past century—that for power two things were necessary, the support of the mob in the forum and the backing of a veteran army. At the time when Cæsar gained Gaul for his province there was a fresh movement towards imperial expansion. Foreign conquest afforded some relief for the chagrins of internal politics. By it Marius, Sulla, and Pompeius had become powerful. If Cæsar wanted to eclipse them all, he must present Rome with a new province, the most powerful of all bribes. It was in this spirit that he set out for Gaul. If his ulterior motive was selfish it is certain that he threw himself heart and soul, with all the burning energy of which his tireless spirit was capable, into the work of conquest and civilisation.

And what a work it was! Archaeology has now shown that the so-called barbarians were by no means always savages. Even the "naked woad-stained" Britons had their arts and industries and political systems. The Gauls, when Cæsar attacked them, were well on the road to civilisation. Town-life was beginning, and there was even a coinage. Agriculture flourished and Italian merchants travelling along the roads and rivers brought up articles of luxury which the natives imitated. The Gallic pottery is by no means destitute of beauty and some of the Gallic bronze-work, inlaid with enamel, is justly famous. As soldiers the Gauls showed many of the qualities of their descendants, a devoted impetuosity in the charge, coupled with a lack of tenacity in resistance which always cost them dear. Much of Cæsar's success was due to his skill in dividing them against themselves, but many of his difficulties arose from their fickle disposition. Mommsen, like a true Bismarckian German, has a fanciful comparison of the ancient Gallic Celt with the modern Irishman. "On the eve", he says, "of parting from this remarkable nation, we may be allowed to call attention to the fact that in the accounts of the ancients as to the Celts on the Loire and the Seine we find almost every one of the characteristic traits which we are accustomed to recognise as marking the Irish. Every feature reappears : the laziness in the culture of the fields; the delight in tippling and brawling; the ostentation . . . the droll humour . . . the hearty delight in singing and reciting the deeds of past ages, and the most decided talent for rhetoric and poetry; the curiosity—no trader was allowed to pass before he had told in the open street what he knew, or did not know, in the shape of news—and the extravagant credulity which acted on such accounts . . . the child-like piety which sees in the priest a father and asks him for advice in all things" (this, by the way, was apparently a characteristic of the contemporary Germans also), "the unsurpassed fervour of national feeling, and the closeness with which those who are fellow-countrymen cling together almost like one family in opposition to the stranger; the inclination to rise in revolt under the first chance leader that presents himself, but at the same time the utter incapacity to preserve a self-reliant courage equally remote from presumption and pusillanimity, to perceive the right time for waiting and for striking, to obtain or even barely to tolerate any organisation, any sort of fixed military or political discipline. It is, and remains, at all times and places the same indolent and poetical, irresolute and fervid, inquisitive, credulous, amiable, clever, but—from a political point of view—thoroughly useless nation; and therefore its fate has been always and everywhere the same."

The internal politics of Gaul seem to have been marked by a division between two parties, one the conservative party of the aristocratic knights, the other a nationalist and popular faction. Cæsar used these divisions for the furtherance of his scheme of conquest. He was not only a consummate general with an instinct for strategy and organisation; but he was also a superb regimental officer in the making of soldiers. By the end of his ten years he had forged a small but invincible army devoted to his interests and entirely confident in his leadership. Personally, moreover, the Roman man-about-town was the best soldier in the army. Physically he was a stranger to weariness or fatigue. He could travel immense distances with incredible rapidity, alone on horse-back, or with a handful of followers. He seemed ubiquitous. In the battle, when his men wavered, he would leap down into the ranks, sword in hand, or snatch the standard from the hand of a cen-turion and fight among the foremost. No detail of fortification or commissariat escaped him, and he, more than any one else, showed the power of engineering in warfare. In the supreme battle against Pompeius he even carried his devotion to the spade beyond reasonable limits when he tried to circumvallate the much larger camp of his enemies. One of his most surprising exploits was when half Gaul, supposed to be pacified, rose in sudden revolt under Vercingetorix. With a much smaller army he chased the rebels into the fortress of Alesia, neglecting for the time all com-munication with his base, and fully aware that a still larger army would soon advance to the relief of the besieged. He therefore entrenched himself outside the gates of the city and kept off the relieving force with one hand while he continued the siege with the other. But while he was capable of brilliant strokes of audacity like this, he was also a cold and cautious organiser of victory, ready to meet his enemies on their own ground and with their own weapons.

In this great war, which ended in the conquest of Gaul, Cæsar's expeditions to Britain were mere episodes. They were summer raids, like his dash across the Rhine, intended for a warning to the barbarians of the hinterland; for it seems that communication to and fro across the channel was continuous. It is probable enough that the persuasions of the Roman traders who swarmed after the eagles across Gaul had their influence also. Undoubtedly the Romans of this generation were keenly alive to commercial openings, and always on the search for mineral wealth. Further, we cannot deny that Cæsar in all his undertakings had one eye upon his political position in Rome itself, and the "conquest of Britain" that almost legendary corner of the earth, concealed in boreal mists and embosomed in the ever-flowing Ocean river, would be a sensational achievement calculated to outshine the Oriental triumphs of Pompeius. One cannot but place among the extravagances of hero-worship Mommsen's belief that Cæsar had a prophetic insight into the true nature of the "German Peril" for Rome. When Cæsar took over the Gallic province there was no tremendous German menace.* There had always been occasional irruptions of the barbarians from across the Rhine, and a steady German penetration of the Netherlands. Cæsar lacked time to lay down any intelligible frontier policy: that was one of the achievements of Augustus. Both in Gaul and in Britain it was simply a forward movement by a general of bold and untiring resolution, backed by an invincible army. The two trips to Britain, like those across the Rhine, were reconnaissances only, and the conquest of the island was one of the legacies which Cæsar intended to reserve for the future. His successor very wisely declined it. There was little immediate profit there, and the Gallic conquests had glutted the Roman market with slaves.

Gaul had submitted easily to a force of less than forty thousand Romans; then it had revolted unsuccessfully. In the end the whole country acknowledged conquest and rapidly began to assimilate Latin civilisation. Meanwhile in the imperial city the Republic was slowly expiring by a natural death. Every winter Cæsar returned to the Cisalpine part of his province to receive intelligence from Rome and secure his position there. Clodius, the most evil of the mob-leaders, was his agent with the popular party. Clodius had managed to hound the respectable Cicero into exile (58) for his share in supressing Catiline, and when Cicero, who was really popular at Rome, had persuaded Pompeius to allow his return (57), the great orator remained thenceforward a timid and reluctant servant of the triumvirate, defending their friends or prosecuting their enemies, with inward reluctance, no doubt, but with unimpaired eloquence. With the astonishing victories in Gaul the star of Julius was rising in the political heavens. The commons

* There may have been no German menace to Rome, but there was to Gaul. The aggression of the German chieftain Ariovistus, combined with the movements of the Helvetii, may suggest that Caesar could reasonably represent his own earliest activities in Gaul as defensive. In view of the continued internal dissensions among the Gallic tribes, it is possible that either Romans or Germans would be drawn in. It was due to Caesar's achievements that the Rhine became the Roman frontier.—EDD

of Rome were not only dazzled by his successes but captivated by his largesses. Meanwhile Pompeius was living on his military reputation and slowly squandering it by his political incapacity. He continued to hold various high offices hitherto unprecendented : he received proconsular authority to manage the corn supply throughout the Roman world, with the right to appoint fifteen legates (from 57 B.C.); he held from 55 B.C. the province of Spain and governed it from Italy through legates; and in 52 he became sole consul. In fact there was scarcely anything in the future position of a Roman emperor which had not its precedent in the career of Pompeius. Had he wished it, or, more probably, had he known how to obtain it, he and not Augustus might easily have been the first Roman emperor. By taste and natural sympathies he was an aristocrat, but the force of circumstances had driven him into an uncomfortable position of alliance with Cæsar the popular leader and Crassus the plutocrat. This was in a large measure the secret of his political helplessness. He, the conqueror of the East, often found himself openly flouted, nay, actually hustled and threatened in the streets, by the organised roughs. Meanwhile there was a small but tenacious opposition party of aristocrats, who had no discipline and therefore no leaders, but among whom Cato and C. and M. Marcellus were the most conspicuous. They had not the strength to offer any consistent resistance to Cæsar's progress, which they watched with growing jealousy and alarm. They had not the sense to rally the respectable elements in the state to their side. Both Cicero and Pompeius would readily have joined them if they had made it possible. Instead of that, they were content to carp at Cæsar's achievements and threaten him with a prosecution as soon as he should return to private life. That was the stupidest mistake, for it made Cæsar resolve at all costs to retain his command, and eventually precipitated the civil war.

As can easily be seen, the coalition between Cæsar and Pompeius was not a natural one : psychologically they had nothing in common, and their interests soon began to diverge. Pompeius could hardly fail to perceive that Cæsar was climbing by his help and at his expense. The old general saw the memory of his great deeds eclipsed by the new one, and there was no lack of mischief-makers to widen the breach. The alliance had been cemented in a striking fashion at a conference at Luca (now Lucca) in 56 B.C. when the conservatives were threatening to recall Cæsar from Gaul. Cæsar had replied by inviting Pompeius and Crassus to meet him in his southern province; he also invited those senators who were his friends to appear at the same time. Two hundred senators had answered the invitation, and for the time being the opposition died away into grumbling. It was arranged that Cæsar's Gallic command should be prolonged for another five years.

But now the breach was growing open to all men's eyes. Cæsar's charming daughter, Julia, who had been married to Pompeius (several years Cæsar's senior) as a pledge of union, and had done much to hold the two chiefs together, died at an early age in the year 54. In the next year Crassus, the mediating third party of the "triumvirate", met his fate at Carrhae. In the next there were more than ordinary disorders over the elections, culminating in a fierce battle in the forum between the rival gangs of Clodius for the triumvirate and Milo for the senate. Clodius was murdered on the Appian Way and the senate house was burnt down soon afterwards. Pompeius then became sole consul, and proceeded, under threat of his army, to introduce a series of laws almost openly aimed at Cæsar. By the Pompeian law of magistrates Cæsar would be compelled to appear in Rome as a private citizen for some months in the year 49, at the mercy of his enemies, while Pompeius himself, by having his titular command in Spain prolonged, would still be master of an army. These laws were passed at the crisis of Cæsar's fate in Gaul, when the whole nation had risen in arms against him. But Cæsar emerged victorious, and was now, in the year 50, free to consider his position in regard to Pompeius and the senate. Cæsar himself maintains that he was reluctant to resort to violence, and I think we may believe him. Though nine legions were still under his command, he could hardly venture to denude the newly conquered province of its garrisons, while Pompeius was master of an equal number of legions, including the veteran Spanish troops, and could levy any number of recruits or reservists in Italy. Cæsar could not have faced the prospect of a civil war with any confidence as to the result, even if he had been the sort of man to provoke it without a scruple. There is a further proof : as late as 50 B.C. he resigned two legions to Pompeius, which would have been madness if he had then intended to "wade through slaughter to a throne". In all the abortive negotiations which preceded the outbreak of the great civil war, Cæsar was prepared to resign everything except the one condition upon which his very life depended, namely, that he should not have to return to Rome as a defenceless private citizen. The civil war was due to the mad folly of the conservatives led by Marcellus, who had convinced themselves that Cæsar meant to sack Rome with his Gallic cavalry and to reign as tyrant over its ashes. In the end they succeeded in communicating their fears to Pompeius.

Conciliatory to the last, Cæsar was driven to show that he was in earnest. Bidden to dismiss his army, and declared a public enemy, in January 49 B.C. he took the decisive step of crossing the little river Rubicon which marked the frontier of Italy. Even then it was only a demonstration of force. Only a single weak legion followed Cæsar to Ariminum and Arretium, and he still offered peace on the most moderate terms. But the panic-stricken and conscience-stricken senators, still believing in the imminent sack of Rome, decided to leave their wives and children there while they saved their precious necks, in headlong flight to Capua, thence to Brundisium, and then to Greece. Pompeius, disconcerted by Cæsar's swift and decisive movements, and thwarted by the obstinate disobedience of the proconsul Domitius who held the legions at Corfinium, decided to give up Italy without a struggle and retire to the East, where all his triumphs had been won. From there he would fight for the lordship of the world.

But meanwhile Cæsar, by his clemency no less than by his bold resolution, was winning all Italy to his side. Few members of his army—apart from his old lieutenant-general Labienus— deserted him, while fresh recruits even from the senatorial party daily joined him. Cool and methodical as ever, he left Rome to recover from its panic, and the East to wait until he had secured his hold upon the West. He knew the value of a veteran army, and therefore turned his march first to Spain. It took him but a short time to secure the capitulation of Pompeius' lieutenants in that province, and then at last he returned to Rome. He was only in the city for eleven days, but in that time he was able to remove the panic and disorder there. He restored credit, assured the supply of corn, and obtained a grant of citizen rights for his faithful provincials of Cisalpine Gaul.

Meanwhile the Pompeian army was gathering in northern Greece, and the senators were breathing death and damnation against Cæsar. The final struggle on the Albanian coast and in Thessaly, which culminated in the great battle of Pharsalus (48 B.C.), decided the fate of the world. Pompeius had the advantage in numbers, but the quality of Cæsar's troops was much higher. They had extraordinary devotion to their general, as he had to his beloved legions. Never was there completer confidence between an army and its leader than between Cæsar and his veterans. He could be merciless in discipline, yet he could recall restless troops to loyalty by a reproach. He shared all their labours, he starved with them, and marched those prodigious forced marches by their side. They trusted in his generalship, and they were not disappointed. Pompeius showed, when at last he roused himself, that he too had not forgotten the military art. It was a battle of giants; Pompeius the more orthodox tactician, Cæsar incredibly bold, rapid, and far-seeing. More than once it was touch and go. Cæsar had terrible difficulties to face, above all in first transporting his army across the wintry Adriatic in face of the enemy when he was short of transports. The feat was accomplished by sheer audacity, and then he had to face and contain a larger army, thoroughly well prepared and supplied, with no base and no communications for his own men. He actually tried to fling a line of earthworks round the Pompeian army while his own men were starving. Yet it was by generalship that the battle of Pharsalus was won.

Pompeius fled to Egypt for refuge, and was murdered there by treacherous Alexandrians and renegade Romans. Cæsar, who had received the submission of the whole provincial world with the exception of King Juba's African realm of Numidia, followed Pompeius to Egypt, and on landing was presented with his rival's head. In Alexandria itself Cæsar had to face one of the most serious crises of his life. For six months he held a royal palace against a host of infuriated Alexandrians. In the palace was Cleopatra, the wife and sister of the reigning Ptolemy, and then a brilliant and fascinating young woman of twenty-two. Let us believe that she was beautiful, and that the portrait-painters and coin-engravers of her day were incompetent or disloyal. If rumour spoke truly, Cæsar was the father of her child, named Caesarion.

When at length Julius Cæsar escaped from the two-fold entanglements of love and battle at Alexandria, he had more fighting still before he could make the earth his footstool. He spent a few days in Syria arranging the affairs of the East, and among other things gave orders to rebuild the wall of Jerusalem, which had been thrown down by the orders of Pompeius. Then he passed over to Asia Minor, and at Zela crushed the rebellion of a Pontic successor of Mithridates. So back to Italy for a few weeks, and there he found all in disorder, and his legions, including the faithful Tenth, mutinying for their pay. He settled the disorder at Rome by his mere presence, enacted laws to relieve the economic distress there, and, having no money to pay his soldiers, quelled their mutiny by sheer sleight of speech. Meanwhile the broken Pompeians had gathered in thousands at the court of King Juba, who himself had a formidable array. As soon as he could find time, the restless conqueror crossed straight to Africa with as many soldiers as he could muster, leaving the main force to follow. That was always Cæsar's way—to dart straight upon the scene of danger was his first instinct. At his coming the marrow oozed out of the very bones of his foes. He had a Scipio and a Cato and a host of notable Romans arrayed against him. At Thapsus on the Tunisian coast, in April of the year 46, he smote them, and slew some ten thousand men. There at Utica, Cato died his famous Stoic death, far the noblest scene of his mistaken life, and so became a theme for the glorification of Stoic Republicanism for all time. Afranius, Scipio, King Juba, Faustus Sulla, and many others, died also. A few stragglers found their way to Spain, to continue the fight there under the two sons of Pompeius. Thither in the next year, so soon as he had leisure, Cæsar followed them, and in a last great battle at Munda he finished the resistance. Only Sextus Pompeius was left of the Pompeian party, and he escaped for a time to begin an interesting career as a gentleman-pirate.

In this manner the amazing Cæsar conquered the world. Now it was unquestionably his. What was he to make of it? This story has been told in vain unless it has shown that the city of Rome was rotten to the core, with few sound elements left in it. Cæsar himself was a solitary prodigy; he had no supporters worthy of his confidence. Labienus had deserted him, Quintus Cicero, another of his legates in Gaul, had also fought against him. Mark Antony was perhaps his right-hand man, but Antony was nothing but a brilliant orator and a fair soldier; of character or reputation he had not a shred. Brutus, to whom Cæsar was personally devoted, had fought against him, and was—in spite of Shakespeare and republican tradition—a vain and shallow egoist. Cæsar had no brother and no legitimate son. Across in Apollonia his young great-nephew Octavius was still at school. Julius Cæsar had to reorganise a broken world alone. For a hundred years there had been little peace in Rome, and little proper government in the empire. Every year of its lingering agony, the Republic had drawn closer to the inevitable issue in Monarchy. Even Cicero, when he tried to console himself for the horrible disorders of Roman life by depicting an ideal commonwealth, had been compelled to build it round a *princeps* who should maintain order and thus allow liberty to exist. In practice also the last century had seen a succession of *principes*—Gracchus, Marius, Cinna, Sulla, Pompeius—all from the necessity of the case forced into unconstitutional positions. And now Cæsar had succeeded without a rival. Sulla had resigned power, and his work had almost immediately fallen to pieces. There was now, even more clearly than then, no chance of building up a senatorial party, and indeed Cæsar had been the lifelong victim of senatorial arrogance and folly. It was equally impossible to build up a Roman democracy out of the demoralised loungers in the forum.

Obviously monarchy was the solution. Cæsar was in the middle fifties, spent with war and labour, and, as I have said, quite alone. He was a man without beliefs or illusions or scruples. Not a bad man : for he preferred justice and mercy to tyranny and cruelty, and he had a passion for logic and order. He was not the sort of man to make compromises. His brilliant successes had taught him to despise his enemies. He was not, of course, ignorant that the Romans (if there were any true Romans left) had it in their blood to hate the title of Rex. Every Roman schoolboy was brought up to declaim in praise of regicides. But possibly in time they could be accustomed to the hideous idea. For the present, old-fashioned titles like Dictator and Consul would suffice. The title of Rex could wait. Cæsar would feel his way gently.

But patience was not one of his virtues. Actually fortune only left him less than two years, and those broken by tedious campaigns in the Spanish provinces, for the regeneration of Roman society. In that time he restored the finances, rearranged the provincial system, abolished the political clubs which had been the centres of disorder at Rome, reformed the Calendar, dedicated a new forum and new temples, restored and revised the senate, regulated the system of municipal government in Italy, settled his veterans on the land, and was preparing a great expedition to chastise the Parthians.

Most of these acts were wisely done, but in one thing Cæsar miscalculated. His brilliant victories and the adulation with which he was surrounded led him to underrate the opposition. He would not stoop to flatter antiquarian prejudices or to cast a decent veil over his monarchical position. You may treat people as slaves and they will admire you for it, but when you *call* them slaves they will begin to resent it. Cæsar once failed to rise from his chair to receive the senators. In his reformed senate he included representatives of the equestrian class, provincials and even distinguished soldiers of quite humble birth. He allowed his statue to be set up beside those of the Seven Kings of Rome. He accepted a gilt chair, he permanently retained the triumphant general's laurel-crown, partly because he was bald and keenly sensitive about it; and then either through his orders or by their own officiousness his friends began to throw up *ballons d'essai* in the direction of kingship. At the Lupercalia Antony offered him a crown of gold. It was spread abroad that an ancient Sibylline prophecy had foretold that the Parthians could only be conquered by a king and that Cæsar was to adopt the title for the purpose of his Eastern expedition. It was trifles like these, and trivial jealousies, trivial requests declined in the name of justice, that led to the great conspiracy. No doubt the influence of rhetorical patriotism had its effect upon many of the conspirators. An unknown hand wrote "O that thou wert living!" upon the statue of old Brutus the Liberator. It was pique not patriotism that sharpened their daggers. More than sixty Romans conspired together, and on the eve of setting out for Parthia—the Ides of March, 44 B.C.— Julius Cæsar was slain.

And then, having slain the tyrant and liberated the republic, the patriots were helpless. A doctrinaire like Cicero might still dream of restoring the commonwealth; but the only real question was who should succeed. The people only cried for peace. It was not so much the speech of Mark Antony as the funeral of Cæsar, cleverly stage-managed, and the genuine sorrow of his veterans, which gradually turned the popular feeling against the conspirators. The senate did not venture to declare Cæsar a tyrant, they confirmed his acts, but there was no proposal to punish the murderers. The whole conclusion was a feeble compromise.

The man who should have grasped the helm was Mark Antony. He was left sole consul; there was a legion at hand and whole armies in the provinces under arms only waiting the word. The conspirators had only a few gladiators in their pay. The consul had every right to arrest them. But Antony was not the man for the part. With all his talents he was ineffective. He was always dependent on his surroundings and generally under feminine influence. Once it had been the actress Cytheris, at present it was his aggressive wife Fulvia; for a time Octavia almost reformed him, but Cleopatra easily ensnared him. He was a rake and a spendthrift, always in debt. He was responsive to public opinion: just now the aristocratic society in which he moved was prating of tyrannicide. Antony wanted to be in the fashion. There were dramatic embracements between Antony and Brutus.

Now the testament of Cæsar, which had just been confirmed by the senate, named the young Octavius as heir to three-quarters of his estate. At the end was a codicil adopting him as a son. Henceforth until he gets the title of Augustus this young Cæsar should be called Octavianus, though he never accepted that name for himself. The "second heirs" named in case the first should fail or decline to succeed included D. Brutus, one of the murderers, and Mark Antony himself. Whosoever should accept the heirship would be bound by all Roman ideas of honour to undertake the chastisement of the murderers. Antony seems to have assumed that the obscure young man would not come forward to accept the inheritance. He therefore got together all Cæsar's papers, and began to spend Cæsar's immense fortune as only Antony could. He began also to manipulate Cæsar's papers, inserting anything he liked among Cæsar's "acts", selling honours, raising taxes, recalling exiles to please Fulvia. For some time no one ventured to complain. Leading senators like Cicero retired to the country remarking that the tyrant was dead but the tyranny still alive. Then, of course, Antony had to provide himself with a province to ensure his future safety. Moreover, the cry of the veterans for revenge began to move him to play the Cæsarian. Thus Antony was virtually master of the Roman world and the sky was dark with menace.

Into this dangerous arena steps the eighteen-year-old Octavian. His tutor advised him to have nothing to do with his perilous inheritance. Historians have often dubbed him a coward. But alone and unfriended this youth left his tutors at Apollonia and came to Rome to take up his trust. It meant, first, revenge upon the conspirators; and secondly, a quarrel with Antony. It meant, in fact, two more civil wars, and Octavian had seen nothing of warfare. He set to work coolly and warily. There was still a magic in the name of Cæsar, and the veterans rallied to him and besought him to march against Brutus and Cassius. Part of his duties as executor was to pay a million sterling in donations to the Roman people. He sold his property and began to distribute the largesse, man by man, tribe by tribe, until the sum was paid. He gave magnificent games in his "father's" honour, with the lucky star of Julius publicly exhibited. He bought an army of 10,000 men with borrowed money. Two of Antony's legions deserted to him bodily, and the very veterans of Antony's bodyguard offered to murder their general if young Cæsar would give the signal.

But there was no haste in his method. Octavian tried for a time to work with the senate, and even marched against Antony under their orders, but the incredible folly of the senate, who were persuaded by Cicero that "the boy" was negligible, drove him into the famous triple alliance with Antony and Lepidus. These three were appointed under threat of their armies to a kind of dictatorship in commission, "a triumvirate to reorganise the state". Revenge was the explicit motive of this league. They began with the usual terrible proscription of all the senatorial aristocrats who had supported Pompey, to be found in Rome. Antony and Octavian needed vast sums of ready money with which to redeem their lavish promises to their troops. Their creditors and enemies were slain wholesale, and among them, Cicero. Eighteen towns of Italy were robbed to provide lands for the veterans.

Meanwhile the tyrannicides had gathered in the East, and now Antony and the young Cæsar set out in pursuit of them. In the two battles of Philippi the luck of Octavian and the skill of Antony triumphed over their dispirited adversaries. Brutus and Cassius fell. A few of the "patriots" survived and joined Sextus Pompeius who was still at large in the Mediterranean. In the war-

fare at Philippi Octavian's inexperience and want of talent for
generalship had been very apparent in contrast to Antony. Lepidus
was already a nonentity. Antony went off to the East; and while
he was holding his court of justice in Cilicia there sailed into harbour the splendid royal yacht of Cleopatra. The people left the
judgment seat to see the famous Queen, and Antony too was soon
at her feet. Ferrero would have us believe that it was policy, not
love, which soon made Antony join her at Alexandria and dally
there. Policy no doubt was involved, but everything we know of
Antony leads us to believe that he was just the man to be captured by such a woman, particularly if she were also a queen.
Certainly his sojourn in the East lowered his character both as a
politician and as a soldier.

Octavian had returned to Rome and the West. His task was full
of perils but also full of possibilities. The soldiers were mutinous,
he himself was grievously sick, and the redoubtable Fulvia, who
was her husband's real agent at Rome, very soon perceived that
he was an enemy to be fought. Octavian had to fight another
small civil war at Perugia before he could call himself master
even of Italy, and then fight Sextus Pompeius in Sicilian waters.
Luckily he had at his side a splendid soldier—general and admiral
by turns as were all good Roman fighting-men—Marcus Vip-
sanius Agrippa.* He had also as his agent at Rome Maecenas, an
astute diplomatist and man of business. So, though he himself was
often in danger, he accomplished his task and became master of
the West. Thus the lordship of the world was reduced to a plain
duel.

Antony had actually married Cleopatra after the divorce of
Octavia, whom he had married after Fulvia's death, and as consort of the Egyptian queen he reigned in Oriental majesty. He
had marched against the Parthians and failed ignominiously. He
was assigning provinces and princedoms to Cleopatra and her
children. It was easy for Octavian to represent Antony as a renegade Roman threatening to introduce Oriental monarchy into
Rome. When at last it came to the final civil war, Octavian
appeared as fighting in the public cause of Rome against Egypt,
with Antony as a mere deserter on the Egyptian side. The great
naval battle of Actium (31 B.C.), which decided the mastery of
the world for Octavian, was thus a triumph for Roman arms

* Plate 31.

over Orientals. Actually it was a degenerate Antony who sailed
away at the crisis of the battle in the wake of the queen's yacht.
The glory of the day was Agrippa's. The luck as usual was the
young Caesar's. He was able to inaugurate his reign at Rome
by presenting her with Egypt, the richest country in the world.
In 29 B.C. he came home to celebrate a glorious triple triumph
and to open a new era as the first Roman Emperor.

LATE REPUBLICAN CIVILISATION

Such is a brief sketch of the hundred and four years from the
day when Tiberius Gracchus first arose to challenge the senatorial
oligarchy to the day when the Empire was established upon the
ruins of the Republic. It was a terrible century. Rome had become the centre of the world, the only hope for civilisation, and
Rome was filled with bloodshed and corruption. For the provinces
there was little decent government, only a succession of licensed
plunderers. In the city itself there was a long series of personal
struggles for the mastery; politics meant organised rioting by
gangs of roughs, questions were often solved by the dagger or by
the swords of senators. At intervals there came from each side
alternately the murderous proscriptions, in which every man of
spirit or eminence on the opposing side was marked down for
destruction. Often their sons and grandsons perished with them,
and in any case their fortunes were destroyed. Besides the proscriptions there had been of late a series of civil wars on a great
scale in which thousands of the bravest Romans perished by each
other's swords. A successful foreign war may have some com-
pensating effect in stiffening the moral fibre of a nation and exalt-
ing its spirit, but civil war is disastrous in every way; it is only the
meanest who survive, and the evil passions which it arouses have
no compensation.

In such a period it is wonderful that civilisation should have
been able to make any advances at all. But in spite of the public
turmoil private citizens were amassing enormous fortunes out of
the plunder of the world, and living, though always on the edge
of a volcano, in state and luxury like kings. It is now our task to
see something of private life and culture in the Rome of the expiring Republic.

Money was easily made in those days and lavishly spent. Even an honest man like Cicero, governing a comparatively poor province like Cilicia, made one half a million *denarii* by his year of office, while he remitted to the provincials a quarter-million which, as he says, any governor of average morality would have retained. Legacies were a very frequent source of revenue, especially to pleaders, and it was customary for a rich testator at Rome to make large bequests to his friends. Cicero gained five million *denarii* by such legacies. Foreign kings and states paid handsomely for legal advice or support. Although a barrister was supposed to give his services for nothing, yet gifts and legacies were not refused. For the financier or business man there were many channels to affluence. There were mines all over the empire to be financed and exploited. Although apart from building there was not much industry at Rome, yet the training and use of slaves for various undertakings was a lucrative business. Crassus trained a salvage brigade for Rome and went about to fires with them in order to make bids for the purchase of the burning property. Atticus trained a company of copying clerks and made money by the sale of books. He also kept gladiators and hired them out to magistrates for the games. Fortunes were made, as in the case of Crassus, by buying up the confiscated property of the proscribed. Land speculation was rendered extremely profitable by the frequent assignation of farm-lands to veteran soldiers, who were often glad to sell them at once. The extravagance of the Roman nobles led to a very brisk traffic in loans at high interest. There was a great deal of genuine commercial speculation in ships and cargoes, generally by companies, and Cato advises the investor to put his money in fifty different enterprises rather than in one at a time. Commerce over-seas was, however, forbidden to the senators by the Claudian law of 218 B.C., and these speculated chiefly in land, on which they made a profit by slave-labour. But the most profitable business of all was tax-farming, in which the equestrian classes joined together in capitalist rings. In these and other ways prodigious fortunes were accumulated. The stored-up capital of the Roman world is astounding in its magnitude. The real property of Crassus was at one time estimated at 50 million *denarii*, that of Pompeius sold for a similar sum, and Cæsar's estate is reckoned by Plutarch as 25 million. The property of the popular actor Aesopus did not reach these vast figures, but he left a large fortune.

But all the wealth of the Roman empire was shared by a very narrow circle. The gulf between rich and poor was far deeper than it is to-day. We hear of poor nobles and rich upstarts, but of a respectable middle class with traditions of its own there is little trace. There is an aristocracy of a few thousand families, and little else but a vast proletariat, inarticulate and hungry, dependent on their bounty, bribed with money, bribed with free corn, and bribed with bloody spectacles. They lived miserably in huge tenement blocks or in hovels on the outskirts of the city. They had little to do but lounge in the streets, gape at gladiators and actors, and shout for the most generous politicians of the day. No doubt there were honest citizen cobblers, but Roman history is silent about them.

That section of the city which is to be styled Society was as proud and reckless as the French aristocracy before the Revolution. The senate had now become almost literally an hereditary rank. A child born into one of these princely houses was tended by a multitude of slaves. By this time there was some attempt at a liberal education. Attended by a slave pedagogue the boy would go daily to the school of some ill-paid Greek, who would teach him his letters and his figures. The staple of education was the delivery of artificial declamation on the model of Isocrates or Demosthenes. After this stage a young man would commonly be sent abroad to Athens, or Rhodes, to finish his education with a little philosophy or mathematics, but chiefly with oratory. Returned to Rome, his destiny placed him in a circle of foppish youths, who devoted their principal attention to dress and manicure. Bejewelled and scented, they practised every vice, natural and unnatural. In due course, with no effort but a few bribes from the parental purse, they became priests and augurs, thus entering what were in reality aristocratic dining-clubs. Dining was now the principal art of Rome. Macrobius has preserved the menu of one of these priestly dinners of the Republic, at which the priests and vestals were present. The party began with a prolusion like the Russian or Swedish system of *hors d'œuvres,* in which seventeen dishes of fish and game were presented. The main dinner itself contained ten more courses, "sow's udder, boar's head, fish-pasties, boar-pasties, ducks, boiled teals, hares, roasted fowls, starch-pastry, Pontic-pastry". Such was the State religion of Rome in the first century before Christ. At intervals the young

33.

MAUSOLEUM OF
AUGUSTUS;
Family Tomb in the
Campus Martius.

34.

THE ARA
PACIS (Altar
of Peace).

35. *(opposite)*
AUGUSTUS'
FAMILY.
From the

36.
SACRIFI-
CIAL
SCENE.
From the
Ara Pacis.

37.
TERRA
MATER
(Mother
Earth)
GROUP.
From the
Ara Pacis.

38. THEATRE OF MARCELLUS erected by Augustus
as a monument to his nephew.

39.

PORTICO OF
OCTAVIA
erected by
Augustus in
honour of his
sister.

40. FORUM BOARIUM (Cattle Market) with round temple of Portunus and temple of Mater Matuta.

41. PAINTING FROM THE VILLA OF LIVIA AT ROME (1st Century B.C.).

42. **ARRETINE VASE.** This fine ware of lustrous red colour
belongs to the time of Augustus and his immediate successors.

43. SILVERWARE FROM BOSCOREALE NEAR POMPEII.

44-47. COIN PORTRAITS OF (A) AUGUSTUS, (B) TIBERIUS, opposite (left) CLAUDIUS, (right) NERO, on plate 46 (left) VESPASIAN, (right) DOMITIAN, on plate 47 (left) NERVA, (right) TRAJAN.

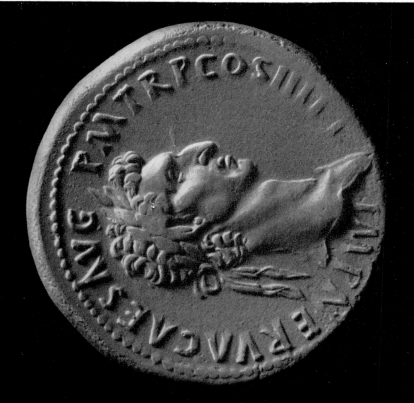

47.

48. BUSTS OF (A) HADRIAN, (B) ANTINOUS.

noble's father's friends would invite him to join their staff on foreign service. If he had the good fortune to serve with Pompeius or Lucullus in the East or with Cæsar in Gaul, he might get a taste of real manliness, and serve his country as tribune of the soldiers. But more often in a peaceful province like Sicily or Africa he was merely initiated into the arts of extortion, and enjoyed all the vicious opportunities of the younger sons of princes. Thus fortified by experience he would return to Rome to seek the suffrages of his fellow-citizens for the quæstorship, the first rung on the ladder of office. Votes were to be won by bribery, direct or indirect. One candidate would spread a banquet for a whole tribe; another would seek to outshine his rivals by providing strange beasts from Africa or Asia—in Cicero's correspondence there are urgent appeals from Caelius for Asiatic panthers to be slain in the Arena—or by dressing his gladiators in silver armour. Similar requirements accompanied his progress through all the stages of office on a progressively lavish scale. As quaestor he would be a judge or a comptroller of the treasury for a single year. Then as ædile he would conduct the public festivals, preside in the ædile's court, control the markets and streets of Rome. So he rose to be praetor and then consul, commander of legions and then in due course governor of a province. From his quæstorship onwards his seat in the senate was assured.

In his home the noble Roman lived like a king, waited upon by an enormous retinue. There was much luxury and little comfort. The houses of the Romans were on a far more luxurious scale than those of the Greeks. The only genuine Roman taste that can be called liberal was the hobby of collecting beautiful town houses and country seats. Cicero, a man of relatively modest income and tastes, seems to have possessed nearly a dozen residences, and gave nearly 900,000 *denarii* for his town house. The qualities prized in the choice of a mansion were space and coolness, and the Romans of this age were by no means insensible to the charms of scenery. The coast round Naples and Baiae was dotted with sumptuous villas, and the gay world spent its summer there in much the same way as the cosmopolitan crowds at Biarritz. Besides his great town house and his family mansion at Arpinum, and his country houses at Tusculum and elsewhere, Cicero had marine villas all along the coast at Antium, Formiae, Cumae, Puteoli, and Pompeii, and along the Campanian road

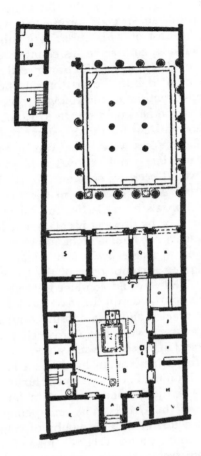

Ground-plan of a small house at Pompeii*

* *A* is the entrance corridor leading to *B*, the atrium; this receives its light from a central opening in the roof under which is the water-tank or *impluvium*, *C*. *D* is a stone table set against the impluvium. *G* is the porter's room, *H* to *N* work and sleeping rooms; the staircase is in *L*. The master's strongbox is at *F*, at the back of the atrium, where are also the two *alae*, *O*, extensions of the atrium, and the *tablinum* or reception room, *P*. *Q* is a corridor giving access to the peristyle, or second courtyard, in the centre of which is a garden. *R* and *S* are dining rooms, *U* slaves' apartments. This is a small house; larger establishments would have the peristyle surrounded by rooms, and behind it still another garden court.

were his private "inns", where he lodged on his journeys. His favourite villa was the one at Tusculum, the scene of many of his literary labours, and, among others, of the famous Tusculan Disputations. It had previously belonged to Sulla and was adorned with paintings in commemoration of Sulla's victories. It was situated on the top of a hill along with many other villas of the aristocracy, and commanded a delightful view of the city about twelve miles away. The park attached to it was extensive, and through it there ran a broad canal. He had books everywhere, but his principal library was kept at Antium. At Puteoli he constructed a cloister and a grove on the model of Plato's Academy.

The principal feature of the Roman house was its large atrium or internal hall, with a roof open in the middle to admit light and air. The roof sloped inwards, and allowed the rain to fall into a

Houses at Ostia; shops below, flats above

central tank, a method no doubt delightful for the coolness it afforded. In old days the atrium had been the common room of the Roman family. It still retained a symbolical marriage-bed, a symbolical spinning-wheel, the portraits of the ancestors, and the ceremonial altar to the family gods, who were represented by statuettes in a little niche above. Most of the rooms opened directly out of the atrium. As they are seen in the ruins of Roman villas, they appear to have been comparatively small and ill-lighted. At the back the atrium opened into a colonnaded garden with a fountain, flower-beds, and shrubbery. The larger houses themselves were generally built of local stone with facings of stucco, though the greater part of Rome was still in this first century B.C. constructed of sun-baked bricks. It was considered unheard-of luxury when Mamurra faced his walls with marble slabs. The floors were generally tessellated. A noble's house would spread over the ground regardless of space, but the bedrooms and sometimes the dining-room were upstairs. The Roman house thus resembled the Greek in facing inwards, but some attention was now paid to the exterior; a colonnaded fore-court would be added to a noble mansion; and country villas were beginning to show external porticos, from which the owner might enjoy the distant prospect. The poorer classes lived in blocks of flats, built up to four or more storeys with shops on the ground floor, very like the houses in an Italian town of to-day. Such blocks were highly characteristic of large towns under the Empire. Even Pompeii was by no means the single-storied garden city described in the old text-books. The more recent excavations have successfully regained for us the upper stories, often with hanging balconies* of almost mediæval aspect.

As the Roman's house was built mainly with a view to coolness, so his daily life was that of a southerner. Rome was never a healthy city in the summer, and all who could afford it fled to the country or the sea-side. A surprising number of the Romans known to us in literature were either invalids or valetudinarians. Malarial fever in its periodic form was widely spread, and most of our distinguished friends pursued a medical regimen. Cæsar was subject to fits of epilepsy, Cicero was of weak constitution, Horace was a martyr to ophthalmia as well as malaria, Augustus was always ailing and often at death's door. The Roman's most amiable idiosyncrasy was his devotion to the bath. Every considerable house had an elaborate bathing department with at least a hot room built over a furnace, and a cold room with a swimming-tank. But

* Plate 72.

there were also public baths, on an ever-increasing scale of magnificence. In 33 B.C. there were 170 of them at Rome. Rich and poor alike made it their daily practice to bathe after exercise, just before their principal meal in the early afternoon. The custom of the noontide siesta was universal, except with prodigies of industry like Cicero. A great deal of time was spent in lounging abroad through the streets or under shady colonnades. The streets of Rome, as of all ancient cities, were extremely narrow, but in the busy parts of the city wheeled traffic was forbidden; the rich were carried about in litters or sedan-chairs.

The wealthy Romans have a name for abominable luxury and gluttony. As to the general question of its influence in destroying the morality of Rome I have already ventured to express disbelief in the popular view. From all that we read, it does not appear that the ordinary Roman was naturally addicted to intemperance either in eating or in drinking. The praise of wine in Horace seems a literary pose; he had a poor head and a poor stomach. The Italian is not, and probably never was, a great eater or drinker judged by northern standards. But rhetoricians and satirists have delighted to dwell upon the immensity of Roman dinner-parties lasting all day and including a hideous series of curious and exotic dainties. This was the form which, in default of any nobler ideals, wealth at Rome had chosen for its display. Time hung heavily on this slave-tended aristocracy: to dine from noon to twilight was one of the ways of killing it. So the guests reclined on their couches, dancers jigged before them, musicians played, occasionally a tumbler or a tight-rope walker would appear, in literary households a slave would read philosophy; and all the time the soft-footed slaves were coming and going with dishes of strange morsels gathered from the ends of the earth and rare wines from the four corners of the globe. A dish of nightingales' tongues is not the sort of thing to please one who is a *gourmet* by conviction or natural taste. Eating was for most of these poor starved imaginations the only form of culture they understood. It was, however, conducted with tremendous ceremony. There was a "tricliniarch" to marshal his "decuries" of slaves as each dish came into the room. There was a special "structor" to arrange the dishes, a special "analecta" to pick up the fragments that the diners dropped. Carving was a science with various branches, as in old England, and the skilful carver had his scheme of gesticulations for each kind of dish. There was another slave specially appointed to cry out the name and quality of each *plat*. In addition to these every guest had his own footman standing behind his couch. The most characteristic and the most unpleasant feature of a Roman banquet was the manner in which the diners assisted nature to provide them with an appetite. Emetics were taken not only as a regimen of health.*

The public shows, which formed the chief recreation of rich and poor alike, grew yearly more brutal and bloody. As they were the means by which ambitious candidates for office sought to canvass popularity, the principal aim was to present something novel and startling. No doubt the more refined spectators regarded the butchery of wild beasts or paid gladiators with disgust, but the populace at large only shouted for more blood. Five hundred lions were slaughtered on one day at games given by Pompeius. Cicero writes that the wholesale destruction of elephants in the arena actually moved the people to pity.† There were still some real theatrical performances in Rome. Actors and mimics, indeed, if they were handsome and graceful, made large fortunes. Roman nobles of a literary bent amused themselves with writing tragedies. Cicero's soldier brother composed four in little over a fortnight when in Gaul. But these were only employed to bore one's friends at dinner. Original literary dramas were even less often staged at Rome than they are in London. Plautus and Terence for comedy, and Ennius, Pacuvius, and Accius for tragedy, had already become classics and were still regularly performed. The drama had died at birth at Rome.

Historians of Rome, fortified by Juvenal and Petronius, love to depict the vices of the emperors and the imperial period. The later Republic can show us a morality no more exalted. The fragments of Varro's satires written in the heyday of the Republic show the same strain of despondency as do the satires of Juvenal.

---

* The reader must not suppose that the description of a banquet is typical of even the most luxurious of the Roman nobles of the Republic. The fact that the words 'tricliniarch', 'structor', and 'analeata' are found only in post-Augustan literature suggests that the description applies better to a later age, one known to us in part through the satire of Petronius and Juvenal.– EDD.

† *Ad Fam.* VII. 1.3 (55 B.C.). Pliny the Elder says the crowd broke into tears and cursed Pompeius.—EDD.

For him, too, virtue is a thing of the past. Sober fact compels us to see that the aristocratic society of Republican Rome was hideously immoral. Voluntary celibacy and "race-suicide" were already rife. The family was a decaying institution, divorce was common, and the sterility of wickedness had long been at work to sap the ranks of the nobility. Even Cicero divorced his wife Terentia upon a trivial pretext after a long period of happy conjugal life in order to marry an heiress. Cæsar had three wives, without begetting a single legitimate son. Cato, the strict censor of morals, having been jilted in his youth, married a wife, divorced her for adultery after she had borne him two sons, married another, lent her for six years to the orator Hortensius, and on his death resumed her again. Mark Antony married Fadia, then Antonia, then divorced her and lived publicly with Cytheris the actress, then married Fulvia, who had already been twice a widow, then married Octavia, then Cleopatra. These marriages were made and dissolved freely for political reasons. A large part of Roman politics was carried on in the *salons* of the Roman ladies, and, if half of what Cicero alleges be true, Messalina herself had her Republican prototypes in women like Clodia and Fulvia. Beside almost promiscuous relations between the sexes, homosexuality was prevalent in the fashionable society of Rome.

Religion was almost purely formal or political. Augurships and priesthoods still existed as the perquisite of aristocratic families. People still uttered the formulæ of oaths and vows. There was still some belief in omens and prodigies, the altars still smoked with sacrifice when triumphant generals went up to the Capitol, but few prayers ascended to Jupiter in sincerity. Instead the importation of strange deities continued. In this first century before Christ the senate tried to expel the worship of Isis from the precincts of Rome, but it always returned, and eventually the triumvirs planned a temple to Isis and Serapis as a measure to court popular favour. The Magna Mater of the Phrygian corybants had long been firmly established at Rome.

I think it was general materialism and immorality that killed the old State religion at Rome. Greek philosophy had generally been able to exist amicably by the side of religion. It now came in to fill up the gap left by the absence of real religious feeling. But at Rome, though Stoicism afterwards became a powerful force of inspiration to the noblest minds, philosophy was in the main a form of literary activity for dilettantists. Cato of Utica was a Stoic by temperament before he became one by doctrine. Cicero amused his leisure by recasting and combining the doctrines of the leading Greek schools in a Roman form of dialogue, in imitation of Plato; but with him it was more of a literary exercise than anything else, and Cicero has added little or nothing to the world's stock of philosophical ideas. Only in the poet Lucretius does the fire of philosophy burn with genuine ardour. Lucretius had before him the task of proselytising at Rome for the doctrines of Epicurus and Democritus. People accustomed to the modern associations of the word "epicure" may wonder what there was to arouse the enthusiasm of a poet in the philosophy of Epicurus. That creed offered a rational explanation of the universe. With its theory of spontaneous atomic creation, and its foreshadowing of some of the ideas of natural selection and evolution, it claimed to satisfy the intellect of mankind and to drive out all the grovelling superstition and empty rites which took the place of religion at Rome. All the enthusiasm with which the nineteenth century approached the new discoveries of science glowed in the heart of this ruggedly majestic poet of the first century before Christ. "Voluptas" was his *summum bonum,* but it was no vulgar pleasure of the body upon earth. It was the spirit soaring to freedom and knowledge. This Epicurean rationalist had attitudes and purposes that we associate with a religious man. He explains the nature of lightning in order that his fellow-creatures may not live in fear of thunderbolts. He explains with the same confident logic the nature of death in order that they may not fear the natural resolution of body and soul into their primordial atoms. He is moved almost to tears by the folly and sorrow of his brother-men, and he pleads with them to suffer the sacred lamp of philosophy to shine upon their darkened minds :

> at nisi purgatum est pectus, quæ proelia nobis
> atque pericula tumst ingratis insinuandum !
> quantæ tum scindunt hominem cuppedinis acres
> sollicitum curæ quantique perinde timores !
> quidue superbia, spurcitia ac petulantia? quantas
> efficiunt clades ! quid luxus desidiæque?
> hæc igitur qui cuncta subegerit, ex animoque

expulerit dictis, non armis, nonne decebit
hunc hominem numero diuom dignarier esse?*

His doctrine is medicine for the feverish unrest of the day :

exit sæpe foras magnis ex ædibus ille
esse domi quem pertæsum est, subitoque reuertit,
quippe foris nilo melius qui sentiat esse.
currit agens mannos ad uillam præcipitanter
auxilium tectis quasi ferre ardentibus instans :
oscitat extemplo tetigit quom limina uillæ
aut abit in somnum grauis atque obliuia quærit,
aut etiam properans urbem petit atque reuisit.
hoc se quisque modo fugit . . .†

He has a compassionate scorn for the mourner :

aufer abhinc lacrumas, balatro, et compesce querelas . . .
cedit enim rerum nouitate extrusa uetustas
semper et ex aliis aliud reparare necesse est;
nec quisquam in barathrum nec Tartara deditur atra.
materies opus est ut crescant postera sæcla;
quae tamen omnia te, uita perfuncta, sequentur :
nec minus ergo ante hæc quam tu cecidere, cadentque.
sic alid ex alio numquam desistet oriri;
uitaque mancipio nulli datur, omnibus usu.‡

* But unless the mind is purged, what conflicts and dangers must
we then encounter in our own despite! What poignant cares inspired by
lust then rend the tormented man, and then also what mighty fears! and
pride, impurity, and brutality! What disasters are caused by these, and by
luxury and all sorts of sloth! He therefore who has subdued all these and
banished them from the mind by words, not arms, shall he not have a just
title to be ranked among the gods? (v. 43-51).

† The man who is sick of staying at home often issues forth from his
large mansion, and as suddenly comes back to it, finding as he does that
he is no better off abroad. He races to his country house, driving his ponies
in headlong haste, as if hurrying to bring help to a house on fire; he yawns
the moment he has reached the door of his country house, or sinks heavily
into sleep and seeks forgetfulness, or even in haste goes back again to town.
In this way each man flies from himself. (III. 1060-8).

‡ Away with your tears, fool; a truce to your complainings . . . For old
things give way and are supplanted by new without fail, and one thing
must ever be replenished out of other things; and no one is delivered over
to the pit and black Tartarus. Matter is needed for after generations to
grow, all of which will nevertheless follow you when they have finished
their term of life; and all these no less than you have before this come to an
end and hereafter will. Thus one thing will never cease to rise out of another;
and life is granted to none in freehold, to all on lease. (III. 955, 964-71).

For him death has no sting :

> numquid ibi horribile apparet? num triste uidetur
> quidquam? non omni somno securius exstat?*

His poem consists of didactic argument with occasional dig-
ressions, and he strings his points together with the plain tran-
sitional words and phrases of argumentative prose. But in virility
of thought and expression, even in majesty of sound and force of
vivid imagery, he is, when he cares to be, on a plane quite above
and away from the ordinary sphere of classic Latin poetry. Almost
alone among Roman writers he has a message of his own to deliver.
His fellow-countrymen thought little of him,† and failed to preserve any details of his biography. The monks of the Middle Ages
consigned him to the hell he had flouted, and Jerome provided
him, five hundred years after his death, with an end edifying to
piety, but quite incredible to any one who had read his work with
sympathy. He was said to have been maddened by a love-potion,
to have composed his poem in the intervals of insanity, and to
have ended his own life. He appears to have lived between 100
and 50 B.C.

In addition to the tragedies and epics which noblemen threw
off as an elegant pastime for their superfluous leisure hours, love-
poetry, pasquinades, and *vers de société* travelled merrily from
salon to *salon*. If Lucretius carries the heaviest metal of Latin
poets, Catullus has by far the lightest touch. He writes with an
ease which makes Horace seem laboured, and with a simplicity
which makes Propertius and even Ovid look like pedants, though
Catullus himself, when following his Alexandrian models, showed
himself a *doctus poeta* who was by no means averse to learned
allusions. Catullus' increasing popularity in the modern schoolroom is no doubt due to the realisation that he possesses much
more of the vital spark of poetry than Horace. Roman poetry,
perhaps because it is mainly second-hand, is on the whole lacking
in the quality of fresh youth which we enjoy in such writers as
Chaucer and the early Elizabethan singers. We do find it in

---

* Is there anything there that looks appalling, anything that wears an
aspect of gloom? Is it not more peaceful than any sleep? (III. 976-7).

† Cicero possibly excepted, but the brief allusion to the poet in one of
Cicero's letters (*ad Quint. Fratr.* II.9.3.) is variously interpreted, though
now generally admitted to be laudatory. Ovid admired him.

Catullus; yet he is by no means unsophisticated. On the contrary, this young native of Verona is a clever son of the *forum*—a boulevardier, one might say—with a pretty but savage wit. But, with his truly Italian scurrility, he combines the quintessence of Italian charm. When the inspiration takes him he is simple, direct, and natural like Herrick or a Greek lyric poet. Indeed, the shorter poems of Catullus reveal the writer's innermost feelings more spontaneously than any work in Latin literature. We have the innocent pleading of the April lover in

> soles occidere et redire possunt :
> nobis cum semel occidit breuis lux
> nox est perpetua una dormienda.
> da mi basia mille, deinde centum,
> dein mille altera, dein secunda centum,
> deinde usque altera mille, deinde centum,*

and the awful simplicity of his wrath at betrayal:

> Cæli, Lesbia nostra, Lesbia illa,
> illa Lesbia, quam Catullus unam
> plus quam se atque suos amauit omnes,
> nunc in quadriuiis et angiportis
> glubit magnanimos Remi nepotes.†

We have a more genuine-sounding love of nature in his praises of Sirmio (XXXI), and a more natural pathos in the famous lament for his brother (CI), than any other Latin poet can give us. In one species of composition, the Epithalamium, he is supreme. For example :

> flere desine; non tibi, Au-
> runculeia, periculum est
> nequa femina pulchrior
> clarum ab Oceano diem
> uiderit uenientem.

---

* Suns may set and rise again; for us, when our brief light has waned but once, one endless night of sleep remains. Give me a thousand kisses, and then a hundred, and another thousand, and a hundred to follow; then yet another thousand—and then a hundred! (V. 4-9).
    † LVIII.

talis in uario solet
diuitis domini hortulo
stare flos hyacinthinus.
sed moraris, abit dies :
prodeas, noua nupta.

prodeas, noua nupta, si
iam uidetur, et audias
nostra uerba. uiden? faces
aureas quatiunt comas :
prodeas, noua nupta.*

The music of this, with its beautiful imagery and refrains, is no doubt based upon a Greek foundation. But it is also distinctively Italian, and the greatest of modern Italian poets, Carducci, writes like a legitimate descendant of Catullus. Catullus would have had as little biography as Lucretius had he not given us some hints of his life in his poems. He must have died at an early age in the fifties B.C. He was an aristocrat who lived in the innermost circles of Roman society; he complains of his poverty, the fashionable complaint of the age, but we need not take him too seriously seeing that he had a town house and two villas, one at Sirmio on Lake Garda and one at Tivoli. He hated Cæsar and loved Cicero. That his "Lesbia" was the infamous Clodia is commonly asserted.

These two poets, Lucretius and Catullus, stand almost alone as representatives of Republican Roman literature on the poetical side. Both are Romanising various Alexandrian Greek modes, but both have something genuinely Roman, a quality which we may best describe as virility, to add to their originals. This was the point from which a genuine Roman literature might have taken its departure. Instead of that, the next era is that of a courtly school of classicists, largely writing to order, who gave to Latin its distinctively classical bent.

Cicero, the most classical of all classics, is, however, far the greatest literary product of the Republic.† He is, indeed, far too vast a figure for these modest pages. By his colossal industry and

* Cease to weep, Aurunculeia: you need not fear that any lovelier woman should see the bright day coming from Ocean.
Even so a hyacinth is wont to bloom in a rich man's many-coloured garden. But you linger. The day is passing. Come forth, young bride.
Come forth, young bride, if now you will, and hear our song. Look how the torches shake their golden hair! Come forth, young bride. (LXI., 82-96).
† Plate 25.

immense fertility of genius his influence dominates the whole field of Latin prose literature. He is not only the greatest of all orators, but he stands as the type of the orator in life as in literature. We of this century, who live in the eclipse of rhetoric, do not find it easy to be just to him. Faced with such gifts of eloquence, such a power of uttering tremendous phrases about duty and patriotism, we cannot but feel affronted at his political incapacity. Mommsen, who is all for action, peppers him with contemptuous expressions —"a statesman without insight, opinion or purpose"; "a short-sighted egoist"; "a journalist of the worst description"; "his lawyer's talent of finding excuses—or, at any rate, words—for everything". And indeed, among men like Cæsar with legions at their backs, or creatures like Clodius with their packs of hooligans, a man of golden words and honest principles does cut a sorry figure on the pages of history—so much the worse for history! He had, as we have seen, a policy, his talents made him a leader among the moderates of the senate, and his character made him genuinely popular among all the more respectable classes of society. Cicero's nature was soft and sympathetic. He turns his coat at a word from Pompeius, utters brave words one day and eats them the next, publishes magnificent denunciations which he has not had the courage to deliver. Moreover, we see his intimate thoughts revealed in all the frankness of an unexpurgated private correspondence—and there are few statesmen, certainly very few orators, whose reputations can sustain that test. Thus the golden words often ring hollow. His vanity is often ludicrous, as when he writes to Lucceius (*Epp. ad Fam.* V.12), to beseech a conspicuous place in his history, even if the truth has to be distorted for the purpose; or when he loiters at Brundisium, with his lictors' rods continually wreathed in laurel for the futile hope of a triumph. Certainly he was an egoist. Probably in their private correspondence all men are. But he was also a gentleman, one of the few Romans of his day with whom one would care to shake hands in Elysium.

To Mommsen, Cæsar is the "sole creative genius" of Roman history. We may well ask what he created. Certainly not the Empire, for that fell to pieces at his death, and had to be re-created on a new plan by his successor. Not even the Gallic province, for though he conquered it, he left the problem of its organisation to Augustus. But Cicero created Latin prose out of next to nothing and left it to the world as its grandest form of literary expression. The splendid Latin period, with its clear logical order, its chain of dependent clauses each in its place with absolute precision, a thought built of words as a temple is built of marble, is the best expression of Roman grandeur, as typical and as enduring as a Roman road or wall. It was not mere art. It was the natural expression of a Roman mind trained in law and rhetoric. It was perhaps the finest thing the Romans ever made, and the Latin period is the true justification for retaining Latin in its place for the education of young barbarians accustomed to string their random ideas together like dish-clouts on a line. Although it was the result of long training under all the most distinguished masters of Rome and Greece, and was perfected with infinite labour, Cicero's style, when once achieved, was extraordinarily rapid and fluent, as the number of his works can testify. It is true that, like many great stylists—Dryden, for example—, he came to believe that style was everything. He was prepared to write a geography of the world or a history of Rome. He only wanted a few notes from his brother Quintus to write an account of Britain. His multitudinous philosophical works were, as we have seen, more style than philosophy, composed in a few months to while away the time at his Tusculan villa at intervals when the temperature of Rome, literally or politically, was too high to suit his health. In such work he may fairly be called an amateur, though a very great one. When he writes of a subject he really understands, such as rhetoric, he is at his best. Again, in his forensic speeches or writings he is much better as an advocate than as a lawyer. His mind is not capable of juristic precision, he is neither deep nor subtle, and so far his influence is wholly detrimental in the history of Roman law. He would probably infuriate a trained judge; but give him a jury, and, if possible, a large Italian one, and he is irresistible, now with translucent rapid narrative, now with clever mystification, breaking off into thundering appeals to conscience or heaven, or again with passionate denunciation of his opponent or majestic encomium for his client. In the senate he is not at his best. We are told that a few blunt words from Cato had more power to move that assembly of practical men than all the Catilinarian orations. But if Rome had been governed, as Greece was, by orations in the market-place, Cicero would have been in Cæsar's place as dictator of the world. Imagine the Roman mob assembling in 63 B.C. to hear their consul's account of Catiline's flight—

tandem aliquando, Quirites, L. Catilinam, furentem audacia, scelus anhelantem, pestem patriæ nefarie molientem, uobis atque huic urbi ferro flammaque minitantem, ex urbe uel eiecimus uel emisimus uel ipsum egredientem uerbis prosecuti sumus. abiit, excessit, euasit, erupit. nulla iam pernicies a monstro illo atque prodigio moenibus ipsis intra moenia comparabitur ... non enim iam inter latera nostra sica illa uersabitur : non in campo, non in foro, non in curia, non denique intra domesticos parietes, pertimescemus.*

—his voice screams with passion, or sinks into pathos; presently he drops into the tones of calm reason or fluent narrative; as he nears his climax his eyes flash, his hands gesticulate, his body sways from side to side, his foot stamps the ground, he seems to foam at the mouth :

dolebam, dolebam, patres conscripti, rempublicam uestris quondam meisque consiliis conseruatam breui tempore esse perituram†

"Why, you did not even stamp your foot!" he exclaims in rebuking the coolness of an opposing counsel. It is true that there were purists of the severer school of Roman oratory who thought such vehemence meretricious and undignified. The true Roman eloquence of the old school is to be found in that ambassador who came to the Carthaginian senate with "peace or war" gathered in the folds of his mantle and briefly commanded them to choose; or that other who drew a circle in the dust round Antiochus the Fourth and demanded an answer before he left the circle. Cicero

* At last, Fellow Citizens of Rome, at last we are quit of Lucius Catiline. Mad as he is with audacity, panting with iniquity, infamously contriving destruction for the fatherland, menacing you and our city with fire and slaughter, we have cast him forth or let him go or escorted him forth on his way with salutations. Gone, vanished, absconded, escaped! No more shall disaster be plotted against our bulwarks from within by that monster, that prodigy of wickedness. No more shall that knife be pointed at our ribs. No more in the Campus, nor in the forum, nor in the senate-house, nor within the walls of our own homes, shall he fill us with panic and alarm. (Cat. II. 1).

† I was grieved, Senators, grieved that the republic once saved by your exertions and mine should be doomed so shortly to perish. (Phil. II. 37; a speech that was never actually delivered).

had studied his art both in the flowery Asiatic and the severer Attic schools. There was still, his critics complained, too much Asia in his style. But that was part of the tendency of his age. The austerity of Cato, with his simple formulæ, was gone for ever. The Romans of this age are more emotional, more sentimental, more characteristically Southern.

If we reproach Cicero with weakness and cowardice in his political life, the story of his end may atone for it. After Cæsar's murder, when Antony was master of Rome, a man utterly unscrupulous and wedded to a still more unscrupulous wife, Cicero flung away all his timidity and hesitation. Convinced that the consul was trying to re-establish a monarchy, the old orator came down to the senate and launched at him the series of ferocious and most eloquent Philippics. Some were spoken, some merely written and published. It was courting death in the cause of liberty. Cicero was not blind to the danger he was running. But he is probably sincere when he says that life has no more attractions for him.

defendi rempublicam adulescens, non deseram senex : contempsi Catilinæ gladios, non pertimescam tuos. quin etiam corpus libenter obtulerim, si repræsentari morte mea libertas ciuitatis potest, ut aliquando dolor populi Romani pariat quod iamdiu parturit. etenim si abhinc annos prope uiginti hoc ipso in templo negaui posse mortem immaturam esse consulari, quanto uerius nunc negabo seni! mihi uero, patres conscripti, iam etiam optanda mors est, perfuncto rebus eis quas adeptus sum quasque gessi. duo modo hæc opto : unum, ut moriens populum Romanum liberum relinquam; hoc mihi maius a dis immortalibus dari nihil potest : alterum, ut ita cuique eueniat ut de republica quisque mereatur.*

As he foresaw so plainly, the Philippics caused his doom. When

* In my youth I defended the state; I will not fail it in my old age: I scorned the swords of Catiline; I will not tremble at yours. Nay, sirs, I would gladly give my body to death, if that could assure the liberty of our country and help the pains of the Roman people to bring the fruit of its long travailing to birth. Why, nearly twenty years ago in this very temple I declared that death would not come untimely to a man who had enjoyed a consulship. With how much more truth can I say that now in my old age! To me death is already covetable; I have had my fill alike of rewards and of exploits. Only these two prayers I make: one, that at my death I may leave the Roman people free (than this nothing greater could be granted to me by the heavenly powers), and, secondly, that every man may so be requited as he deserves at the hands of the republic! (*Phil.* II. 118-9).

the triumvirate drew up its proscription-lists, Octavian is said to have pleaded for his life. But Antony's wrath was implacable. Cicero's head and his hands were nailed to the rostra from which he had so often poured out his rhetoric, and Fulvia, so the story goes, thrust her needle through his tongue. As well as his numerous orations and works on philosophy and oratory he left behind a magnificent collection of Letters, written to various relatives, friends and acquaintances, and much poetry which, to judge by the surviving fragments, contained work of considerable quality.

Julius Cæsar, beside being a competent grammarian and no mean poet, was reputed the second of Roman orators. Of that we have little means of judging. Certainly he could quell a mutiny by a speech, and his Commentaries were not the least wonderful of his achievements. They are mere despatches intended to inform the senate and the world of the progress of his campaigns. They were written at odd moments in a prodigiously active life. Their style is so simple and so correct that we cast them as pearls before the fourth-form schoolboy. Yet they are in reality a triumphant product of the rhetorical art; so simple, they must be honest; so modest, they must be candid. You would scarcely think that they are a defence or a vindication. In the same easy flow of narrative breathless escapes are concealed. Who remembers from his school days Cæsar's description of that moment, so pregnant with human destiny, when the eagle first alighted on our shores in the hands of the gallant centurion of the Tenth Legion? Cæsar seems more like a Greek than a Roman in his directness as in his reticence. Fortunately for history Cæsar had far more natural curiosity than most of the Romans. It is surprising how little Cicero really tells us of Roman or Cilician life in all his voluminous correspondence. But Cæsar went out to explore as well as to conquer. It may even be true that his visit to Britain was, as he asserts, partly due to curiosity. He notes our little insular peculiarities—our custom of sharing wives, our habit of keeping the hare, the hen, and the goose as pets though our religion forbids us to eat them. He sees the superior civilisation of Kent. He observes our clothing of skins, our dyeing ourselves blue with woad, our long hair and moustaches, our horsemen and charioteers, our innumerable population and crowded buildings, our plenteous store of cattle, our metals—bronze, iron, and tin. He is equally observant in Gaul and Germany. The debt that history owes to him for these records is incalculable.

Lesser lights such as Sallust and Nepos dabbled in history and have had the good fortune to survive. Livy, though he wrote under Augustus, is a true Republican in mind and sympathy. His majestic history of Rome is the work of a rhetorician setting out to extol the glories of the Republic. Although he sometimes displays a rudimentary critical instinct in comparing his authorities, his main task was to latinise Polybius and to embellish with Augustan style the dry annals of such writers as Fabius Pictor and Licinius Macer. It is not the least of our many grievances against the monks that they allowed so much of Livy to disappear.

The golden age of classical literature covers this last half-century of the Republic and the first half-century of the Empire. There is, on the whole, little trace of division between the general character of Republican and Imperial letters except that with Augustus the principal writers are definitely engaged under the Emperor's banner of reform. The main characteristic of both is rhetoric and convention. It is to Alexandria and its state-fostered writing-club that the world owes convention in literature. The Romans drew their inspiration from Greece but mainly from Alexandria, and as literature at Rome was now chiefly in the hands of the upper classes it was possible for a classical style to grow strong there. Cicero and his friends evolved a style, not only of literature but even of thought, which could pronounce itself as "urbane", and all else as barbarian or rustic. Roman literature of the first centuries before and after Christ was as much under the domination of epithets like "urbane" and "humane" as was the literature of the eighteenth century under "elegant" and "ingenious". Even Livy as an outsider, a provincial from Patavium (Padua), was accused of mingling "Patavinity" with his Latinity. It is the aristocracies of literature, such as the court of Louis XIV or of Charles II, or such as the coffee-house cliques of Addison's day or the Johnsonian clubs, which create and maintain our periods of classical convention.

Literature, as we have already seen occasion to remark, since it works in the most plastic medium, is generally the first of the arts to develop; and literature is only yet beginning. But then Rome borrowed her arts wholesale from Greece, and thus her culture has no true infancy. The controversial problem of Roman originality in Art must be reserved until we reach the Augustan Age. For the present we must still deny the existence of any really spontaneous art growth at Rome during the Republic. Where native art may be looked for with the highest probability of finding it is in architecture, portrait-sculpture, and painting; in architecture, partly because the Romans had a natural passion for building and partly because their religious and social habits called for quite distinct types of construction in palaces, halls, amphitheatres, triumphal arches, *fora,* and other secular buildings upon which the Greeks had wasted little of their attention; in portraiture, because it was a peculiar custom at Rome to make and display images of their ancestors, whereas the Greeks in their love of the ideal had until latterly shrunk from the presentation of casual human lineaments and still idealised them as far as possible, and also because the Etruscans, who were the first nurses of Roman culture, had developed a realistic tendency in their renderings of the Greek ideal types; and in painting, partly owing to the same Etruscan influence and partly because the Romans, using inferior building materials such as brick, limestone, and terra-cotta covered with stucco, were naturally drawn to mural painting for the sake of ornament. But if we look for originality here we are disappointed. Undoubtedly hundreds of magnificent villas were being run up all over Italy from Como to Sorrento, but a Roman villa was more an affair of landscape gardening than of architecture. It consisted mainly of a series of courts and colonnades sprawling at large over the ground. The walls were built of coarse tufa or peperino; they were only just beginning to be incrusted with marble slabs. As a city much of Rome was still contemptible—the poorer quarters consisting of a huddled mass of narrow, tortuous alleys. There were of course ancient temples, venerable with dignity, and no doubt to us they would have seemed beautiful with the picturesqueness of antiquity. But with Gracchans and Marians and Clodians rioting at large through the city, many of these venerable shrines were destroyed by fire. The Roman ruins as seen by the modern traveller are mainly of Imperial times. The great Temple of Jupiter on the Capitol was rebuilt four times. The round Temple of Vesta was frequently destroyed and restored. Although for religious reasons the plan of the original was generally preserved in these rebuildings, the details were in accordance with the style of the day. Nevertheless the plans are interesting. The round shrines of Vesta,* Hercules and Portunus† are clearly an architectural development from a round hut constructed of wood with a thatched roof. Indeed the Temple of Vesta is said to have been modelled on the hut of Romulus.‡ It was perhaps originally the king's house in which the princesses tended the sacred fire. The Temple of Jupiter Capitolinus also was, if we may trust the coins, built on an un-Greek plan with three naves, instead of a single nave with aisles; the plan as well as the habit of uniting three deities under one roof is Etruscan, as we have already seen. It stood on a high plat-form measuring nearly 200 ft. each way, a testimony to the wealth of Rome under its Kings. Not until the Empire was any temple approaching it in scale attempted; a group of Republican shrines, of which the foundations have been laid bare in the Largo Argentina, illustrate how far the Republic was from equalling the grandeur of the Regal period.

The only considerable remains of Republican architecture, apart from the temples in the Argentina, are the Tabularium or Record Office overlooking the Forum, which dates from 78 B.C., and the Ionic temple near the Tiber, which is now generally thought to be that of Mater Matuta,§ and which is some years later. In that period, when Rome had just discovered Greek culture, when the armies of Sulla and Lucullus came home laden with Greek spoil, there was a temporary outburst of artistic activity at Rome. It was, however, entirely in the hands of foreign artists. About 146 Metellus, the victor of Macedonia, built the first marble temple at Rome in the Campus Martius. Sulla himself carried off the huge columns of the unfinished Temple of Olympian Zeus at Athens to adorn the Roman Capitol. The Cyprian Greek Hermodorus was employed to construct temples and docks. The Romans had indeed their native principles of building, which from a merely constructive point of view were in advance of anything that the Greeks had evolved for themselves. Greek architecture of the best period had been primarily devoted to the service of religion. Their efforts were almost limited to the perfecting of the Doric and Ionic temple, and when they had to build a secular building like the gate-way of the Acropolis, they were still content with a mere adaptation of the Doric temple to their new purpose. Their building material was marble, and with

* Plate 17.   † Plate 40.   ‡ See fig. on p. 12.   § Plate 40.

their peculiar artistic discretion the Greeks saw that marble was at its best in the austere lines of pediment and columns. But the Romans, before they imported marble, had made a beginning with brick and cement, which require quite different methods of architecture. In early days they had discovered or learnt from the Etruscans the use of the vault and arch, at any rate for tunnels, but they were slow to make extensive architectural use of these important principles. The triumphal arch seems to have been a Roman invention, and several triumphal arches were built in republican days, but unfortunately we have little information as to their style. The Sullan revival of art was purely an importation of foreign models. In the Temple of Mater Matuta, built about 50 B.C., we see how the Romans used their imported architecture.* The graceful Ionic columns support nothing. They are used for ornament. The Greeks had indeed used engaged columns, as in the Erechtheum, to complete the design where there was no space for a free colonnade, but the Romans built them into their walls for the sake of ornament. This is typical. Culture was to the Greeks a vital part of their existence, to the Romans it was an embellishment.

†The use of new building materials, however, opened up fresh possibilities for Roman architecture. The earliest use of concrete (third century B.C.?) was modest, but it prepared the way for a revolution in constructional methods and made possible the great domes and vaults of the Empire. While the Greeks had fitted their theatres into the solid rock of hill-sides, Italian architects could now begin to experiment in building amphitheatres and masonry auditoria raised on vaults. Further, the appearance of the city was brightened by the use of an attractive limestone from Tibur, known as Travertine, and by white marble from Carrara and coloured marbles from abroad.

†Although a lull for nearly a century followed the building activities of the earlier second century, the monumental centre of Rome received much attention and embellishment from Sulla, Pompey and Cæsar. Though the poorer quarters might remain squalid, the outskirts also were improved by the turning of the gardens of Lucullus and Sallust in the north and of Cæsar's across the Tiber into public parks. Sulla was the first to try to systematize

* Plate 40.
† Paragraphs added by EDD.

large areas, using the new Tabularium as a means to link Forum and Capitol into an architectural unit. He reconstructed the temple of Jupiter Capitolinus and enlarged the Senate-house. One of his most magnificent works was his rebuilding of the great sanctuary of Fortuna Primigenia at Praeneste after the civil war of 83-82 B.C., the extent of which has been revealed only as a result of damage caused in the Second World War and of subsequent investigation and reconstruction. Other relics of the Sullan period are Jupiter's temple at Terracina, two Italic temples at Cori, and the temple of Vesta and Sanctuary of Hercules at Tivoli. Pompey's contribution to the city was to set a new fashion in theatres and porticos: he gave Rome its first stone theatre, a splendid building with an adjoining portico (where the Senate met Cæsar on the Ides of March). Cæsar's chief works were the new Forum Iulium, to the north-west of the old Forum, with its shops and the temple of Venus Genetrix, and the new Basilica Iulia, which Augustus later completed. Cæsar also restored the Basilica Aemilia, reconstructed the Senate-house, which had been burned in 52 B.C., and built a covered enclosure, the Saepta, for voters in the Popular Assemblies. Thus the work of some of the *principes* of the late Republic prepared the way for the later improvements by Augustus.

It was much the same with the other arts. Take the coins, for example. The clumsy copper As, with the head of Janus on the obverse and the prow of a ship on the reverse,* had weighed 12 ounces when it was first introduced in the first half of the third century B.C. Throughout the course of its history it was gradually shrinking, until in 89 B.C. it was fixed at half an ounce. When it was fixed at two ounces about 187 B.C., the old method of casting was abandoned and a neater piece was produced by striking. As we have remarked, silver was not coined, though no doubt it circulated, at Rome before 268 B.C. From 187 onwards silver became the real standard of value, and about 80 B.C. the copper coinage ceased altogether for a time. The earliest coinage at Rome was produced under Greek influence, and there are traces of good style in the artistic conception and execution. Thereafter for some time there is a decline, which lasted until the end of the second century. Soon afterwards, however, artistic merit increased and reached a very high level, particularly from about 70 to 50 B.C.;

* See page 31.

Lucullus and Pompey almost certainly brought back with them to Rome from the East Greek artists who made a permanent contribution to the style of the Roman mint. But if much of the merit in Republican coinage was due to the example of Greece, something peculiarly Italian can be detected in the hard and precise style of some of the later *denarii*. In one sphere the Romans attained great success, namely in the coin portraiture of the late Republic and early Empire. Here again there were magnificent Greek exemplars in the fine series of portraits of the various Hellenistic monarchs, but the low level to which even a Greek workman could sink is illustrated in the coins of Antony and Cleopatra issued at Antioch, interesting though they are historically. But, however varying its artistic level, the Roman coinage of the last century of the Republic has a wealth of interest with its religious, personal, historical, architectural and other types.

In sculpture the most ardent supporters of Roman originality can find little to comfort them in the closing century of the Republic. We have seen how the victories of Mummius and his successors had created a taste and a market for Greek works of art. With those of Sulla and Lucullus immense quantities of loot had crossed the Adriatic, and Rome began to be what New York is now, the home of connoisseurs and collectors. As connoisseurs sometimes do, the Roman millionaires studied commercial values rather than artistic qualities. No doubt in time their taste improved from the days when Mummius had warned his men that any of the Greek masterpieces destroyed in transit would have to be replaced by new ones. But they still went very largely by the names of the artists: a genuine Praxiteles or Scopas was worth immense sums. Every villa now required statues for its adornment—Greek originals, if possible; if not, copies. For the most part they were reckoned purely as objects of value along with handsome tables, vases, bowls, and signet-rings. When Cicero buys Greek statues he prefers Muses to Bacchantes as being more appropriate to his studies. The result was the appearance of regular workshops of copyists which set themselves to supply the demand for sculptural decoration; and on the Græco-Roman copies thus produced we are often forced to rely for our knowledge of masterpieces of the great Greek artists, whose own work has perished. Many of the "archaistic" works in our museums belong to this period of production; they imitate the primitive stiffness of the early Greek period, and as decoration many of them are extremely charming. The most famous sculptor of this age was Pasiteles, an Italian Greek who obtained Roman citizenship after the Social War in 87 B.C. He came to Rome and won a reputation by making statues for temples. He was a metal worker by training and his work is like that of Cellini, more decorative than creative. An example of his school is the group by his pupil Stephanus at Naples, sometimes called "Orestes and Electra";* it is really a meaningless group, made by setting together two stock Greek types of mid-fifth century B.C.; the drapery of the woman has been changed into the transparent clinging style of a later age, and the whole is served up as an original composition. The claim of originality will more readily be conceded to those contemporary sculptors who endeavoured to continue unbroken the Greek tradition even if their labours resulted in nothing better than the writhing horrors of the Laocoön or the confusion of the Dirce group.† Examples of this school too are not lacking in Rome; witness the Belvedere Torso or the bronze boxer,‡ both by the same man Apollonius. There is a vigour about them that is refreshing after the banalities of the Pasitelean school.

We know from history that portrait statues had long been common at Rome. The Forum was full of them. We saw in an earlier chapter how the old Etruscans had placed terra-cotta representations of the deceased upon their tombs, and how the old Romans preserved wax images of their fore-fathers for use at funerals. Most primitive peoples have an instinctive dread of portraiture as a sort of blasphemy. Perhaps the early growth of facial portraiture at Rome was helped by the worship of a man's *genius,* his luck, his spirit, his guardian angel. The genius naturally was depicted in the likeness of the man himself. So the *imagines* in a Roman atrium were no mere portraits of defunct ancestors. Rather they were visible presentments of invisible presences. Unfortunately very few unquestionably genuine examples of republican portraiture have survived. Portraits of ancient celebrities were freely constructed in later days, and it is not easy to date them. Nor are we helped by the anxiety of our grandfathers to find a historical name with which to christen a likely-looking bust; many

* Plate 21.
† See *The Glory that was Greece,* p. 293, Pl. 97.
‡ Plate 22.

of the Scipios, Sullas, Brutuses, etc., which still appear in text-books are fanciful identifications. There are no portraits of the republic surviving of a date earlier than the first century B.C., and nearly all of them we must perforce be content to leave anonymous.* Most show a hard realistic style, often of undeni-able power. Portraits of Julius Cæsar† are less common than they are said to be and none is contemporary. Nearest to him perhaps is a head in Naples which recalls the hard republican style. The bust of Pompey‡ may also be identified by comparison with the coins. That of Cicero is known from an inscribed bust in Apsley House.§

This art of realistic portraiture, then, is claimed as the great contribution of ancient Rome to artistic progress. It yet remains to be shown that any part of the work was done by native artists. At present the evidence is all in favour of Greek authorship. But the Romans may claim the credit of demanding or even inspiring realism. Roman archæologists, especially those who, like Wickhoff and Mrs Strong, are concerned to plead the cause of Roman originality in art, often seem to assume that the Greeks of the best period could not express individuality, in fact that the ideal tendency of their statues, portraits included, is due to convention if not to the sheer limitations of their craftsmanship. Elsewhere we have seen that much of the apparent simplicity of Greek work of the best period is really elaborate self-restraint. All their reli-gious ideas forbade them to express divinity with any marks of time or place upon face or feature. So when it came—as it came slowly--to portraying a statesman like Pericles, or a monarch like Alexander, they deliberately honoured them by idealising them and smoothing away the accidentals. Thus they concealed the inordinately long skull of Pericles by depicting him in a helmet. They could be realistic enough when they chose to be, but that was never in the adornment of temples except just so far as to indicate the barbarity of Centaurs or Giants in contrast to the perfection of the Greek. Myron's Cow has perished without off-spring, but the slave-boys on the tombstones are realistic enough

* Except the contemporary coin portrait of Flamininus minted in Greece (c. 195 B.C.) and the still earlier portrait on a coin from Carthago Nova in Spain which probably depicts Scipio Africanus Maior.—EDD.
   † Plate 23.
   ‡ Plate 24.
   § Plate 25.

—to say nothing of the Ludovisi Reliefs. Realism was no new discovery of the Romans. On the contrary, so far as it was an
innovation it was an act of indulgence, a breaking down of self-
imposed barriers. Even then it was not inspired entirely by
abstract passion for the naked truth, such as moved Cromwell
to command his portrait-painter to include the warts. The
Romans were a rhetorical, not a realistic people. I believe that
Roman realism in portraiture is chiefly due to the national custom
of preserving the *imagines* of the illustrious dead. On Greek soil
the Greek artists were still idealising their portraits—witness the
fine head of Mithridates on the coins of Pontus; but when their
Roman sitters asked for realism they gave it—gave it sometimes
with the unexpected thoroughness of Sargent. Besides coins and
statues there are very fine portraits on the gems of the first century
B.C.

Towards painting too the Romans may have inherited from
Etruscan times some traditional bent. We hear of Greek painters
highly esteemed at Rome in this period as well as of imported
Greek pictures fetching enormous prices. The Romans loved
colour, and their villa walls were commonly stuccoed and painted,
if not incrusted with marble, while their floors began to be inlaid
with pictorial mosaic. But we have little or nothing of this date to
show. It should, however, be noted that the graphic taste of the
Romans, together with their habit of treating art as mere decoration, was now leading to a new phase of pictorial sculpture which
will have important effects in the bas-relief work of the Augustan
period.

IV

AUGUSTUS

ultima Cumaei uenit iam carminis ætas;
magnus ab integro sæclorum nascitur ordo.
iam redit et Virgo, redeunt Saturnia regna;
iam noua progenies cælo demittitur alto.

V I R G I L

V I R G I L ' S Fourth Eclogue, from which my text is quoted, is often called the "Messianic Eclogue". It is a strange poem. In the midst of a book of pastoral eclogues closely modelled on the Idylls of Theocritus, the young poet from Mantua inserts one in which he invites the Sicilian Muses, that is, the Muses of Theocritus, to assist him in a loftier strain than usual. His poem is a vision, a prophecy of a return of the Golden Age to accompany the birth of a child. It is not easy to determine what child. The poem was written for the consulship of Pollio, who had helped Virgil after he lost his paternal farm. Thus it is possible that the poem was really a piece of delicate flattery directed to a patron. Nevertheless, the prophecies of peace on earth which it foreshadows chime so strangely with the Messianic language of Isaiah that the scholars of the Middle Ages alternatively placed Virgil among the prophets or condemned him as a wizard. But apart from that approaching event to be witnessed in an obscure village of the client-princedom of Judaea, there was even in secular history a general expectation of better days to come. The Virgin Justice did in sober fact soon return to the Roman world, when Octavian, in 29 B.C., came home to celebrate his triumph over the three continents.

I make high claims for Octavian*—or, as he may now be called by anticipation, "Augustus"—in history. Julius Cæsar has usurped

* Frontispiece, and Plates 27 and 28.

the credit of inventing that wonderful system, the Roman Empire. The credit really belongs to Augustus. Monarchy, indeed, had for two generations at the least become inevitable at Rome, as everybody, from Catiline to Cicero, was bound to admit. In the scramble to realise it Julius Cæsar had won the day, but he died before his plans were perfected and we have no means of knowing his inner purpose. But we know that he had spurned the dignity of the senate, had taken some of the paraphernalia of royalty and set up his statue alongside of the old kings of Rome. His plans for the future had failed, because he had not reckoned with the tyrannicidal sentiment of the Roman nobles. His assassination was no mere episode or accident. It was impossible to live like an autocrat in the republican city without a personal bodyguard. Julius Cæsar had failed through pride. When he fell, the whole dreary round of proscriptions, triumvirate, and civil wars had to begin again. The inevitable monarchy had to be devised afresh on a different basis : that was the task of Augustus. He devised it in such a manner that it lasted in the West for just five centuries and in the East for nearly fifteen. Judged by results then, the work of Augustus was clearly a consummate piece of statesmanship. When we consider the methods by which that result was obtained we shall, I think, esteem Augustus as the greatest statesman in the history of the world.*

Augustus has never been a popular hero. The pure statesman who has few dashing feats of arms to his credit, and who has left us no records of impassioned eloquence, does not lend himself to idealisation. Augustus had no contemporary biographer, nor even any very great historian ancient or modern. The early Empire is in the gap between the end of Mommsen and the beginning of Gibbon. Gardthausen collected all the available material about Augustus but scarcely succeeded in making him clear or real to us as a man. Tacitus touched him off in a few satirical epigrams as the crafty tyrant who "bribed the army with gifts, the populace with cheap corn, and the world with the blessings of peace, and so grew greater by degrees while he concentrated in his own hands the functions of the senate, the magistrates, and the laws". For biographical particulars we have to go to Suetonius' *Lives of the Twelve Cæsars,* a most unsatisfactory source. Suetonius' pages

* For a less favourable view of Augustus see R. Syme, *The Roman Revolution* (1939)—EDD.

teem with human interest, but for purposes of history they are
provoking and baffling. He is a patient bookworm who compiles
systematic biographies with little biographical sense. As imperial
librarian he had access to most valuable sources of information
but he lacked critical instinct in using them. He simply collected
scraps from various sources and grouped them under headings.
For a list of virtues he would go to a courtier's panegyrics and
then turn to a seditious pamphlet for a catalogue of vices. His
own instinctive preference being for scandal, he has touched nothing which he has not defiled. It is chiefly due to Suetonius that
Augustus appears as a selfish hypocrite, Tiberius as a libidinous
tyrant, Caligula as a maniac, Claudius as a pedantic clown, and
Nero as a monster of wickedness. And yet under these five reigns
the Empire was growing steadily in peace and prosperity. The
rulers who were omnipotent cannot have been altogether such as
they are described. The factious senators who still dreamed of unreal republican glories and still treasured the memories of Cato
as a saint and Brutus as a martyr were not, of course, allowed
free criticism of their monarchs. They revenged themselves by
writing secret libels, many but not all of which logic and common
sense can easily disprove. When it came to popular reigns like those
of Vespasian or Hadrian the censorship of the press was removed
for a time, and then the senatorial Republicans like Tacitus and
Juvenal took ample revenge upon the dead. The scurrilous pam-
phlets were unearthed and exalted into historical documents and
so passed down to our historians as history. It is a suspicious and
thankless task to attempt the rehabilitation of these emperors. The
world is rightly sceptical of the process which it calls "white-
washing". Moreover the necessary data are wanting. We can only
allow our imaginations to suggest how different the story would
look if it had been told from a sympathetic point of view.

It is very difficult to form any complete idea of the character
of Augustus as a man. He had shown daring and ambition when
as an obscure lad he had crossed to Italy in 44 B.C. to take up his
perilous inheritance as Cæsar's heir. He had been cool and diplomatic even in those earliest days in the way he intrigued with
the senate against Antony, and then with Antony and Lepidus
against the senate. He had had extraordinary luck when both
the consuls died in the engagements round Mutina and left him,
the pro-praetor, in charge of a great army. Then we have the

infamous acts of the triumvirate, when the unfortunate senators and knights were proscribed in hundreds, and Cicero, with whom the young Cæsar had been on friendly terms, was handed over without apparent compunction to Antony's vengeance. Admirers said that in this he was overborne by his older colleague, and yielded reluctantly to a stern necessity for destroying the tyrannicide party. Enemies declared that, even if he had been reluctant to begin the bloodshed, he was the most cruel of persecutors when it started. In the fourteen years of civil war that followed, he had succeeded in winning his way through to victory more by coolness and luck than by any display of generalship. I do not think that we can fairly accuse him of cowardice. It was a bold act when he rode alone and unarmed into the camp of the rebellious and hostile Lepidus, and took his legions away from him without a blow. He had not the dashing gallantry of Antony, or the fiery vigour of Julius, but he must have had the gift of nerve and coolness. He had certainly come through the most terrible difficulties and dangers from open enemies and rebellious armies by land and sea. In the last duel with Antony luck had been with him once more. Like the rake and gambler that he was, Antony had thrown away his game for the sake of Eastern ambitions and Eastern dalliance. Then there was that last scene of Cleopatra's tragedy, when the conqueror came to her palace after Antony had committed suicide. She tried to win him by the same arts that had won his "father" and his rival. Dressed in her finest robes she came weeping to him and displayed the picture and the letters of Julius wet with her tears. He judged her splendour coldly as a future ornament for his triumph at Rome, and when she disappointed him of that by a suicide staged as all her life had been for theatrical effect, he hunted down her two elder children with the same cold ferocity as before.* Policy forbade them to survive. That was all he thought of.

And now at the age of thirty-four, with this record behind him, he had come back to Rome to celebrate his many triumphs. No doubt the few remaining nobles at Rome trembled at his coming. Remembering the proscriptions some of them might well tremble, especially those who had sided with his enemies,

* Alternatively there is some evidence to suggest that Octavian may have connived at Cleopatra's suicide: what he wanted was her Treasury, not her person for his triumph.—EDD.

with Sextus Pompeius, or with L. Antonius, or with Marcus. On the other hand, some might remember the clemency which Julius Cæsar had displayed in his hour of triumph.

Augustus had to restore confidence and order in a shattered world. He had to deal with provinces ruined and desolate, a form of government visibly obsolete, an aristocracy with immense traditions of pride and power now thoroughly corrupt and effete, a Roman mob which still called itself lord of the world, but which was in a political sense hopeless, armies which were dangerous to the state, conscious of their power and destitute of real patriotism. He had at his side a trusty general in Agrippa,* who had won many battles for him, though that in itself was generally a dangerous circumstance, and an astute diplomat in Maecenas, who for the past ten years had been controlling Rome in Octavian's name without holdng any official position. But beyond these two it was hard to know where to turn for support. The civil wars and proscriptions had almost destroyed the race of Brutus; all that was left of the aristocracy was still jealous and hostile under a cover of abject sycophancy, ready to stab him with their tongues if they had not the courage to use the stiletto. Nevertheless, Augustus had one great asset. The Roman world, exhausted with a whole generation's civil war, was longing for repose. It was ready to fall down and worship the man who would give it that. Thus the broad outlines of his policy were clear before him. He must undertake the work of healing. The fall of Julius warned him that he must not be openly a monarch, but the failure of Sulla and the actual state of Rome were equally eloquent to prove that he must retain the power in his own hands. In the lassitude following upon grave illness—for the dangers and exposure of the civil wars had weakened his health—he may have cherished occasional thoughts of a real abdication. But in his mind he must have known that it was impossible. It was, of course, equally impossible for him to govern the whole world directly without help. For that purpose the machinery of the whole constitution with its senate and magistracies had to be preserved, at any rate for the present. These were the broad lines upon which his policy was shaped.

The splendour of Octavian's triumph must have confirmed the Romans' impression that they had now a king. For three days

* Plate 31.

they saw a constant procession of prisoners, emblems of captured cities and conquered princes. Some of Cleopatra's surviving children were among his train. The three days were apportioned to the three continents, the first for the Illyrian war of 34, the second for Actium, and the third for Egypt. Cartloads of money from the Egyptian treasury rolled along the streets, and the rate of interest on loans at Rome fell instantly from eleven to four per cent. There was one significant change. In old republican days the victor had been led into the city by his colleague and the senators, now they followed humbly in the rear. Lavish triumphal gifts were distributed : 250 *denarii* to every soldier, and about 100 to every citizen. Even the boys got a present in the name of Octavian's dear young nephew Marcellus. Thus Octavian passed in his gold-embroidered purple toga, with a laurel branch in his hand, while a slave stood behind holding a golden crown of victory over his head. Of the horses that drew the chariot one was mounted by the fourteen-year-old Marcellus, famous for his early death and for Virgil's beautiful lines about him, and the other by his still younger stepson, Tiberius. Thus he was drawn up to the Capitol to deposit his laurels and his costly offerings at the feet of Jupiter.

There were festivities on many a day to follow. Temples were dedicated, one to the deified Julius and one to Venus, the goddess mother of the Julian house. There were games in which the foreign captives fought to the death. On another day the boys of the nobility fought a Battle of Troy in the circus. On another there was a great beast-hunt of strange animals from Egypt when the rhinoceros made its first historical appearance in Europe; the hippopotamus had been seen first at Rome in 58 B.C. For the first time for nearly two centuries the temple of the war-god Janus was solemnly closed. *L'Empire c'est la paix.* There are many signs of the earnest longing for Peace in the Roman world. "Pax" and "Irene" became common names in the West and East; "Pax" was the legend on coins. The Romans had now drunk their fill of bloodshed in those dreary civil wars. It was upon this new condition of things that Octavian had the wisdom to build his monarchy. The army was greatly reduced at once, from 60 to not more than 28 legions. Fortunately the treasury of Egypt enabled them to be dismissed without dissatisfaction. A change in the *imperator's* form of address to his troops indicated that they were now subject to the civil rule of a constitutional state : hence forth they were not "fellow-soldiers" but "soldiers".*

And now the work of reconstruction began in earnest. Acting merely as one of the two consuls and empowered by the senate and comitia, Octavian restored the depleted ranks of the patrician order. It is true that the patricians had no political privileges but they still had significance in the domain of religion, and their restoration as the first official act of the new regime marked a deliberate desire to conciliate the aristocracy and enlist its services in support of order. Then a census of the Roman citizens was taken for the first time for forty years. The number found was 4,063,000 heads, which was to be increased by 170,000 in the next twenty years. The census and purification of the people was accompanied by a revision of the senate-roll. Here already Octavian showed his intention to break away from the policy of Julius. Whereas Julius had aroused the most bitter resentment by introducing provincials and common soldiers into the ranks of the senate, and Antony also had secured the appointment of all sorts of disreputable friends of his own, Octavian with infinite caution and tact reduced, strengthened, and purified the roll. Then since the numbers had been reduced and it was necessary to secure full attendances for the transaction of business, the senate was induced to pass a standing order that its members must not go abroad even to the provinces without permission of its president. As Octavian was the *princeps* of the senate it meant a concentration of all the possible leaders of opposition at Rome and under his eye. During this same year, 28 B.C., the other side of his rule came into prominence, the splendid liberality which turned Rome from a city of brick into a city of marble and made this epoch to stand out next to that of Pericles as an age of brilliant culture. No fewer than eighty-two temples were built or restored in that year. Among the rest a magnificent marble temple to Apollo with a public library annexed to it was erected on the Palatine. Libraries were new and significant things at Rome. The first had been built by Virgil's patron Asinius Pollio only nine years earlier.

The time was now ripe for the all-important settlement of the constitution which historians have agreed to call the establishment of the Empire. It is important to narrate the actual proceedings, at this point, somewhat more fully than the scope of this work

* Suetonius, *Diu. Aug.* 25. See also *Diu. Iul.* 67.

generally allows. The establishment of the Empire was such a delicate and equivocal act that it has been open to various interpretations ever since. Probably in the clever brain of Octavian it was intended to be equivocal from the first, so that republican aristocrats at Rome might still believe themselves to be free, while the populace had a prince to whom they might look for their patron, and the provincials, particularly those of the orient, might have a splendid monarch for their instincts of adulation.

Towards the close of the year 28 Octavian had issued a proclamation formally reversing all the illegal acts of himself and his colleagues during the Triumvirate. It would not call the dead back to life, it would not restore Cicero to the senate, it did not even give back the land to the burghers of those eighteen confiscated townships.* But it marked contrition, and restitution of some sort was to follow. At the beginning of his seventh consulship on January 13, 27 B.C., Octavian convened a meeting of the senate and made them a long speech in which he spoke with pride of his own and his "deified father's" benefactions to the state. At the end, with a true Italian instinct for the theatre, he turned to the astonished fathers and exclaimed: "And now I give back the Republic into your keeping. The laws, the troops, the treasury, the provinces are all restored to you. May you guard them worthily". Dio Cassius, who has given us a long speech certainly of his own composition, paints the mingled feelings of the audience, the indifference of those who were in the secret, the uneasiness of those who feared that it was another trap to catch the unwary, and the joy of those who believed and hoped. The immediate reply of the senate was, it appears, to grant him further honours—the "civic crown" of oak leaves† awarded to one who had saved the life of a fellow-citizen, in token that Octavian had saved the lives of all his countrymen, and laurel trees to be planted at his gate in sign of perpetual victory; and a golden shield was set up in the Senate-house, commemorating his "valour, clemency, justice and piety". Then they conducted a long and solemn debate upon the proper title to be conferred upon their saviour and at length decided upon the name "Augustus". In these proceedings we have the measure of the Augustan senate. Already they had the instinct of courtiers. Augustus knew it, and

* See p. 114.
† See frontispiece.

therefore knew what he was about in this dramatic "restoration of the Republic". An official calendar at Praeneste records that Augustus "rem publicam populo Romano restituit", and Ovid, though a courtier, was free to say :

> redditaque est omnis populo prouincia nostro
> et tuus Augusto nomine dictus auus.*

Augustus himself records this occurrence in the great inscription (*Monumentum Ancyranum*), in which he afterwards described his achievements: "In my sixth and seventh consulship, when ... by universal consent I had acquired complete dominion over everything, I restored the State from my own control into the hands of the Senate and People".

The Senate decided upon its answer, no doubt concocted at the suggestion of Augustus. It accepted the restitution of most of the provinces, and undertook to govern them for the future by means of senatorial magistrates very much as they had been governed of old. But three provinces which were still unsettled, and required soldiers, and money, and a general, called for special treatment. Augustus was therefore entreated to take for his province Syria, Gaul, and Spain for a period of ten years. Gaul was not yet completely organised; besides, Julius had left to his successor the task of adding Britain to it. Syria was of the utmost importance, because the Parthians were still "riding unavenged" flushed with fresh victories over Antony. This was another of the legacies of Julius. Part of Spain was still largely unconquered and in great disorder. Military needs were more powerful than economic motives in the selection of these provinces. It is to be noted that there was no question of the restitution of Egypt. Augustus had never given this kingdom to the state. He still kept it for the sake of its treasures, as a private domain, and governed it through an agent, a mere knight, not even a senator. Augustus could govern these three great provinces by means of subordinate legates, much as Pompeius had governed Spain in 52 B.C., and for this purpose either his consular *imperium* (he was consul in 27 B.C. and for the next four years) was extended beyond Italy or else he received a special grant of proconsular *imperium* for ten years. The ingenious nature of the whole compromise will be manifest when it is perceived that this arrangement of provinces left the senate

* *Fasti* I, 589-90.

with but few legions under its command, while the bulk of the
Roman army was concentrated in Augustus' provinces.

Now let us consider the constitutional position of Augustus in
these years from 27 to 23, when a slight rearrangement was
effected. He continued each year to be elected consul with a
colleague for one year, until he had far outstripped even the record
of Marius. In addition to this he had *imperium* over his enormous
province, which included most of the armies of the state. That
power was ostensibly granted for ten years, but as a matter of
fact it was renewed with some ceremony at intervals of ten or
five years throughout the reign. Constitutionally he was by no
means master of the world although, of course, he was so in reality.
He says himself: "I excelled all in prestige (*auctoritas*), but of
magisterial power (*potestas*) I had no more than my colleagues in
each office". For the maintenance of his domestic dignity, he had
in addition to the consulship various privileges of tribunician
authority. His person was protected by the sanctity of that office,
and it is probable that all prosecutions for treason were taken on
that point. He also became chief priest in 11 B.C., when the Pontifex Maximus died. He was also *princeps senatus,* but that simply
meant that his name came first on the roll of senators, so that he
had the right to speak first. However, when Augustus said "aye",
it would be a bold man who would say "no".

For the lawyer this exhausts his titles to power, but in reality
he was something very much more than consul with tribunician
powers. The one word that embraces all his authority is the word
"princeps". "Princeps" is not the title of any office, it merely
expresses dignity. He is "the chief", he is "Cæsar the August, the
son of the God Julius, ten times hailed as general". It is historically
misleading to speak of these early *principes* as "Emperors", for
that word implies notions of purple and crowns really foreign to
their position. Any stout republican who chose to be deceived
could still boast that he was governed by senate and comitia, by
consuls, praetors, ædiles, tribunes, and the rest of them. It is even
historically false to believe that the senate and magistrates had
ceased to exist for practical purposes. They had, as we shall presently see, a very real function in the state, especially when
Augustus was abroad, as in the earlier years of his rule he constantly was. It was impossible for one man to govern the whole
empire. Little by little, when a complete imperial bureaucracy

was evolved, the senate really sank into insignificance, but for the present Augustus and the senate were to some extent colleagues in the government of the empire.

It is equally unhistorical to assert, with some historians, that this "Restoration" was a genuine abdication, and that Augustus only continued to act as the senate's executive officer. Sometimes he did act in that capacity, often he made a pretence of so acting. Especially, when there was anything disagreeable to be done, he liked to get it authorised by a decree of the senate. But no intelligent Roman can have failed to perceive that there was no real equilibrium between Augustus and senate. He had not only the control of nearly all the legions, but he had the only troops in Italy, the prætorian guard which he established, at his beck and call. Roman generals had always had their life-guards. The law forbade the presence of an army at Rome, but Augustus had shown his usual ingenuity in circumventing the spirit of the law, while respecting its letter. An army meant a legion, and a legion consisted of ten cohorts generally of six hundred men each. Very well, Augustus would only have nine cohorts. But each consisted of a thousand men; and to these he added eleven other cohorts which were not reckoned as part of the prætorians; four were "urban" to police Rome, seven were the "watch cohorts" to act as a fire brigade. Thus he found himself in command of twenty thousand men, more than equal to three legions, the majority in permanent quarters within the city. If he thus had the men, he had the money too. He had the enormous treasury of Egypt in his pocket, Spain was rich in undeveloped mines, and Gaul had great possibilities as yet unexploited. Moreover, Augustus had inherited an immense patrimony from Julius, and the legacies of admiring friends also increased his wealth. Thus it came about that the senatorial treasury simply could not exist without help from the imperial purse. His private wealth, too, enabled him to keep the Roman mob happy with cheap or free corn, public shows, and handsome buildings, and to satisfy the troops with lavish bounties. There was no real equilibrium.

On the other hand, Augustus was very careful not to wound republican sensibilities. He was himself of a distinctly historical and antiquarian turn of mind. He never performed a function or assumed an office without assuring himself that it was not new to the constitution. Thus when he was asked to undertake cen-

sorial duties he perhaps declined the "censorial authority", which
the senate conferred upon him, and carried out the duties by
virtue of his power as consul, having assured himself that in the
olden times consuls had performed the duties of the censor. He
was also most punctilious in his use of forms. We shall see later
something of the republican simplicity of his mode of life. He
never failed, as his "divine father" Julius had done, to treat the
senate with outward marks of respect. Call him a "crafty tyrant"
if you will. It is much more just to call him a diplomatic reformer
engaged in a necessary work of repair, working it with infinite
patience, tact, and subtlety, by the ingenious system of compromises.

In the year 23 B.C. there was a readjustment of the constitutional situation. After his return from a troublesome war in
Spain, and after a very serious illness which had brought him to
the brink of death, he formally abdicated the consulship, alleging
his ill-health as the motive. It was, indeed, more than a pretence.
The continual tenure of the consulship involved a continual series
of ceremonial duties, which added to the immense burdens of his
position. But there were political motives as well. He was now
in his eleventh consulship, and for a nation of antiquarians it was
distinctly improper that any man should compile a list of this
magnitude. Moreover, the consul had to have an apparently equal
colleague, and there was no longer at Rome an unlimited supply
of nobles suitable to be Augustus' colleagues. Besides, it blocked
the road to honour; it was difficult to find men of consular rank
for the consular provinces. More than all, it was unnecessary.
Therefore in order that he might not be molested with reproaches
he retired to his Alban Villa, and sent a letter to the senate not
only renouncing the consulship, but suggesting as his successor a
notorious republican who had fought for Brutus against him and
still honoured the memory of Brutus as a martyr in the cause of
liberty.

That this was another solemn farce, or rather another deep
stroke of statecraft, is quite clear. The senate replied by offering
him the very powers he needed to maintain his real position unimpaired. The consular power over the provinces was continued,
without any new enactment, as "proconsular". He already possessed the authority of a tribune, but from now on he begins to
make fuller use of the powers inherent in the tribunate, and hence-

forth dates his years of rule not by consulships, but years of tribunician power. His *imperium* over the provinces was defined as "superior" to that of other magistrates, and he received the special right which belonged to the consuls of proposing the first motion at any meeting of the senate. Practically, then, he was relieved of some tiresome duties, his position was made to look more republican, and at the same time he had increased rather than diminished his authority.

By this time the principate had taken its permanent form. Its powers varied considerably with the varying force of the individual emperors, and it tended by mere prescription as well as by the development of an administrative hierarchy of officials to grow more absolute as the years advance. But constitutionally very little change was made in the course of the next two centuries. It always remained a compromise, and something of illegitimacy always clung to it. From time to time the senate actually remembered that it was a governing council. It had always to be reckoned with. As for the comitia of the Populus Romanus, they continued to exist both for legislation and elections as long as Augustus was alive. But in reality the princeps had taken the place of the people in the government of Rome. Tiberius, the next successor of Augustus, virtually suppressed the comitia as unnecessary, and though once or twice in later times an antiquarian emperor might get a plebiscite passed for the sake of old times, the Populus Romanus was extinct. It perished without a groan.

The personality of a monarch had been thrust almost surreptitiously into the frame of a republican constitution. Skilfully as it had been done, the illegitimacy of the proceedings entailed certain awkward consequences. There could be no open talk of a succession. Thus when Augustus recovered from his grave illness in 23 B.C. he offered to read his will to the senate to prove that he had nominated no successor. On the contrary, he had formally handed to Piso, the other consul, a written statement of the disposition of the forces and the moneys in the treasury. That was true enough, but he had handed his signet ring, the ring by virtue of which Mæcenas had controlled Rome for ten years, to Agrippa, the man who would certainly have taken his place if he had died at that time. In reality there is little doubt that in his own mind Augustus at that time planned to make young Marcellus, the brilliant child of his beloved sister Octavia, his heir and successor. That this ultimate intention was plain to Agrippa when Augustus recovered is shown by Agrippa's sulky retirement into private life. Although Augustus could not directly or legally nominate a successor, he could train a young prince for the succession, and in his own lifetime raise him to such a point of honour that he would naturally step into the vacant place. The newly born Empire had the great good fortune that Augustus, in spite of his feeble health, lived to a ripe age and held the principate for forty-one years. But unfortunately, for various reasons, neither he nor his successors managed to establish a dynasty. Not for a hundred years, until Titus, did a son succeed his father. Augustus had nephews, stepchildren, and grandchildren, but, he had only one child, a daughter, although thrice married. All his life long he was vexed with tiresome dynastic problems, and each youth whom he selected for his successor seemed to be destined to a premature death. At the last he was driven, sorely against his will, to nominate his stepson Tiberius, whom he disliked. This fact is mentioned here because it was a vital fact in determining the future of the principate. If each of the first half-dozen holders of that office had been surrounded by a large family, it is likely that the principate would have settled down quietly into a hereditary monarchy. As it was, the whole system was upset by continual intrigues for the succession, sometimes leading to actual warfare. Thus the army and the prætorian guard came to acquire a fatal domination over Roman politics.

THE SENATE

For all his moderation Augustus had successfully gathered all the strings of policy into his own hands. In his repeated revisions of the senate-list he succeeded in securing a body subservient to his wishes, and the only trouble it caused him was by its excess of zeal for his dignity. As a rule it merely registered his decrees, conferred honours on the kinsmen he delighted to honour, and sometimes shouldered the responsibility for an unpopular proposal. It was to some extent a safety-valve for the expression of public opinion, but the more tyrannical emperors kept a very tight hand upon it, and Augustus undoubtedly became more absolute as his system developed. When an embassy came from an independent foreign power, such as Parthia, it went first to a powerful senator, just as in republican days, to seek a *patronus* or champion. Now that champion was, of course, none other than the princeps. By him the ambassadors were introduced to the senate, who heard their case and deliberated upon it. As of old, they would necessarily entrust the settlement of the matter to a commissioner chosen from their own body. Again, the commissioner was of course the princeps. The senate sometimes undertook state impeachments as a high court of justice, but now it was only Augustus' enemies whom they impeached, and in one case—that of the prefect of Egypt—they displayed an excess of zeal in Augustus' cause which brought down a rebuke upon their heads. The senate was often used as a medium of publication. Augustus would go down to the house and read a speech to them when he intended to reach a wider public. When he was abroad, he would send regular reports and despatches to them. Augustus, like all Roman magistrates, had his *consilium* or board of advisers. This was now organised to consist of so many representative senators. Towards the end, when Augustus grew old and infirm, this committee of senators sitting in the palace, and reinforced with members of the imperial family and with nominated members of the equestrian order, acted as a privy council and was competent to transact business even without senatorial confirmation. But as a rule he was very careful to respect the senatorial traditions. Decrees of the senate and laws were passed with all the old formalities (the senate was indeed virtually given the right to issue legally-binding decrees), but now they were all in reality Augustus' laws and Augustus' decrees. On the whole, however, we may well believe that the senate's decline into impotence was largely its own fault. The Augustan senate displayed little trace of spirit or, if that is too much to expect, even of initiative. There was grumbling and a little feeble plotting, but if the senate had chosen to take Augustus at his word whenever he spoke of abdication, they might have recovered real power, though indeed they could not have done without a princeps. For one thing the mob would not have suffered it. Augustus was, and remained, the patron of the inarticulate commons. When we speak of unpopular emperors such as Nero or Domitian, we generally mean only that they were unpopular with the notables of the senate. If they failed to retain the regard of the common people and the common soldiers, their reigns speedily came to an end. Augustus' resignation from the consul-

ship in 23 B.C. was shortly afterwards followed by a famine at
Rome and the populace besieged the senate-house, threatening it
with fire unless fresh powers were conferred upon their champion.

German historians have used the term Dyarchy to describe the
balance of power between Augustus and senate. The government
of Rome had always been to some extent a Dyarchy of senate and
people as its title shows—"Senatus Populusque Romanus". In
many respects the princeps had taken the place of the people.
But such a description loses sight of reality. You cannot in this
whole period show an army set in motion by a senatorial governor
without authority from Augustus, save in the case of the governor
of Macedonia, M. Primus, when it was instantly followed by a
prosecution (23 B.C.); not a single tax imposed, nor a law so much
as proposed without Augustus' authority, nor a treaty made otherwise than in accordance with his suggestion. The true relation
between them is practically that of a monarch and his council.
Augustus frequently revised the roll of the senate, reducing it
from a thousand members to six hundred, and for all his tact and
ingenuity arousing the fiercest resentment. There were violent
scenes in the house, and Augustus wore a shirt of mail and went
accompanied by ten stalwart senators. It is clear that he was
purging the house of his opponents just as Cromwell did. On
other occasions he would present his friends with the amount of
property needed to complete their qualification for the senate.
Thus it is no exaggeration to call the senate his council of state.
If it is objected that the senate still governed rich and important
provinces, that is more apparent than true. No longer did the
governor of a senatorial province go out girt with the sword that
signifies *imperium* or wearing the military cloak. Now he goes
in his toga as a mere civilian functionary. That little change must
have been bitterly galling to the proud aristocracy. Augustus had
persuaded the senate to pass an ordinance forbidding its members
to go abroad without his permission. He made them fine their
members for non-attendance, and it is highly significant that it
was difficult to keep a quorum of the senate for public business.
He chose his own order for asking their opinions and thus pro-
moted them in honour or degraded them as he pleased. It was
mainly the peaceful and contented provinces that had fallen to
their share. Asia was the richest and most important, but almost
throughout the period there is some member of the imperial

house with a general control over the affairs of the East. There is an inscription in Cyprus which proves that even when that island was under senatorial government a proconsul was re-appointed "By the authority of Augustus Cæsar and a decree of the senate" to restore order. Finally by the end of the reign the senate had become so feeble and unreal that a score of its members sitting in Augustus' house were able to pass decrees which had the full validity of the old sovereign council of Rome.

These considerations are enough to prove that Monarchy is the only term which can properly describe the real nature of the new government. Nevertheless, here as elsewhere in this system of compromise and half-way houses, we must walk warily between two fallacies. The senate is there and will always be there. When Constantine made a new Rome he made a new senate. As we study the subsequent progress of the Empire we shall sometimes find the senate really active. It chose Galba and Nerva (A.D. 68 and 96). It dared to depose Maximin (A.D. 238). It exercised control through Tacitus and Probus (A.D. 275-82). It was its constant aim to get its members declared immune from prosecution and sometimes it succeeded; but more often it served as a whipping-stock when the emperor was in a bad temper. Only in this sense is there any meaning in the term Dyarchy: if we take the whole period of the principate from Augustus to Diocletian there is some trace of equilibrium, faint though it be. And we must not fall into the error of despising the letter of a constitution for the sake of its spirit. Though a king of England never refuses a bill in practice, it nevertheless remains important that he may. The letter is always there for reference, if not for use, and the spirit is always liable to be brought up for trial before it. The practice depends upon personal forces which are transitory, the theory is always there awaiting its opportunity.

THE PEOPLE AND THE MAGISTRATES

Nevertheless, if it is to the letter of the constitution that one appeals, we must not forget the existence of a third element in the constitution of Augustus—the People. As we have seen, the plebiscite and the lex were still formally passed. The plebiscite had of late republican years become a weapon of opposition to the senate. Yet even under Augustus we can point to a few measures passed in this form. None were of much importance—one was merely the conferring of the new title of "Father of his Country" upon Augustus. Another concerned aqueducts. The judicial functions of the populus were entirely abrogated by Augustus, and there only remained that which, after all, had always been its most important function, the elections. Popular election in the comitia was still under Augustus the chief path to the senate and the magistracies.* It is true that the magistracies had all paled into insignificance before the new and mighty office of the princeps. For this reason, perhaps, Augustus did not deprive them of what they regarded not only as an ancient right, but still more as a source of income. He had, moreover, two direct methods of securing the return of his nominees. In virtue of his consulship, he had acquired the right to draw up the list of candidates, a right which he retained after 27 B.C., and in the second place it had always been the practice for candidates to put forward the names of their principal supporters. Augustus in his early days of strict deference to constitutional etiquette used to go down to the forum and personally canvass for his friends; afterwards, however, he reverted to the brusquer methods of Julius, and merely issued a fly-sheet to the electors bearing the names of those he commended. Augustus seems to have acted with moderation: unlike later emperors he did not nominate the same number of candidates as there were vacancies, nor did he normally "commend" men for the higher offices, using his influence rather to get the right sort of men in the lower offices and so start them on their careers. But the elections became more and more a form, and Tiberius transferred them to the senate without arousing much opposition. In the whole period of Augustus we have only one instance of his failure to pass a law which he desired, and then it was due to the organised opposition of the knights, who demanded its rejection publicly in the theatre.

The equestrian order still remained the stronghold of the wealthy bourgeoisie. Owing to their wealth and their want of political recognition, they had always been somewhat of a danger

---

* Through the discovery of an inscription at Heba in Etruria, we now know that by a law of A.D.5 the first stage in the elections was put into the hands of a special electoral body drawn from the senatorial and equestrian orders; the names chosen by this body then probably had to be confirmed formally by the Comitia until Tiberius deprived the people of this formality.—EDD.

to the republican constitution. It is typical of the skilful statesmanship of Augustus that he saw this and provided an honourable outlet for their ambitions as well as utilising their services on behalf of the state. He had begun his period of rule by putting a mere *eques* into the seat of the Ptolemies as his prefect of Egypt. Subsequently the other great præfects (Prætorian, Corn supply, Vigiles, etc.), the governors (procurators) of some of the smaller imperial provinces (as Judaea) and the fiscal agents (procurators) in the imperial provinces were chosen from this order. In finance he made great use of them, and along with a certain number of clever Greek freedmen they filled the greater part of the new bureaucracy which he gradually created. Mæcenas himself, who was probably at the head of the whole great system, and who acted almost as prime minister to Augustus until he fell out of favour, was content with equestrian rank. Social honours such as rich men love were freely bestowed upon them. The young princes of the imperial house rode at the head of the knights with silver lances as "Princes of the Youth". Sometimes Augustus treated the equestrian order as if it were a third limb of the constitution on an equality with the senate and people.

It was chiefly to the senators and knights that Augustus turned for the administration of the empire. One of the reasons for the collapse of the Republic had been the lack of an adequate civil service; Augustus took steps to ensure that the empire should not suffer the same fate. The prerequisite was to build up a pool of able and upright men from which the administrators could be drawn. Augustus therefore reorganised the conditions for entry into the senatorial and equestrian orders and arranged a graded system of posts and promotion for members of each of the two orders; in general governorships of provinces and the higher military commands were reserved for senators. These new officials continued to work from year to year, many of them making administration their life-work. Thus a professional body of public servants gradually came into being. Further, it was part of the system of Augustus to provide careers for talent in every class. Even the slaves and freedmen had considerable opportunities in Cæsar's bureaux. For the freedmen in the country towns, where they were often the richest inhabitants, he invented the special titular distinction of "Augustales", their principal duty being to give dinners and festivals in his honour, precisely the sort of duty to flatter their pride without doing any harm.

As for the ancient magistracies of the Roman people, while they were strictly preserved, they were utterly disarmed. Consulships remain important only as leading to a subsequent governorship of a province. The prætors still sat in their courts of justice but really important cases came up to Cæsar on appeal. The tribunes were of no account beside their mighty colleague. Magistracies were bestowed as marks of imperial favour. The consuls no longer held office for the full term of a year, but were replaced by others halfway; under later emperors they were changed every few months. Augustus himself would sometimes deign to take a consulship when he wished to honour a colleague or a relative. Here again, however, the impotence of the magistracies was very largely due to the intellectual bankruptcy of the Roman nobility. They could not perform an administrative task such as the charge of the corn-supply without the assistance of Augustus. But on one occasion when a certain ædile* organised a fire-brigade of his own and became very zealous in extinguishing fires, he received a hint that his zeal was unwelcome in the highest quarters. Thus the magistracies declined little by little into mere decorations, or became once more what they had been in the beginning, municipal officers for the city of Rome. But even there they were superseded by the organising activity of the princeps. He resuscitated the ancient office of city prefect and put him in charge of the new police while two other new prefects commanded the prætorian guards. These two officers soon began to over-shadow the old magistracies.

ARMY AND TREASURY

Dio Cassius rightly asserts that the real power of Augustus rested upon two things—the control of the army and of the finances. We have already seen that in the so-called abdications of Augustus there was no surrender of these and no suggestion of their surrender. In view of a tendency among some historians to attach

* Egnatus Rufus, aedile in 20 B.C., who won popularity by organising his fire-brigade, and was at once elected prætor, without the usual interval between offices prescribed by custom. This turned his head; he tried to become consul and launched a plot to murder Augustus, but was apprehended and executed.—F.N.P.

real importance to the restoration of the Republic in 27 B.C. and again in 23 B.C., it is all the more important to remember that the 27 or 28 legions which with the auxiliaries and reserves formed the entire military force of the Roman Empire took their oath solely to Augustus and were with one exception stationed exclusively in his provinces, fought under his auspices and took their orders from no other but Augustus and his legates. Beyond these he had a prætorian corps of 9000 men in permanent cantonments within striking distance of Rome, as well as a drilled bodyguard of slaves in his own house. In view of these facts it is absurd to limit our conception of the power of Augustus to a survey of the constitutional offices which he held. It is only in the language of lawyers and pedants that his authority rested upon proconsular and tribunician powers. Everybody knew that a letter sealed with Augustus' sphinx was backed by the swords of 150,000 legionaries. The military situation of Augustus is therefore of the utmost importance.

Augustus was, as we have seen, a statesman and not a soldier. The stories of his cowardice, repeated by Suetonius, are confessedly drawn from the venomous letters of his enemy, Antony. Augustus had emerged successfully through five civil wars, had shown personal mercy in the Illyrian war, had faced mutinous armies and every sort of hardship. But all his instincts were for peace and statecraft. We have seen that it was the need of a standing army at Rome which led to the need of permanent generals, and this to the downfall of the old Roman constitution. When Cæsar built his throne on the ruins of the Republic the plain fact was that the general had become monarch. Thus, in spite of the fact that Augustus was not of a military character, and in spite of all his efforts to prevent it, the monarchy of the Roman Empire was eventually revealed as a military despotism. It was the irony of fate that such a man as Augustus should have founded such a monarchy.

But for the present the ugly fact that the army had bestowed the purple was decently concealed. Augustus from the very beginning of his power did his best to reduce the military element in the state. During the civil wars, and indeed for fifty years before they began, the troops had made and unmade consuls, there had been constant mutinies and blackmail in the army. Cæsar's own first consulship had been obtained in this way. A centurion had marched into the senate-house and cried, "If you will not make him consul, *this*"—and he tapped the hilt of his sword—"this shall". But now the older discipline was revived. Agrippa in particular was a stern disciplinarian of the old school. The soldiers were flattered no longer. For an honour a legion was allowed to call itself Augusta, for a punishment the title was revoked. The highest military distinction, the triumph, was gradually reserved for the princeps and the members of his house alone. Even when the title of Imperator was earned by a victorious general it was transferred to the princeps. But it was his aim to see that no private citizen should have the opportunity of securing high military honours. Agrippa might have been dangerous and accordingly he was brought into the family by marriage with Augustus' daughter. But for the rest the conduct of important operations was almost always confided to one of the young princes—to Tiberius, or Drusus, or Germanicus. And they were generally victorious. When Quinctilius Varus, a general of humbler birth, was allowed to lead a great army, he conveniently pointed the moral by a signal failure. No senatorial governor might now levy troops or declare war on his own account.

The only hand that the senate still had in military affairs was that a "senatus consultum" was generally sought for a new levy of troops. This was probably because it concerned the state treasury, but partly because it served to shift an unpleasant responsibility off the shoulders of the princeps. It is not likely that Augustus had forgone the right to levy.

It still remained the legal duty of every Roman citizen to serve in the army. But since the days of Marius that duty had become obsolete; no one wanted the city riff-raff in the legions. Soldiering had become a profession, and there was never now any general levy of the kind involved in modern conscription. There must have been some compulsion upon the upper classes to serve as officers, for Suetonius tells of a Roman knight who was sold into slavery because he had chopped off his sons' thumbs to enable them to evade military service.* Normally, however, numbers were kept up by voluntary enlistment. The legions, which now became permanent units with numbers and titles, were mainly recruited from Italy and the western provinces. The only people in the East who were enrolled in the legions were the Galatians,

* *Diu. Aug.* 24.

49.
AQUEDUCT OF
CLAUDIUS (c. A.D.
50). Serving Rome.

50.

ARCH OF
TITUS.
(A.D.70) in
Roman
Forum.

51.   (opposite)
Relief from
the Arch
showing
triumphal
scene.

51.

52.
ARCH OF
TITUS.
Relief show-
ing sacred
vessels.

53.
THE
COLOSSEUM.
Late 1st
Century A.D.

54. THE COLOSSEUM. Interior.

55. TRAJAN'S FORUM. The Market building.

56. (*Above*) TRAJAN'S COLUMN. Spiral reliefs illustrating
his conquests.

57. (*Opposite*) BASE OF THE COLUMN.

58 and *59* (*opposite*).   SCENES FROM TRAJAN'S COLUMN.

60. SCENE FROM TRAJAN'S COLUMN.

61.

THE PANTHEON
built by Augustus'
minister Agrippa.
Rebuilt by Hadrian
(2nd Century A.D.).

62.

HADRIAN'S
VILLA near
Tivoli (begun
A.D. 126).

63.

HADRIAN'S
MAUSOLEUM
by the Tiber
(Castel S.
Angelo).

64. TEMPLE OF THE DEIFIED HADRIAN (A.D. 145).

65. (*Opposite*) PALATINE HILL AND FORUM.

who were Gauls by ancestry. Normally recruits were Roman citizens, though in case of need others might join : at the crisis of the Pannonian revolt even some liberated slaves were enrolled in special companies. Although there were probably over four million full Roman citizens, there were probably only some 150,000 men in the ranks of the legions, and as the normal period of service was twenty years, it follows that only a moderate number of recruits would be wanted every year. The legionaries were, however, supplemented by another body of men, in number not far short of the same total. These were the "auxiliaries", levies drawn from the non-Roman subjects of the empire, who patrolled the frontiers; their organization was quite separate from that of the legions. The provinces would contribute in proportion to their warlike activity : for instance, since the horsemen of Holland were famous, the Batavians had to supply large contributions of cavalry. This army of some 300,000 men was certainly not too large in relation to the needs of the empire; indeed it may seem to have been dangerously small to hold such vast frontiers.

Augustus was successful in reducing the enormous rate of pay which had prevailed during the civil wars. After the death of Augustus the troops mutinied and demanded an increase of their pay to a denarius a day. Augustus established a special military chest to provide pensions for his veterans in place of the farms which they were still accustomed to expect.

How greatly—how dangerously—Augustus had reduced the size of the army may be seen from the fact that there were over sixty legions after Actium (31 B.C.) and only twenty-five at his death. These troops were for the most part stationed along the northern and eastern frontiers;

In Spain	3 legions
Upper Germany	4 ,,
Lower Germany	4 ,,
Pannonia	3 ,,
Dalmatia	2 ,,
Mœsia	2 ,,
Syria	4 ,,
Egypt	2 ,,
Africa	1 ,,

To these must be added the 9000 men of the prætorian guard, who enjoyed shorter service (sixteen years) and double pay. The prætorians had to be genuine Italians, and when inside the walls of Rome wore civilian dress. There were also four "urban cohorts" as police—a new and most salutary invention—and seven "cohorts of watchmen" for the prevention of fire. Obviously with a service of twenty years there could be no reserve. But some of the veterans of the prætorian guard were used as paymasters or engineers. There were also colonies of time-expired soldiers planted as garrisons in dangerous country.

The legions themselves were stationed in great fortified camps along the frontiers of the various provinces. There were thus huge spaces of country totally without military forces. For warfare on the shores of the Black Sea troops had to be summoned from Syria. There was no such thing as a readily mobilised striking force in Italy. This was an inconvenience and a danger, but Augustus did not mean to organise a military monarchy. Gardthausen has a clever comparison of the problems before the Roman army with those faced by the British Empire. The problems were remarkably similar, for greater speed of transport counteracts the greater distances. Both peoples made great use of the system of drilling native troops. But the Romans would have been saved much trouble if they had been able to adopt the British system of a compact and highly trained expeditionary force backed by a citizen army for home defence. To be sure, the Romans now lived in a state of peace far more profound than any that the world has enjoyed before or since. For long their wars were of their own making. Within the circle of the armed frontiers the Pax Romana reigned supreme.

The creation of a standing fleet was not the least of Augustus' achievements. The Mediterranean was now properly policed and commerce was free to circulate. The Italian navy was divided into two flotillas, one for the Western Mediterranean and one for the Adriatic. Great artificial docks were constructed for them, one for the Mediterranean fleet at Misenum by opening up a connection between the Avernus and Lucrine lakes and the sea and thus creating a land-locked harbour which was used for exercising the rowers in rough weather. The construction of this Portus Julius, which was carried out by Agrippa with a lofty disregard both of the gastronomic fame of the Lucrine oysters and of the mythological celebrity of the lake of Avernus as the gateway to the underworld, excited a wonder which has been reflected in a fine passage of Virgil.*

* *Georg.* II. 161-4.

Similarly a base for the Adriatic fleet was constructed by great engineering works at Ravenna. A third harbour was created on the coast of Gaul at Fréjus (Forum Iulii). The Tiber was dredged and restored to navigation. Flotillas of small vessels were maintained on the Rhine.

The navy, however, did not even in these days attain to anything like the status of the army. It was equipped and maintained by the emperor, and manned by slaves, freedmen or provincials. Even the "prefects of the fleet", were generally freedmen. A Roman admiral, as Mommsen remarks, ranked below a procurator or a tax-collector. After the Julio-Claudian period, however, the servile element disappeared, and the status of the prefect improved. But the Romans never to the end of their days realised the meaning or importance of sea-power. Their navy was only for police work and on several occasions, as for example in the Dalmatian War, they failed to perceive that naval operations might have been of the greatest assistance to their army. It is true that there were no hostile navies in the world, but the Empire was so distributed that marine communication might have been of very great value.

The control of finance was a necessary corollary to the control of the troops. The Republic had been shipwrecked on finance almost as much as on the military system, and there is some truth in Mommsen's epigram : "the Romans had bartered their liberty for the corn-ships of Egypt". Perhaps the most sinister light in which we can regard the statesmanship of Augustus is that suggested by Tacitus. He was buying the support of all classes in the state systematically. But to that the Republic had already accustomed them.

We must clear our minds of the modern idea of a budget and a coherent public system of finance. The Romans had never paid regular taxes, at most an occasional *tributum* in time of emergency, and their financial administration had rested in the hands of young men just beginning their public career as quæstors. This was because finance was a comparatively recent idea at Rome. It was not part of the *mos maiorum* at Rome to have a financial policy, and Rome had always been a military and not a commercial state. Even now it was a cheap empire. If we except the corn-supply and civil service salaries, the pay of the army was the only large head of expenditure. On the whole, one with another, the provinces were more than self-supporting, and as time went on a prudent policy of development made them extremely profitable. As we shall see later, the encouragement of natural resources and the exploitation of minerals all over the Empire added enormously to Roman wealth. Officials and magistrates had generally been expected not only to give their services for nothing but even to pay for their honours handsomely with public works and entertainments. Public works undertaken by the state were generally carried out by slaves or soldiers. When marble was needed it was usually requisitioned from Greece or Numidia. But it was inevitable that the man who controlled the army should also possess the revenues. Julius Cæsar had simply appropriated the treasury. Augustus as usual reached the same end by a more devious path.

The enormous treasures which he disbursed were his favourite weapons of statecraft. If he had to get a friend into the senate he would simply make him a present of the necessary income. To retain the goodwill of the commons he scattered those immense largesses which he has recorded on the Ancyran monument.* To the Roman plebs he distributed the sum of about 150 million *denarii* in seven donations. On another occasion of financial stress he lent 15 million without interest. When the soldiers had to be rewarded after Actium he was able to save himself from the unpopular necessity of confiscation by finding 150 million in cash to buy them land. There was scarcely a town in the Empire which had not some splendid building to bear witness of its debt to Augustus' generosity, and we shall see how he transformed the whole aspect of the metropolis. In addition to all this he often replenished the state treasury out of his own resources. Nearly 40 million was thus transferred. In all, he gave to the Treasury, to the Roman plebs, and to discharged soldiers the sum of 600 million *denarii*. No wonder that a man who could thus pour his gold into the treasury should come to regard it as his own.

To the Roman mind it was unbecoming to a free gentleman to be asked to pay taxes in a free country. Moreover it was one of the limitations of the power of Augustus that he had no constitutional right to impose taxation on Italy. Twice indeed he proposed to inflict a property-tax on Roman citizens. In A.D. 4

---

* This is an inscription on the wall of the Temple of Augustus and Rome at Ankara. It is a copy of the official record, drawn up by Augustus himself, of the principal events of his life. (*Res Gestae*. cf. p. 229).

and 13 he took a census of all properties above 50,000 *denarii* as a preliminary measure, but on the second occasion at least it is explained by the historian as a shrewd stroke of diplomacy to make people acquiesce in the existing death-duties. The serious financial embarrassment of these years was caused by the expense of the gratuities paid to time-expired soldiers. The soldier's daily pay of less than a *denarius* was only pocket-money; he had always expected a farm on his discharge. Under Augustus this allowance of land was commuted for a bounty of about 3000 *denarii* for the legionary, or 5000 for the prætorian guard. Of course, with a service of twenty years and constant fighting, the number of veterans discharged each year must have fallen considerably below the 20,000 recruits enrolled, but still it was a heavy expense. In some cases the veterans were retained under the colours and in some cases land in new countries was still given. But this burden led to the establishment of a new military chest in A.D. 6. This was filled in the first instance by a donation of over forty millions from Augustus and Tiberius, but it was maintained by two indirect taxes which fell upon the Roman citizens—very much to their annoyance. One was a tax of one per cent. on all objects bought and sold, the other a five per cent. tax on legacies. The latter was not imposed purely for revenue. It was intended, along with other laws, to discourage celibacy, since it only fell upon those who died without heirs of kin. A tax of four per cent. upon the sale of slaves was used for the maintenance of the vigiles.

The other large head of expenditure was that of the Roman corn-supply. Two hundred thousand people received free corn and the rest of the citizens always expected to buy it very cheaply. Most of this corn came from Egypt and Sicily as taxation paid in kind. The control of the supply was in the hands of an old department, *cura annonæ*, but owing to its mismanagement there were several periods of famine, on which occasions either Augustus himself or some member of his family had to step in and put things straight. In the end he appointed a new *præfectus annonæ*, of equestrian rank, who counted as one of the leading imperial officials.

The general expenses of administering the Empire were not as great as modern analogies would lead us to suppose. No doubt the imperial legates and procurators received wages from the emperor's resources. It is commonly stated that all provincial magistrates now received a fixed salary instead of being left to plunder the provincials. The truth is that the higher magistrates of Rome never had received and did not for a long time yet receive a salary. But they had always claimed an allowance for their travelling expenses technically called "mule and tent money", and this had been fixed on a generous scale which really amounted in practice to a salary. The only change was that instead of allowing these fees to be subject to contract on the regular contract system of the republican treasury, the governors now received a fixed grant calculated according to the necessary scale of expenses in the various provinces. For the provinces an immense saving was effected in this manner, but it must have been more expensive to the central treasury.

The finances of the provinces were gradually brought into order and arranged with consummate skill. The little information that we possess tends to show that nowhere was the Augustan reformation more beneficent or more brilliantly successful. In Gaul the land-tax and property-tax were fixed in 27, on a fairly high scale it is true, but the development of commerce and agriculture fostered by the Romans made their incidence a light burden in comparison with the rapidly increasing wealth of the province. Later in the first century Roman lawyers developed a theory, which had little importance in practice, that the emperor or Roman people had *dominium* over all provincial soil. Thus tribute would be regarded as a rent paid to Rome for the continued enjoyment of lands which had passed to her by right of conquest. The tribute was everywhere reassessed upon a new valuation systematically conducted. The main direct tax was a *tributum soli* from all occupiers of land, supplemented by a *tributum capitis* on owners of other property. The chief indirect taxes (*vectigalia*) were harbour-dues (*portoria*) and taxes in kind supplied for the use of governors and their staffs. In the senatorial provinces the old system of tax-farming by contractors survived for a time, but in his own provinces Augustus instituted an imperial board of revenue administered by Roman knights with a staff of slaves and freedmen as his fiscal procurators. We have, indeed, three known cases of embezzlement by native agents. One, Eros, had advertised his insolent rapacity in Egypt by purchasing a celebrated fighting quail for an immense sum of money, and then cooking it for his dinner. Another, Licinus, a native of Gaul set to collect taxes in his own country, disarmed Augustus' wrath by showing rooms full of silver and gold, which he professed to have stored up in his master's interest. In this case it is zealous extortion which is charged against him. One of his methods was to extort fourteen months' taxes in the year by pointing out to the innocent natives that since December was by its very name the tenth month, they had two more monthly contributions to pay before the end of the year. A paymaster, also a slave, who died in Tiberius' reign, was notorious for the retinue of fourteen persons who attended him on his travels. He had his private cooks and physicians. But these are isolated cases. On the whole it is clear that the provinces were rejoicing at their deliverance from the oppression of the Republic. They were always anxious to be transferred from the senate to the emperor. If the tax-gather was still at their door, he was now a man under independent authority with a master who would listen to petitions and appeals. Moreover, they now had a government which assisted them to pay by intelligently developing their resources.

The public treasury of the senate was no longer entrusted to mere quæstors. Augustus at first instituted prefects for this also, but he soon transferred the charge to two prætors. However, he kept an eye upon its administration himself, as is shown by the fact that when he died he left to the state an account of the condition of the treasury.

It is still too early to speak of a definite system of division between the public *ærarium* and the emperor's private *fiscus*. But the budget of the senate would include :

REVENUE	EXPENDITURE
Tribute of Senatorial provinces.*	Administration of senatorial provinces.
Customs and harbour dues.	
Public lands, state mines, etc.	The corn and water supply of Rome.
Intestate estates.	
Mintage of copper.	Public worship and festivals.
	Maintenance of roads, public buildings, etc.

* It is suggested that the *ærarium* received also certain revenues from imperial provinces. The exact distribution of income and out-goings is often doubtful, seeing that in the long run the emperor controlled all three treasuries and increased or diminished their funds as convenience or caprice dictated.

The budget of the emperor would include :

REVENUE

Tribute of provinces.
Family inheritance.
Private domains, mines, etc.
Mintage of gold and silver.
Legacies from individuals.
The *aurum coronarium* (a complimentary gift from cities on accession or other special occasions).

EXPENDITURE

Administration of provinces.
The imperial privy purse.
Largesse and bounties; games and shows; new buildings.
Army and fleet.*

And the military *ærarium,* formed in A.D. 6, comprised:

REVENUE

5% legacy duty.
1% duty on public sales.
Any treasure captured in war.

EXPENDITURE

Pensions of retired soldiers.
Special rewards for valour, etc.

THE PROVINCES

Turning now to a rapid survey of the Roman world from a geographical point of view we shall see the work of restoration and repair proceeding with the same methodical thoroughness which makes this regime one of the most beneficent in the history of civilisation. We have already seen something of the provincial system as it was reorganised in 27 B.C. The provinces which fell to the share of the senate were these :

Asia
Africa
Gallia Narbonensis (transferred to the senate in 22 B.C.)
Hispania Bœtica
Crete with the Cyrenaica
Macedonia with Achaia
Bithynia with Pontus

* It is not improbable that the *ærarium* carried all the regular military expenses of all the provinces, and Augustus presented his accounts to the *ærarium* like an ordinary Roman magistrate. He was probably voted by the senate both regular and supplementary grants; he would draw the money from whatever sources were most convenient, e.g. the *ærarium* (for expenditure in Rome and Italy) or the *fisci* of his own provinces.—EDD.

Cyprus (also transferred to the senate in 22 B.C.)
Dalmatia (until the revolt of 11 B.C.)
Sardinia with Corsica.
Sicily.

These were governed by annual magistrates, chosen by lot from a list selected by the senate—the first two by proconsuls of consular rank, the others also by governors termed proconsuls but actually only of prætorian rank, that is, ex-prætors. Africa was the only one of these provinces which contained troops and the senatorial governors went out in civilian dress as administrators only. Augustus' provinces were :

Spain (except Bætica).
Gaul.
Syria with Cilicia and, until 22 B.C., Cyprus.

To these were gradually added :

Germania.
Illyricum, including Dalmatia and Pannonia.
Galatia, including Lycaonia, Pamphylia, Pisidia, and part of Cilicia, with Paphlagonia added in 5 B.C.

These were all governed by legates of Augustus, commonly chosen from the ranks of the senate, with the title of pro-prætor. They held office for as long as the emperor desired, and were provided with a staff, chosen by him, of trained financiers. In addition to these, other districts under prefects were gradually accumulated :

Egypt.
Mœsia (after c. A.D. 44 under a consular legate).
Alpes Cottiæ.
Alpes Maritimæ.

And others again under procurators :

Judæa (after A.D. 6).
Rhætia.
Noricum.

Further, there were a large number of "allied" or "client" king-doms and republics :

Thrace.	Abilene.
E. Pontus.	Emesa.
Bosporus.	Galilæa and Peræa.
Judæ (till A.D. 6).	Nabatæa.
Commagene.	Batanæa.
Cappadocia.	Mauretania.
Armenia.	
Arabia.	

And the allied states :

Lycia.
Athens, Sparta, Rhodes, and other Greek cities.

In his own provinces Augustus was supreme in all things; he had the right of making peace, war, and alliance, without consulting the senate. Though he governed through legates or procurators, the Roman law had always granted a right of appeal from a lower magistrate to his superior. This was the source of Paul's "appeal unto Cæsar" from the procurator of Judæa. In the senatorial provinces his *imperium,* which had been specially defined as "superior" (*maius*), gave him precedence, and we know from inscriptions from the senatorial province of Cyrene that on occasion he did exert his authority there although with consider-able tact. Further, when his friend Agrippa was given a special commission in the East as the deputy of Augustus, he too inter-vened in senatorial provinces. We hear of Augustus founding colonies in Sicily. Moreover, the princeps had sole authority over the army, and for any military operations it would be necessary to borrow troops from him.

The foundations of this great empire were not hastily or care-lessly laid. Although of feeble constitution and by nature a man of peace, Augustus spent the first half of his long reign more abroad than at home, in fighting rebels and organising or reforming with unwearied energy. To this part of his work we are unable to devote sufficient attention through lack of material. The ancient historians prefer to record small victories over barbarian tribes, or the petty gossip of the Roman streets, while they have little to say about the tireless administration which in one generation transformed the Roman world from a horrible chaos into that scene of peace and prosperity shown to us in the pages of Strabo and Pliny. So while our eyes are fixed upon the sins and follies of Roman emperors and courtiers, until we get an impression of rotten tyranny conducted according to the caprice of monsters and fools, all the time the greater part of Europe was advancing in peace to a state of general culture and civilisation such as it had never known before, and such as it never knew again until the nineteenth century. A casual glance over the inscriptions of a provincial town probably gives us a truer impression than all the rhetoric of the historians. In Pompeii, for example, a small town which scarcely comes into the view of history, we see a busy and useful municipal life carried on in absolute security. There were the councillors (*decuriones*), who corresponded to the Roman senate, and there were two local consuls bearing the title of *duumuiri*. In most cases a small municipality would have its *patronus* also, a local squire, perhaps, who in some measure corresponded to the princeps, and who would represent the interests of the town at Rome or with the Roman prætor. His main business, however, was to equip his town with baths, temples, and colonnades, or to provide it with public banquets. For the rich freedmen, in whose hands was much of the trade of the place, Augustus had provided the new office of *Seuiri Augustales,* which we have already described.* There were no rates, for private munificence took their place. There was no direct taxation in Italy, and the indirect taxes were inconsiderable. Internal trade was free. The obligation to military service was so widely distributed that it fell very lightly on Italy, and the population accordingly became less and less warlike. All the Italian peoples were now Roman citizens. Trade was greatly assisted by the improvement of communications which took place during this period. The care of roads properly devolved upon the senate, but as they proved inadequate in this department the princeps had to step in and organise a special Board of Roads with a *curator* for each of the trunk lines of communication. Augustus also established an imperial post with a system of stages and relays; the vehicles and horses were maintained by the roadside communities, and imperial messengers who carried a *diploma* or passport were allowed to travel express by this means. The great road to Arimi-

* See p. 163.

num, the Flaminian Way, was repaired by Augustus, who adorned its terminal city with a handsome marble bridge* and triumphal arch, possibly as a compensation for the trouble which he himself had inflicted upon the town during the civil wars. Flourishing historic cities like Turin and Brescia owe their origin to colonies founded by Augustus. Towns like Perugia which had been almost destroyed in the civil wars now grew up again and flourished. In all, Augustus founded twenty-eight colonies in Italy, and supplied 90,000 veterans of the civil wars with land either in Italy or the provinces. That the sea was now safe for trade and fishery must have meant a great deal to the coast towns. Augustus himself wrote an account of the condition of Italy, and Pliny confesses to using it as his authority. In all the long and important history of Italy it is doubtful whether she has ever enjoyed such peace and prosperity as began for her in the reign of Augustus.

A broad view of foreign politics showed Augustus two vital points of danger—the North and the East. To the north the fierce and warlike barbarians of Germany had been checked indeed by Julius, but also exasperated. Tribes more or less akin to them extended southwards across the Danube and even to the Austrian Tyrol, where they were little more than a week's march from Rome. A strong frontier policy was needed here. In the East there were the Parthians, the only possible rival power to Rome. The Romans at Carrhæ noticed that, while the chiefs wore their hair parted and curled and their faces painted in the Persian fashion, the warriors had the unkempt locks of barbarian Thrace. These Parthian bowmen had come down from the eastern shore of the Caspian Sea. They had all the characteristics of northern nomads, but their kings and nobles had a good deal of Hellenic culture. They could boast of a choice collection of Roman eagles captured not only from Crassus at Carrhæ, but from two armies sent against them by Antony. Thousands of Roman prisoners were still working as slaves on the banks of the Euphrates. The task of punishing them had been definitely laid upon Augustus as a legacy from Julius, who had been slain at the moment when he was about to undertake it himself. Moreover, the Romans felt the loss of those standards very acutely, and their feelings are reflected in Horace and other contemporary poets.

The manner in which Augustus satisfied these ardent aspira-

* Plate 96.

tions of national pride is characteristic of him. Instead of the armies and bloody battles which historians demand of their favourites, Augustus achieved his object by luck, diplomacy, and strategy. When he was organising the affairs of the East in 29 B.C., after the conquest of Egypt, he had left the Parthian question unsolved. For this, Mommsen takes him to task, but there is little doubt that it would have been folly to undertake a great and perilous war at that moment while the affairs of Rome were still in disorder. Moreover the attitude of the army compelled him to return home. Instead of fighting, he was content to set up rival powers on the Parthian frontier. The Parthians hated their king Phraates IV and there was a deposed rival in the field, Tiridates, to whom Augustus now gave shelter in the province of Syria, hoping, as indeed happened, that his presence in the neighbourhood would keep Phraates civil. At the same time Augustus set up a buffer kingdom of Lesser Armenia on the Parthian border and in the south strengthened and reinstated Herod the Great. Four or five legions were left to guard Syria.

In 26 B.C. it chanced that Tiridates had managed to kidnap the child of Phraates and was keeping him in custody in the Roman province. It is significant of the changed relations between Parthia and Rome that, instead of marching into Syria to recover the child, Phraates sent an embassy to Rome, whither also Tiridates had gone. The senate made the restoration of the child conditional upon the return of the standards and prisoners. Phraates consented, but there was some delay in carrying out the contract. Finally, however, Augustus who had in 22 B.C. set out on a tour of inspection of the Eastern provinces, marched out with an army and at his mere approach the standards and captives were given up with due formalities (20 B.C.). It was really a Roman triumph, as great as if it had been attained by bloodshed, for all the world could see the humiliation of Parthia. Augustus, that astute tactician, took care that the event should not be allowed to lose its impressiveness for the mere lack of bloodshed. The return of the standards was treated as a Roman triumph. They were placed with every solemnity in the Temple of Mars the Avenger. Coins were struck representing the suppliant Parthian on his knee and the same scene is depicted in relief on the centre of Augustus' breastplate on the famous statue (Plate 27). The poets broke out into dutiful pæans.

> nunc petit Armenius pacem, nunc porrigit arcus
> Parthus eques timida captaque signa manu

cries Ovid (*Trist.* II. 227-8). Virgil, after his manner, speaks of the
Euphrates flowing more quietly.* The odes of Horace and the
elegies of Propertius contain similar loyal allusions. Ferrero, who
regards Augustus as a feeble trickster just as he
regards Julius as a shabby adventurer, has
nothing but contempt for this episode. But, seeing
that the Parthians were now weakened by their
internal feuds and amenable to Rome, it would
have been folly to embark upon their conquest.
That they gave much trouble in the future is true
enough, but that might fairly be left for the
future to deal with. Extermination might have
quieted them for ever, but Augustus had really no excuse for
making war upon them.

Surrender of
the Standards

On the same visit to the East a still more elaborate system of
buffer states forming a double semicircle round Parthia was organised. Armenia yielded to Rome and received at the hands of
Tiberius a new king who had been educated at Rome. Augustus
himself explains that although he might have made Armenia into
a Roman province he preferred to follow the example of "our
ancestors" and give the crown to a native king. Augustus never
pretended to be a world-conqueror. Similarly Media Atropatene
received a new king of Roman education; so did Commagene and
Emesa. These formed the outer ring of buffer states.

The central state behind them was Galatia, an arid highland
district inhabited by the descendants of those Gauls who had burst
into the Greek world under Brennus. Though they had acquired
some tincture of Greek civilisation and had a capital of some
importance at Ancyra, they still spoke a Gaulish language and
were still a warlike race. For these reasons, on the death of their
king, Augustus preferred to turn their country into a province
(25 B.C.). To the north was the very friendly kingdom of Polemo
in Pontus, and to the south other friendly princedoms as well as
the Roman provinces of Cilicia, Syria, and Cyprus.

For all this elaborate bulwark, the Parthian question was not
really settled. They continued to exercise an undue influence in

* *Aen.* VIII. 726.

Armenia, and in A.D. 1 there was another solemn mission to the East and a conference between Phraataces the new Parthian king and Gaius the grandson of Augustus. Once more the Parthian professed submission, and once more the court poets struck their obsequious lyres. When Phraataces died, Orodes who succeeded ruled with such cruelty that he was assassinated. Thereupon the Parthians sent to Rome for a king and Augustus gave them Vonones a son of Phraates, a youth also of Roman education. We note this proceeding as common in the foreign policy of Augustus. He must have had something like a school for young foreign princes at Rome, but whether the lessons that they learnt in Roman society were altogether salutary is doubtful.

Behind this wall the great provinces of Asia, Syria, and Bithynia were wrapped in profound security. Here Greek culture continued to flourish, influenced by oriental religion and philosophy. In every considerable town the Jews formed a great and growing section of the population but even they were half-Greek in their ways of life. The country was rich, lazy and unwarlike. Civilisation had risen to a high pitch and it was probably this part of the world that sent to Rome those artists who contributed to the revival of sculpture. Pretty little epigrams in Greek elegiacs seem to have been their principal literary accomplishment. These provinces have very little history—happily for them—at this period. We know them best from the Acts of the Apostles, where we get a glimpse of their superstitions, their eagerness to embrace new religions. We see the fanaticism of Ephesus with its magnificent Temple of Diana and stately worship, a religion of oriental character overlaid with Greek culture. For these people as for the rest of the world Augustus had his policy. Since worship was their instinctive need and Euhemerism, with its theory that the ancient gods were but men around whom legend had gathered, had accustomed them to worship men, he set up an elaborate cult of himself, or rather, by a subtle distinction without a difference, a cult of "the genius of Augustus". Temples were built to "Rome and Augustus" with an elaborate hierarchy of "High Priests", "Asiarchs", and "Bithyniarchs", which became the highest social distinctions in the society of the day. This was his method of securing the allegiance of nations devoted to religion and flattery. Here in the near future was to be the field of that momentous conflict between this State religion and Christianity, with other oriental faiths, such as Mithraism, also claiming their proselytes.

As for old Greece, the Romans never denied their spiritual debt to her, and accordingly they regarded Greece with something of the veneration which a man feels for his university. Augustus himself had been educated at Apollonia; he sent his heirs to various Greek cities for their education. It would have seemed sacrilege to educated Romans to put a legate in charge of Athens Hence we find Greece enjoying quite an exceptional position in the Empire, indeed without exception the freest and most favoured part of it. Towns such as Athens, Lacedæmon, Thespiæ, Tanagra, Platæa, Delphi, and Olympia were free and almost sovereign. Athens and other cities were allowed to issue autonomous bronze coinage without the emperor's portrait. Athens elected her own archons and generals, held assemblies and even had a sort of empire extending over all Attica, part of Bœotia and five islands of the Aegean. One Julius Nicanor, her "new Themistocles", purchased the island of Salamis and presented it to his city in the civilised manner of empire-building. Sparta, too, though now shrunken to the size of a village, bore rule over Northern Laconia, while in the south there was a free confederacy to keep her in order. Beside these cities of ancient renown stood the new and splendid creation of Augustus—Nicopolis, the city of victory, founded on the promontory of Actium in commemoration of the great victory of 31. Nicopolis had its great athletic festival like Olympia and ruled over a considerable territory. In addition to these free cities there were some Roman colonies. Corinth rose again from her ashes as an important commercial city founded by Julius Cæsar. Patras, on the Corinthian Gulf, a new foundation of Augustus, became one of the most important cities of Greece, as it is to-day. The rest of Southern Greece, consisting mainly of obscure villages, formed the new senatorial province of Achaia and was governed by a proconsul at Corinth. It was a poor unmilitary province. The northern part formed the senatorial province of Macedonia. Thessalonica and Apollonia were the principal centres of government and civilisation in this region. In Greece, as elsewhere, Augustus made it his aim to focus a national unity upon religion. The old Achæan league was revived as a religious gathering with Argos for its centre, and the Delphic Amphictyony became the basis of a Panhellenic con-

AUGUSTUS   **183**

federacy which met annually for religious purposes under Roman
patronage, a sort of Eisteddfod combining religion with culture.
It sacrificed to Augustus, and here later we find a president called
"Helladarch". But although Greece had liberty and peace, something was amiss with her. Her shrunken population continued to
decline. In Strabo's *Geography* Thebes is a mere village.

Crossing the water, we find that the newly conquered kingdom
of Egypt was the key to the whole position of Augustus. It was
the wealth of Egypt which had reconciled Rome to monarchy
and it was by means of that wealth that he continued to hold the
allegiance of his subjects. Like Greece it had an ancient civilisation which impressed the Romans as something beyond their com-
prehension. Alexandria, in particular, as the gateway to the wealth
of Egypt and as the greatest existing centre of Greek culture, not
to mention its huge population and commercial advantages,
seemed to the Romans a dangerous rival. The fear of that rivalry
had been felt very acutely at Rome when news came of the ambitious schemes of Cleopatra and the subservience of Antony. Augustus was heading something like a national crusade when he declared war upon them. The same fears now actuated him in
settling the treatment of Egypt as a province. Though he writes
"I added Egypt to the Roman Empire", he treated it rather
as an imperial domain under a prefect or viceroy closely attached
to his interests. Its first prefect was Cornelius Gallus, a knight
from the Gallic colony of Forum Iulii (Fréjus), a poet himself
and a friend of Virgil. Cornelius Gallus was the hero of Virgil's
famous eclogue: *neget quis carmina Gallo*? It was specially or-
dained that no senator might visit Egypt without the express permission of Augustus. The native Egyptians were already overriden
by a Greek aristocracy dating from Alexander's conquest. They
had no rights, and no nationality was designed for them as it had
been elsewhere. Augustus accepted the elaborate bureaucratic
system which he had found in existence when he came. The Greek
aristocracy lived almost exclusively in Alexandria, possessing a
municipal constitution, magistracy, and priesthood of their own.
The *ecclesia* was stopped, but otherwise there was no attempt to
romanise Egypt. The old Egyptian worship of Isis and Osiris had
conquered all its conquerors and continued to make inroads even
into Rome itself, where Augustus was forced to accept it as irresistible. All that had happened in Egypt was that Augustus had taken

G.W.R.—14

the place of the Ptolemies in the official religion. It was the motive of fear which led to the appointment of a mere knight as viceroy, though he had three legions under his command. The officials under him were knights or freedmen. The taxes remained very heavy, as was necessary, but now the Egyptians were placed in a better position to pay them. Even before the civil war was quite ended in 29 B.C. Augustus had employed his soldiers to clear the canals and raise the level of the dams which ensure the Egyptian harvests. This process continued, and Egypt never had such prosperity again until Lord Cromer came to resume the work of Augustus. The harvest depended simply on the height to which the Nile rose. The ancient Nilometer at Elephantine records that the Nile rose to an unprecedented height in the latter days of Augustus. Formerly a level of eight ells had meant famine; now it ensured a tolerable harvest. Another inscription found at Coptos gives us the names of the Roman soldiers who built reservoirs of water along the great roads. Then the trade with India along the Red Sea first began to grow great. Strabo, writing under Augustus, says that 120 merchantmen would sail to the East from Red Sea ports in a single season. Taxes on exports and imports returned a huge revenue to the imperial purse.

The prefect who represented his master on the throne of the Ptolemies was in a difficult position. To Rome he was a mere servant, to the Egyptians something like a god. Against these flattering influences Gallus the poet had not strength to resist. He allowed statues to be erected to him and even had his own achievements engraved upon the pyramids. A traitorous friend reported these indiscretions at Rome. Augustus was content to recall him and forbid him to live in the provinces or to enter his presence. But the officious senate voted his condemnation to banishment, and confiscated all his property to Augustus, whereby Gallus was driven to suicide. Then Augustus was sorry and complained that it was hard not to be able to scold one's friends like a private man. This was the first case of that disease known as *delatio* (informing) which was afterwards to become such a pest under the Empire. It is satisfactory to learn that the informer was very rudely treated in Roman society. From Egypt, as a base, expeditions were made in the time of Augustus to Arabia and the Sudan. Arabia Felix was to the Romans a kind of Eldorado of boundless wealth, as Horace writes to a friend who was joining the campaign. The

Arabs brought their incense into the Syrian markets and already traded with India from Aden, but the natural wealth of the country was exaggerated and its difficulties unknown. This expedition of 25 B.C. was on a very large scale and included contingents from Judæa, but it failed in the burning and trackless deserts. The other campaign against the black Aethiopians of the Sudan under their warlike but one-eyed queen Candace was more successful. Petronius the prefect penetrated as far as the Second Cataract and sent a thousand prisoners to Rome, but Augustus seems to have been content to make the First Cataract his southern frontier.

The neighbouring client kingdom of Judæa is of importance not only because the days of Augustus saw the birth of that Child in Bethlehem who was destined to conquer Rome and through Rome the world, but because its throne was occupied by one of the ablest and most remarkable men in the whole Empire. Herod the Great, an Edomite by birth, had succeeded to the throne of the Maccabees in 37 B.C. He was not only a daring warrior but a singularly skilful diplomat who was able to cover up his crimes by adroit flattery and a fascinating manner. He was very successful in trimming between the rivals throughout the civil wars and even resisted with fair success the political intrigues of Cleopatra. In these ways he increased his domains by the addition of Gadara, Samaria, and the Philistine coast towns. In compliment to Augustus he refounded Samaria with great splendour as the Greek city of Sebaste and built Greek theatres, Roman amphitheatres, and baths in Jerusalem itself. He even instituted quinquennial games there, wherein naked athletes performed to the infinite disgust of the Jews. He took his sons to Rome for their education and there he met and fascinated both Augustus and Agrippa. He even persuaded Agrippa to visit Jerusalem for the opening of his magnificent new temple in 15 B.C. Agrippa came and sacrificed a whole hecatomb to Jehovah, to the apparent delight of the people. Later on Herod made a grand tour of Asia Minor, scattering lavish gifts everywhere and receiving complimentary inscriptions in return. He succeeded in obtaining valuable privileges for his Jewish co-religionists scattered abroad in these regions. Henceforth they were not forced to render military service and had special permission to keep the Sabbath.

In 9 and 8 B.C., however, he got into trouble with Augustus

for conducting a military expedition against the Arabs without permission. This was the greatest offence that a client king could commit, and Augustus declared that henceforth he would treat Herod not as a friend, but as a subject. But in the next year a humble embassy was sent to Rome with the historian Nicolaus as its spokesman. Herod received the gracious permission to deal with his rebellious sons as he thought fit, and accordingly strangled two of them. Herod's family history is a deplorable record of crimes and intrigues. He seems to have had ten wives, and on his death in 4 B.C., he left three sons between whom Augustus had to decide. Seeing that Judæa was so rich and powerful as to be a possible source of danger, he decided to split it up into three. Then began a whole series of troubles, in the course of which the Jews of Jerusalem actually attacked a Roman legion. In revenge the legate of Syria, Quinctilius Varus, crucified 2000 of the inhabitants. In the final award Judæa fell to Archelaus, Galilee to Herod Antipas. Ten years later, however, the infamous Archelaus was deposed at the petition of his subjects, and Judæa was made a Roman province with a procurator of its own. Herod Antipas continued to rule his petty kingdom until about A.D. 39 when it was united to the province. He is the Herod whom Christ denounced as "that fox", and he is the Herod of Christ's Judgment, when he happened to be at Jerusalem on a visit to Pontius Pilatus, the Roman procurator. Pilate was a Roman knight, but Felix, one of his successors, was only a freedman. The seat of the Roman government was not at Jerusalem, but at Cæsarea, so that the *prætorium* in which the trial of Jesus took place must have been the temporary headquarters of Pilate in the palace built by Herod the Great. The procurator only commanded auxiliary troops, and nearly all the "Roman soldiers" mentioned in the Gospels must have been of non-Italian origin, not Romans. As soon as it was a province, but not before, Judæa had to pay tribute to Cæsar. Hence the existence of a "chief of the publicans" like Zacchæus. As usual, the Romans preserved what they could of native institutions, and the Sanhedrin continued to act as a national council, so far as could be permitted. Thus it might try Jesus, but it could not pronounce the death sentence. On the other hand, another procurator, Festus, committed Paul to the Sanhedrin for judgment. The fact is that the Jewish law was so peculiarly national that a bewildered and well-intentioned Roman knight like Pilate might often say "take ye Him and judge Him according to your law". The Roman government was so tolerant of the religion of its subjects that even a Roman citizen who dared to enter the Court of the Israelites was put to death. The Jewish religion was expressly under Roman protection. Agrippa, as we have seen, had sacrificed to Jehovah, but later on we find Augustus commending his grandson Gaius for not having worshipped Jehovah. As a matter of fact, with the spread of the newer forms of Hellenic philosophy the religious feeling of the world, which had long ago given up its faith in the Olympian mythology, was turning more and more towards monotheism and a mystical system of ethics. The higher Pharisaism, which Paul had learnt at the feet of Gamaliel, was decidedly influenced by Stoicism. Hence the Jewish religion even before its Christian development was extremely fascinating to the Roman mind, and it had to be forbidden in the capital. Even at Jerusalem the Jews were expected to sacrifice, not *to* but *for* "Cæsar and the Roman People" every day. Augustus paid for this ritual out of his own pocket. In deference to the feeling of the Jews, the coins struck by the Roman procurators for Judæa bore no portrait of the emperor, and even the standards, because they bore portraits, were ordered not to be carried into the Holy City. It is likely that the Roman silver denarius from other provinces would circulate in Judæa to some extent, and it is of such a coin that Christ was speaking when He asked: "Whose image and superscription is this?"

The province of Africa with Numidia was handed over to the senate as peaceful in 27 B.C., and it was one of the only two Roman provinces which Augustus never visited. Nominally it stretched from the boundary of the kingdom of Mauretania at the river Ampsaga on the west to the borders of the Cyrenaica on the east. But actually it consisted of the fertile districts on the Tunisian coast. Carthage had been colonised by Julius Cæsar and Augustus. There was no inland frontier. In the desert behind the mountains there still flourished the wild Gætulian nomads who occasionally descended upon the peaceful province and provided a Roman triumph. This was the reason why a legion was still kept in Africa. The neighbouring kingdom of Mauretania was assigned to an interesting young royal couple. The husband was Juba, a descendant of Masinissa, who had been educated as a Roman, had served in the Roman army and was so complete a Greek scholar that he wrote among many other works a history of the Drama. The wife was a daughter of Cleopatra by Antony, and had ridden in Cæsar's triumph at Rome. Mauretania, together with its eastern neighbour Numidia which had been added to the Roman province, now settled down to wealth and happiness under the Roman rule. The splendid ruins which still survive indicate a prosperity in marked contrast to present conditions.*

Cyrene, where the descendants of the Romans carved out a province for themselves in 1911, though geographically a part of the African continent, was historically regarded as a Greek island, and united in one province with Crete. It consisted of a group of five Greek cities with a large inter-mixture of Jews. Cyrene has no history in this period, but during the widespread Jewish revolt of A.D. 116 it witnessed a terrible outburst of Jewish fanaticism. Thousands of Roman citizens were tortured and slain.

Perhaps no country in the world has had such a chequered and miserable history as the pleasant island of Sicily with its rich volcanic soil. For four hundred years it had been mainly Greek. The eastern end, at least, had been scattered with important city-states which, under the leadership of Syracuse, had waged incessant conflict with the Carthaginian invaders in their western strongholds. We have seen how the Romans finally drove out the Semitic element and conquered the Greeks. During the latter part of republican history the island had been of vital importance to Rome as supplying through its tribute the chief part of the corn-supply. At the same time it had been cruelly exploited and oppressed by Roman governors like Verres. Then during the civil wars Sextus Pompeius had made it his head-quarters, and it had been laid under heavy contributions by both sides. Messina, its richest town, had been the scene of a sack and massacre. No country had more to hope from the Pax Augusta, and it now began to enjoy one of its brief periods of rest. Augustus, who spent the winter of 22 in Sicily at the beginning of his tour in Greece, founded colonies at six famous cities of old.

So far we have been surveying the treatment of that part of the Roman world which was already quite civilised and mainly Greek. We now turn to the barbarian West and North, mainly consisting of newly conquered imperial provinces. In these

* See Norman Douglas, *Fountains in the Sand* (1912).—EDD.

quarters, the nearer parts of Spain and the Narbonensian province of Gaul were the only regions which could be called civilised. As soon as the provisional settlement of 27 B.C. was effected, Augustus hurried away to Gaul. It was generally thought that he was on his way to conquer Britain, for that was the second of the two tasks which Julius had left to his successor. Accordingly the loyal Horace dutifully prays :

> serues iturum Cæsarem in ultimos
> orbis Britannos.*

But this was not the time, and Augustus was not the man, for dazzling conquests. "Make haste slowly" was his favourite motto, and his empire policy was founded on the same principle. For the present the Ocean, then called British, was boundary enough. Augustus was reducing the army, and Britain would have taken more than one legion to keep it quiet. So Britain had to delay its prospects of civilisation until Gaul and Spain were organised and the German frontier settled. We have the record of British chiefs coming to Rome with unknown petitions during the period, but beyond that little is known concerning our island. As for Gaul, Julius had done the work of conquest thoroughly enough, and the Gauls as an adaptable people were taking to Roman civilisation with avidity. There were indeed corners of it not yet enlightened and the whole government required organisation. Augustus went straight to the capital of the old province, Narbonne, and there he arranged a census and a land register, not, as Ferrero observes, out of mere statistical curiosity. Probably no tribute had come in from Gaul during the civil wars, and Augustus was much concerned with finance. For the moment an outbreak in Spain called the emperor away, but five years later he returned to complete his work. The old province, which has passed into history as Provence, was now handed back to the senate as completely pacified, and the rest of Gaul was eventually divided into three parts : Aquitania, the half-Spanish south-west; Lugdunensis, the east and centre stretching right across France, with its capital Lyons or Lugdunum on its eastern border; and Belgica, the

* Mayst thou (Fortune) preserve Cæser, about to march against the Britons at the ends of the earth. (*Odes*, I. XXXV. 29-30).

northern part, with Trier—Augusta Treverorum, not yet founded —and Rheims as its chief towns. This division was mainly, though not entirely, based on racial considerations. Together the three formed one of Augustus' provinces as Gallia Comata.

The treatment of the conquered land was wise and humane. The druidical religion, already a waning force, was at first permitted to exist, though it included human sacrifice and was hostile to the Romans, but in the reign of Claudius it was forbidden. But other native deities were actually encouraged by the state, and Augustus himself built an altar to some strange Gallic spirits. Side by side with the native religion he fostered the new cult, as in Asia, of "Rome and Augustus". There had always been tribal councils which culminated in a great national gathering at Lugdunum once a year. Apparently the presiding priests had been elected from the well-born natives and were in opposition to the Druids. Augustus made skilful use of this organisation and fostered it in order to make it a centre for Roman patriotism. He set up a great altar at Lugdunum inscribed "to Rome and Augustus". It was constructed in a sacred grove, and was surrounded by statues emblematic of the sixty Gallic tribes. The elected priest had to be a Roman citizen of Gallic birth. It soon became a distinction coveted by the grandsons of those who had fought against Julius. This is very characteristic of the systematic empire-building which went on in the days of Augustus. Lugdunum rose to be a great imperial city, the only city in Gaul which possessed in full Roman citizenship; it was the centre for the imperial mint. From it a great and elaborate road system radiated to all parts of Gaul, very much in the same directions as the modern railways. Schools were founded and the study of Latin encouraged though not enforced. The Gauls took very ardently to their new studies, displaying in particular a remarkable faculty for rhetoric. The principle came into force that when a town or district could show that it spoke Latin it received important rights of citizenship, including that great privilege, the use of Roman law. The land system of Gaul differed essentially from that of Italy in that it was based on tribes and cantons instead of cities. Already the towns were growing as centres for the tribes, but to this day many of the names of French cities are those of tribes rather than towns: thus Lutetia of the Parisii is Paris, Durocortorum of the Remi is Rheims, Divodurum of the Mediomatrici is Metz, and Agedincum of the Senones is Sens. The tribute ultimately fixed was a high one but on the whole justly regulated. It is probable that the ugly story of Licinus and his extortions (15 B.C.) is told as an exceptional occurrence. In any case Gaul was taught how to grow rich and prosperous. Mines of silver and gold were successfully exploited, the culture of flax was encouraged, and the soil was found to be admirably suited to cereal crops. Gaul became a hive of industry and a source of ever-increasing wealth. Italian industrialists and manufacturers flocked into the country to establish factories; in pottery especially with such success that by the middle of the first century Gaul began to capture the market, even in Italy. She purchased oil and wine from Italy as well as the articles of Eastern luxury which passed through the hands of Roman merchants. A 2½ per cent. duty was charged at the frontier both on imports and exports. Such were some of the methods by which the romanisation of Gaul was effected, and the foundations so well and truly laid that through all the invasions of Franks and Burgundians, Gaul remained Roman in speech and thought, and remains so to this day.*

Of all the momentous problems which Augustus had to face, the delimitation of the northern frontier was the weightiest. It has always been one of the disputed questions of Roman history, why Augustus, who was generally so cautious and so unwilling to embark upon adventures, deliberately chose to cross the Rhine and plunge into those impenetrable forests of whose dangers and difficulties Julius Cæsar had left so clear a warning. Was it his aim to forestall the danger of a German invasion of Gaul? On the other hand, the Rhine might well seem a sufficient frontier, as indeed for many centuries it was. Was it his aim to exercise his troops in difficult warfare and perhaps secure military renown for the young men whom he had destined for the succession? These are scarcely adequate motives for a man like Augustus. Did he hope to acquire wealth out of Germany as he had done out of Gaul? He must have known that the virgin forests and undrained morasses of Germany would scarcely balance the difficulties and dangers of a campaign there, and that the Germans were far behind their Gallic cousins in civilisation. The problem seems to me insoluble

* Plates 80, 82, 83, 90 and 91.

unless we accept the theory that the whole scheme was part of the search for a natural strategic frontier.*

This penetration of Germany and its ultimate failure was a fact of vast consequence in the history of Europe. From one point of view the history of Europe may be described as a record of the various relations between the Roman and the German elements, with occasional incursions from the Celtic or Turanian fringes. It is one long contest between Latin and Teutonic race, religion, language, law, and ideas political and economic. Hence it is impossible to overrate the importance of the moment when the first round of that age-long contest was fought and settled. Hidden among the forests in those mysterious wildernesses beyond the Rhine were the numerous tribes who were destined one day to form the nations of Europe. Here were the Saxons of Saxony and England, the Swabians, the Franks, the Vandals, the Burgundians, the Goths, the Lombards, and many others, yet unnamed, the germs of the nations.

History has recorded several alarming incursions of northern barbarians, and in a general sense the story of the Mediterranean peoples shows how wave after wave of strong warriors from the North descended upon the fertile peninsulas of the South, which always absorbed and assimilated them, until finally they became a prey to the enervating influences of climate, melted into the native strain, and had to make room for a fresh wave of untamed northerners. Read in this light, extraordinary interest attaches to the moment when all-conquering Rome attempted to conquer the wilds which sheltered these mighty tribes. If she had succeeded in taming and romanising the Germans also, as she had done with the Spaniards and Gauls, the course of history might have been very different. But even then, though she knew it not, behind the Teutonic peoples lay the Slavs, and behind them the Tartars and the Huns. The task of civilising the world from a single centre was impossible. Augustus would have been wiser to choose a strong

* Augustus decided to advance the Balkan frontier northwards to the line of the Danube from Lake Constance to the Black Sea. If the Gallic frontier remained on the Rhine, this would leave an awkward re-entrant angle in the Black Forest area between the sources of the two rivers. Augustus therefore decided to advance over the Rhine to the Elbe and then by reducing the Marcomanni to link the Elbe frontier with the Danube, thus greatly shortening the lines of communication and strengthening the whole northern frontier. How near to success he came—the Pannonian revolt occurred at a critical moment—is described below.—EDD.

frontier first and then proceed gradually by peaceful penetration. Probably he judged that the policy of buffer states which he had applied in the East was not applicable to barbarians; perhaps he judged Germany a favourable field in which his young relatives, destined to be his heirs, might win military renown. As it was, conquest was the method he selected, contrary to his usual custom and contrary to his natural inclination. Herein success led to over-confidence and so to disaster.

We always term the people over the wall "barbarians", but the Germans had their various political and social systems and some of their tribes were more civilised than others. By comparing the *Commentaries* of Cæsar with the *Germania* of Tacitus we get a fairly comprehensive notion of German institutions, which, it must be remembered, were those of our own ancestors. They had no cities. Like the Gauls they were grouped in tribes and the tribes were subdivided into cantons, the cantons into villages. They lived on the produce of their flocks and herds, on the chase, and on a primitive type of "extensive" agriculture, which involved fresh ploughlands every year and thus caused continual unrest and jostling of tribe against tribe. This was what made them such troublesome neighbours to the Gauls, and led to those gigantic "treks" which meet us from time to time in history. Their only political system was a fighting organisation; hereditary chiefs and princes led them in battle and the general in a large movement was elected from amongst the princes by the freemen of the tribe. In peace there was no general magistracy, but the elders and priests administered justice in the villages. Among the warriors there was a rough freedom and equality. The free warrior had very con-siderable rights, but only as a warrior. Among the Suevi, accord-ing to Cæsar, there were a hundred cantons, each of which fur-nished a thousand men to the army for a year's service while the rest stayed at home to carry on agriculture and hunting. But this seems, if it is accurate, to be an exceptional degree of organisation. The chastity, the patriotism, the honesty of these barbarians as well as their courage and gigantic stature were favourite themes for Roman eloquence. It is likely enough that Tacitus heightened their virtues with his satirical instinct in order to point a moral to his fellow-countrymen.

Julius Cæsar had left the Rhine as the frontier of his Gallic provinces, though he had crossed it twice by way of reconnaissance. At the beginning of Augustus' reign, the Suevi had had tc be chased back across the Rhine, and the Treveri across the Moselle. At this time, Germany was still for administrative purposes a part of the Gallic provinces, and as a rule there was the same high officer in charge of both. The Rhine was not impassable to the barbarians, and moreover there were Germanic tribes on both sides of it, such as the Treveri of Trier* and the Ubii of Cologne, who were in frequent intercourse with their neighbours on the other side. This made the river a somewhat insufficient boundary. There were inroads of German barbarians in 29 and again in 17 B.C. In the last case a Roman legate was surprised and defeated, and the eagle of the Fifth Legion carried off in triumph.

This brought Augustus to the spot, and he spent two years in studying the problems of Gaul and Germany. In 12 B.C. the first campaign was undertaken under the command of Drusus, his younger stepson. Drusus, who was not yet twenty-seven, was the most brilliant figure of his day, brave, handsome, virtuous, adored by the soldiers, and a thoroughly capable general. On this occasion he crossed the Rhine and descended into Dutch territory, laying waste the lands of the Sugambri and the other hostile tribes who had provoked these punitive measures. He accepted the submission of the Frisians who lived on the coast of North Holland. During the winter his troops seem to have been employed in cutting a canal from the Rhine to the Zuyder Zee. Next year he crossed again, marched on, and built a bridge across the Lippe, crossed the territory of the Cherusci—the most warlike of all the tribes—and halted on the banks of the Weser. He built a great fort on the Lippe, possibly at Haltern, and cut a highway along the river banks to join the new fort Aliso with a great camp on the Rhine near Xanten. In the next year there was more building and settling, and in 9 B.C. came the great effort. Drusus marched out into Swabia and Cheruscia, crossed the Weser, ravaging everywhere, and reached the Elbe. This river he essayed to cross, but he could not, and, as the historians put it, omens appeared to forbid further progress. This then was the Roman limit. Somewhere between the Saale and the Weser, Drusus fell from his horse and sustained injuries which resulted in his death. Augustus,

* The Treveri were probably a Gallic tribe with strong Germanic admixtures.—EDD.

though greatly grieved, determined to continue his operations. Tiberius was sent to continue the work, and 40,000 Sugambrians were transported into Roman territory. We know little of the work of the next dozen years. Another legate reached the Elbe. A great viaduct was constructed between the Ems and the Rhine. During this period the pacification was apparently proceeding with rapidity. Many of the young Germans came into the Roman camp and learnt Roman ways and Latin speech. The headquarters were still at Vetera Castra near Xanten and at Mogontiacum (Mainz), with summer quarters at Aliso. In A.D. 4 fresh campaigns were undertaken by Tiberius. In A.D. 5 the greatest expedition of all was undertaken. There was a great "durbar" at which the wild Chauci and Cherusci handed in their weapons and did obeisance to the Roman general. The Longobardi—later known as the Lombards—submitted, and Tiberius crossed the Elbe itself, while the fleet which had "circumnavigated the recesses of the Ocean" sailed up the river to meet the army with supplies. All seemed to be going well: Germany was nearly conquered. There only remained the powerful kingdom of the Marcomanni under King Maroboduus, who dwelt in the fastnesses of Bohemia. Maroboduus was an able ruler who alone in Germany had succeeded in establishing a strong throne, and had drilled a powerful army of 70,000 foot and 4000 horse. As the historian Velleius observes, his Alpine boundaries were only two hundred miles from Italy, and this formidable power was a real menace to the safety of the Empire. Accordingly elaborate plans were made for his destruction by an invasion from three sides at once. Unfortunately just at the moment when the armies were converging upon their prey, there broke out the great Pannonian and Illyrian revolt of A.D. 6, which brought all the tribes of Austria down upon the Romans. It was one of the most dangerous moments in Roman history. Fifteen legions were employed against them and the military resources of the Empire were strained almost to breaking-point. Luckily for Rome, Maroboduus made no attempt to join the revolt, and the barbarians were under divided leadership. Germanicus, the son of Drusus, helped Tiberius to crush them, but it took three or four years to accomplish it.

Meanwhile Quinctilius Varus, legate of the Rhine army, perhaps underestimated the tranquility of Germany. He is said to

have gone about founding cities, holding
assizes, collecting tribute and giving
justice according to Roman law precisely
"as if he had been a city prætor in the
forum at Rome and not a general in the
German forests". But in A.D. 9 he was
treacherously attacked by the Cherusci in
the Saltus Teutoburgiensis where he
perished with some 20,000 men.

Portrait of Varus

In itself the disaster was not over-
whelming. Three legions had perished, but fifteen more,
flushed with their recent victory over the Illyrians, were at
hand to avenge them. The Cheruscans immediately submitted
and Germanicus found no serious opposition when he penetrated Germany on an errand of chastisement. But for Augustus
the reverse was decisive. He was now an old enfeebled man.
When he heard of the disaster he beat his head against the
door and was often heard to cry: "Varus, give me back
my legions". He saw that there was no end to these adventures in the forest. Therefore he abandoned hope of a frontier on
the Elbe and accepted the Rhine as his frontier. Henceforth Rhine
and Danube, with roads and forts along them, and with special
arrangements to strengthen the angle where the rivers run small
—that should be bulwark enough for the present. And so it was.

The patriotism of German historians has made of this defeat
of Varus rather more than it deserves. Arminius, the young
Cheruscan patriot, who led the attack, was a traitor from the
Roman point of view. He had been, says Velleius, a faithful ally
in previous campaigns and had even attained Roman citizenship
and equestrian rank. He spoke Latin fluently. His very name is
most probably a Latin *cognomen,* though the patriotism of the
Germans will call him "Hermann". So the German student of
to-day sings over his beer:

> Dann zieh'n wir aus zur Hermannschlacht
> Und wollen Rache haben.

It was not half so gallant an act of revolt as that of our British
heroine, Boudicca, but it had the merit of success.

Under Tiberius ample revenge was taken for the defeat of

Varus, and Germanicus again swept through Germany to the Elbe. He might very well have reversed the result of the Varus disaster, had the Emperor Tiberius been less cautious. The Cheruscans and Arminius were defeated in a tremendous battle at Idistavisus near Minden on the Weser in A.D. 16. But on the way back the Roman fleet was ship-wrecked and a great many prisoners fell into the hands of the Germans. Some of these were sold as slaves to the Britons and many eventually returned to Rome bringing back marvellous stories of their adventures. Tiberius decided to revert to Augustus' final frontier of the Rhine, anticipating rightly that the German tribes would quickly quarrel among themselves. Soon Maroboduus was defeated in a battle with the Cheruscans and took refuge on Roman soil, where he lived for eighteen years at Ravenna. Arminius, his conqueror, was slain by the treachery of his kinsmen at the age of thirty-seven. His wife Thusnelda and his son had long ago fallen into the hands of the Romans and the boy grew up as a Roman citizen.

Four legions were stationed on the Middle Rhine in three permanent camps at Vetera (Xanten), Novæsium (Neuss) and Bonna (Bonn), and four more on the Upper Rhine at Moguntiacum (Mainz), Argentorate (Strasbourg) and Vindonissa (Windisch, near Basle). The two areas formed two military frontier districts, styled Lower and Upper Germany, and extending from the Rhine to the Ardennes and the Vosges. For civil purposes these districts were at first left as parts of Belgic Gaul, but towards the end of the first century they became independent provinces.

In order to create an adequate frontier to link up with the Rhine—or with the Elbe, as he had first planned—Augustus decided on a great advance northwards beyond the Alps, and beyond the mountains of the Balkans as far as the Danube. In the extreme west the Alpine passes were secured by the reduction of the Salassi and the construction of a road from Turin over the Little St. Bernard with a colony at Aosta (Augusta Prætoria) to guard it, while the coastal strip of Liguria was made into the little province of Alpes Maritimæ. A fine monument to Augustus at La Turbie on the heights above Monaco enumerates forty-six Alpine tribes made subject to Rome. Farther east Tiberius and his brother Drusus in a campaign in 15 B.C. reduced Rætia (E. Switzerland and the Tyrol), and about the same time Noricum (roughly Austria) was also subdued. Both these areas were soon organised as imperial provinces, though no troops were stationed in them. Thus the Danube frontier was won as far east as Vienna. To the east the Pannonians (in western Hungary) gave trouble and were reduced by Tiberius in 12 B.C. Farther south Illyria was turbulent, and so two new imperial provinces were made, Pannonia and Dalmatia (the latter being old Illyria, i.e. Western Yugoslavia). The violent revolt of these two provinces in A.D. 6 was crushed in three years, but, as we have seen, it had serious repercussions on Augustus' policy towards the Marcomanni and on the Rhine. Lastly there were disturbances in Thrace and Mœsia. Though Thrace was left (until the reign of Claudius) under a client king, Mœsia was annexed as an imperial province, probably by A.D. 6. Thus the Danube frontier was won from the Black Sea to Lake Constance and was protected by the four new provinces of Rætia, Noricum, Pannonia and Mœsia. Communications were soon improved when the emperor Claudius opened up two new roads over the Alps, the great Via Claudia over the Brenner Pass to the Inn valley and that over the Great St. Bernard. Thus, as the result of these vast conquests and with strong legions posted in permanent encampments along the Rhine and Danube, Rome had now a satisfactory northern frontier which only required guarding to keep Rome and Italy in security.

Spain had never been entirely subjugated though it had been in the possession of the Republic for nearly two centuries. Parts of it indeed were almost as Roman as Rome. Gades and Corduba, for example, were centres of learning and literature, and it was soon to produce writers of renown in Seneca, Lucan, Quintilian, and Martial, and an emperor in Trajan—a most distinguished galaxy. But a great part of Spain was still in the hands of wild and chivalrous barbarians. Particularly in the north-west the Cantabrians and Asturians were a menace to the peaceful province. For eight years and more the Romans continued to fight them with brief intervals termed "victories". Augustus himself came over in 26 B.C. The leader of the rebels was a hero-chief called Corocotta who so exasperated the Romans that Augustus offered a large reward for his capture. This the brigand earned by walking into the Roman camp to surrender, and Augustus, charmed at the idea, gave him his liberty as well as the reward. He married a Roman wife and died a Roman citizen as Gaius Julius Caracuttus. Augustus himself fell seriously ill in the course of the long campaign. Both sides increased in ferocity. The Romans crucified their prisoners and the Spaniards mocked them from the cross. Finally Augustus had to send for Agrippa to finish the business, which he did in 19 B.C. Now Spain was really conquered and even the northern highlanders laid down their arms and accepted civilisation. Bætica, the southern part of the peninsula, was given to the senate to govern, and the northern half was divided into the two imperial provinces, Tarraconensis and Lusitania, the latter corresponding roughly to modern Portugal. At Tarraco, the legate's headquarters and a road centre, was established the seat of the worship of Rome and Augustus, and the place where the provincial council met. Many towns were founded, such as Cæsar Augusta (Saragossa), Augusta Emerita (Merida), Pax Julia (Beja), Lucus Asturum (Lugo), Asturica Augusta (Astorga). The Iberian religion and the very language quickly became extinct. Even in the time of Augustus there were fifty communities with full Roman citizenship. New mines were discovered and vigorously worked, new industries, especially in metal, carefully fostered.

This brief and imperfect sketch of the Roman Empire, as it took shape under the all-seeing eye of Augustus, should indicate, more than all the triumphs she won in battle, the real "Grandeur that was Rome". The true greatness of the Roman lies in his indomitable energy and his practical good sense, not to be obscured by the surface of rhetorical culture which had come to overlay it in these later generations. Now that Rome had at last secured for herself a reasonably settled and sensible form of government, she was able to exercise her natural capacity for affairs and to play the part which destiny had assigned to her of propagating civilisation throughout Europe. If the historians would allow us, we should gladly turn away from the wars and proscriptions to study the quiet useful work which she was performing now and henceforth in every corner of her empire. The motive was, no doubt, self-interest, but it was that broad and far-seeing selfishness which in the realm of public affairs is the nearest approach to altruism. The Republic that sucked the blood of her provinces is detestable to all right-thinking men. The autocracy that cleared out the canals in Egypt, planted flax and encouraged pottery in Gaul, irrigated Africa and taught agriculture to the Moorish nomads, set the wild Iberians to mining and weaving, built aqueducts and roads everywhere, established a postal system and policed land and sea so effectively that a man might fare from York to Palmyra, or from Trier to Morocco "with his bosom full of gold", may have been tyranny governing in its own interest, but it brought immense material advantages to the governed.

V

AUGUSTAN ROME

Pater argentarius, ego Corinthiarius.
Anonymous lampoon on Augustus quoted by SUETONIUS

THROUGHOUT his great task of repairing a world which had fallen to pieces Augustus was by no means ignorant of the fact that it is the "spirit that maketh alive". Indeed it was his constant endeavour to alter facts without changing their names. He was well aware that Sulla had failed miserably when he tossed the Romans a constitution and left nothing but an oath to support it. To adjust frontiers and organise new provinces with the help of his trusty and invincible legionaries was probably the pleasantest and the easiest part of Augustus' task. To reform the ancient imperial city with her centuries of proud and brutal tradition was equally essential, but it was desperate work. For the Empire of Augustus was born into the world suffering from degeneration of the heart. The nobility, upon which much that was great and glorious in Roman history depended, was morally corrupt, intellectually inert, spiritually void, and even physically sterile. The civil wars and proscriptions had systematically pruned away all that was virile and spirited in its ranks. The trimmers and nonentities had survived. The women, long since freed from iron control which had kept them in order under the old system of the Roman family, dominated society with an influence that was often evil. The Roman boudoir with its throng of slaves and parasites was not only profligate; it had already begun to produce the type of murderous intriguers that we meet more prominently in the Messalinas and Agrippinas of imperial history. But as there were virtuous exceptions like Octavia and Antonia among the women, so there were among the men nobles of probity and honour who had somehow, probably by hiding themselves away on their country estates, survived all the conflicts of the past generation. But those who read Roman history in the same light as Livy were lovers of the old regime, suspicious and bitterly jealous of the new. We have seen that one of the first official acts of Augustus was to restore the patriciate. But it is easier to make peers than patricians, and we may be sure that there was little love between the old aristocracy and the new. Augustus himself, though the "son of the god Julius" and descended through his mother from Venus and Anchises, was on the father's side only just respectable. By nature and instinct, however, he was an aristocrat. All his life long he strove to win over the aristocracy to the support of his regime. But he failed. Whence throughout the history of the Empire we have in existence more or less prominently a conservative opposition of old nobles, genuine or spurious, sometimes plotting manfully and dying nobly, but more often sneering and writing in secret against the emperors.

But most of the old aristocracy lacked the spirit to oppose Augustus. The few plots which came to light were negligible affairs. Some of the nobles came down to the senate and devoted their intellects to the choice of a new *cognomen* for the new Cæsar, or vied with one another in proposing fresh titles of honour for him. But they soon discovered that flattery was not very lucrative in the face of their chilly and statuesque master. Politics at Rome had lost their savour when there was no chance of blood to follow. The noble senators had to be coerced into attending at the curia; they devoted their gifts to drawing-room battles, they collected *objets de luxe*, they wrote indifferent verses and sometimes bad histories, and they devoted themselves to self-indulgence. In place of the old religion they had smatterings of philosophy. Above all the old Roman family upon which the piers of Roman society had rested was now in ruins. To be the husband of one wife from marriage to death seems to have been a rare exception. This was no innovation of the Empire. For a century or more men had changed their wives without compunction for the sake of a fortune or a political alliance.

Augustus set before himself, as one of the most important phases of his task of regeneration; the moral purification of this society. He had provided the provinces with a new religion, the worship of his own "genius", which involved a new social organisation. But the cloak of republicanism in which he had chosen

to drape his autocracy forbade him to make himself a god in
Rome. On the contrary he steadily forbade extravagant flattery.
He was on no account to be called "dominus". It is true that the
mayors of the new boroughs into which he divided Rome were
allowed to set up altars to the Lares and Genius of Augustus.
Outside the city, temples to Augustus and priests in his service
began to appear. He declined divine honours in Rome, but Julius
Caesar had been formally deified and Augustus regularly styled
himself "diui filius". The title of "Augustus" itself carried the
notion of transcendent power. Thus the emperor stood on the
threshold of heaven, at any rate for the poorer classes, even in
Rome itself. But for the aristocracy something else was needed :
it is of little profit to claim divinity in a society of sceptics. For
Roman society, as typified by Ovid, the gods were little more
than a literary convention, and it would do a respectable man
little credit to be enrolled in their company.

For the reformation of Roman society Augustus had recourse
to three methods—legislation, culture, and example. The legislation consisted of a whole series of laws sponsored by the emperor
himself, and solemnly passed by the comitia in 18 and 17 B.C.;
they were supplemented by some other laws later. There was one
enacting heavier penalties for adultery, another permitting marriage between citizens and freedwomen, designed to meet the circumstance that men outnumbered women in the ranks of the
aristocracy. There were also sumptuary laws to curb extravagance.
There were laws imposing penalties on celibacy and discouraging
the fortune-hunters who lay in wait for the rich bachelor's legacies.
Fiscal privileges were granted to the fathers of families, and
Augustus himself went down to the house and read the senate an
old speech of Metellus on the increase of population. Unfortunately the emperor himself had not set a good example in the matter
of parentage. He had had three wives but only one child, a
daughter. Still he exhibited himself in the theatre in the capacity
of a father by collecting the children of Germanicus about his
knees. Of course legislation proved quite helpless in the matter,
besides arousing a good deal of ill-feeling, which was chiefly displayed in the ranks of the knights.

Augustus was in a very difficult position when it came to setting
an example. The principal evils which his social code was designed
to remedy were the prevalence of adultery, the frequency of

divorce, voluntary celibacy and formal marriages contracted without intention of producing offspring, and finally, as a consequence
of celibacy, the prevalence of a regular profession of fortune-
hunting. There was scarcely one of these necessary reforms to
which Augustus himself came with clean hands. He had begun
his matrimonial career by repudiating his young betrothed; he
had then married an immature virgin, and divorced her for political reasons before the marriage was consummated; in the third
place he had married Scribonia, who had already had two husbands, and whose son was already a man at the time of her
marriage to Augustus. She was many years older than he, and the
marriage was intended to secure a reconciliation with Sextus Pompeius. This third matrimonial venture was terminated in a manner
which shocked even Roman society. On the very day when
Scribonia became a mother by him, Augustus put her away charging her with immorality, though he kept her infant Julia as his
own and only child. He had been fascinated, it seems, by the fair
face and brilliant abilities of Livia Drusilla. Livia was of the
highest ancestry in Rome, a descendant of Appius Claudius, and
attached by adoption to another very noble family, the Livii. Also
she had married another scion of the illustrious Claudian house,
the proudest in Rome, and at the age of fifteen had become the
mother of Tiberius. Her father had chosen the losing side at
Philippi, and committed suicide after the battle. Her husband,
Ti. Claudius Nero, had taken arms against Augustus—or Octavian, as he then was—in the Perusine War, and his life was forfeited. His beautiful wife sued the conqueror for mercy, and mercy
was granted upon conditions. Claudius was compelled not only
to divorce his wife, but to act the part of a father and give her
away in marriage to Augustus. She was then not only the mother
of Tiberius, but just about to become the mother of Drusus, who
was born in the house of Augustus three months after the
marriage. This, then was the model family on the Palatine which
was to set an example to the Roman aristocracy—a daughter
whose mother had been divorced on the day of her birth, a mother
who had been sold by her husband, and two stepsons whose father
had been divorced. The sequel scarcely improved matters. Julia
grew up and was married first to the boy Marcellus, Augustus'
nephew, then to Agrippa, by whom she had a large family. When
Agrippa died, Tiberius was forced to put away his wife, Agrippa's

daughter Vipsania, whom he really loved, and marry the widow Julia, whose immorality he knew and detested. At last the profligacy of Julia grew so open and notorious that Augustus was informed of it and banished her in company with her mother Scribonia, who had survived to see her shame. Later on a second Julia, the daughter of the first, suffered a similar fate.

As for Livia the empress,* if we choose to call her by that title, there is no doubt that she was a singularly beautiful and clever woman, who managed to retain the affections of Augustus for over forty years—in itself a remarkable feat in Roman society. History records in her favour many acts of royal mercy and charity. She seconded her husband's efforts at reform, and established a powerful ascendancy over him and over Tiberius. There is no whisper against her chastity when once she entered the household of Augustus. But on the other hand there are very serious charges of crime made by contemporaries and recorded by Tacitus. The suspicion is that she was fighting all her life long without remorse or scruple for the succession of her son Tiberius. Augustus did not intend to be succeeded by a Claudius. This he showed again and again in the most public manner. His aim, as soon as he knew that he was destined to leave no male offspring of his own body, was to leave the succession in the sacred Julian line, the family descended from Venus, the house of the star. But that could only be secured through the female line. His first choice was the brilliant young Marcellus, son of his sister Octavia. Marcellus, who had been the first husband of Julia, died of a mysterious complaint just as he came of age. Then Augustus married Julia to Agrippa, and two of her sons, Gaius and Lucius, were next chosen for the succession. They grew up and came of age. Just as they were beginning public life, Tiberius having left Rome to make way for them, they too died : Lucius on board ship as he was sailing to Marseilles (A.D. 2), Gaius as the sequel to an assassin's blow given him in Armenia (A.D. 4). In the first case we have no details. In the second, Gaius was recovering from his wound, but he turned aside to an obscure town on the southern coast of Asia Minor, refused the warship which had been sent to convey him home, and begged to be allowed to live there in obscurity. The circumstance is full of suspicion and mystery. Moreover, before his rivals were dead, Tiberius had word, from a well-informed

* Plate 29.

prophet, of their approaching decease, and returned to Rome. He himself, living in banishment, must be acquitted of active complicity in the crime. Julia was banished to a lonely island. Her third son was also put out of sight for no crime but sulkiness and grumbling. Deprived of all his hopes, Augustus with very marked reluctance adopted Tiberius, but in his old age he still cherished the idea of a reconciliation with Julia's third son, Agrippa Postumus, and is said to have visited in secret the remote island where he was interned. But as soon as Augustus was dead—and his death was carefully concealed as long as possible—Agrippa Postumus was murdered, and this time we have direct evidence that the crime was Livia's.* This sort of domestic intrigue, marked by hideous murders, is one of the blackest features of imperial history at Rome. It arose very largely from the illegitimate character of the imperial throne, and the absence of any legalised system of succession.

Nevertheless, out of these unpromising materials Augustus endeavoured to organise a model Roman family of the old style. Livia and Julia were set to work at spinning and weaving. Augustus would wear no cloaks but of their making. Julia was solemnly counselled never to do or say anything which she would be ashamed to write in her diary. Once when she built a palace for herself Augustus had it demolished. His own house on the Palatine was of the simplest character, with a humble portico of the local tufa from Alba and no decorated pavements. In food and drink he was most abstemious, and indeed the prodigious industry of his life left little time for banquets. A slice of bread made from inferior flour, with a relish of pickled fish or dates or olives, often served him for the day. He never drank more than a pint of wine. He slept winter and summer in the same room, and spent most of the year in the city, unless he was travelling. His favourite country seat was on the island of Capri where he could be sure of freedom. His pleasures were simple and almost childish. He liked a little mild gambling, he was fond of playing knuckle-bones with little slave-boys. He attended the circus as a matter of duty and was very strict in enforcing decency of behaviour there. He set his face against changes of fashion and insisted that Roman citizens should

* Few modern historians believe the insinuations that Livia was responsible in any way for the deaths of Marcellus or of the two young Cæsars to be worth serious consideration. Postumus was perhaps removed by Tiberius, or possibly by an order left by Augustus.—EDD.

wear the old-fashioned toga in public. All his instincts seem to have been for simplicity and clemency. He never permitted a freedman to appear at his dinner-table, but when a slave of his once pushed his master into the way of a charging wild boar in order to shield himself Augustus dismissed the matter with a joke. On the other hand, when the tutor and servants of Gaius showed themselves tyrannical and overbearing to the provincials after their young master's death, Augustus had them drowned like rats. Towards personal abuse of himself he was singularly indifferent. It remains difficult to visualise the character of Augustus. Originally he was a typical Roman, as callous towards bloodshed and suffering as the rest of them and quite unscrupulous in his progress towards power. But when he had attained it he had the greatness of mind to perceive that his work of repair could only be done by setting an example of virtuous living and moderation. Self-control was perhaps his most powerful quality.

Twice his self-command broke down. Once when he heard of the defeat of Varus in Germany with the loss of his three legions, and again when some one, probably Livia, revealed to him the scandal concerning Julia. Apart from the blow to his honour as a man, it was the undoing of all his measures for reform and the open publication of their futility. "Her orgies", men said, "had been conducted upon the very rostra whence her father's laws against adultery had been proclaimed." Her accomplices included the flower of the old aristocracy, a Scipio and a Gracchus. Augustus hid himself from the sight of men, banished his daughter to a remote island and officially informed the senate by letter of her disgrace. He was heard to cry out that he envied the father of Phœbe, one of Julia's freedwomen, who had hanged herself when the scandal went abroad. He quoted a Greek verse :

Oh that I had been unwedded and died without a child,

and he spoke of Julia as one of three cancers of his life.*

Legislation was obviously futile, and example had broken down. It was only from within that Roman society could be reformed, only by supplying a spiritual influence which could counter the materialism and immorality of the day. Augustus had tried in the provinces to raise up a new religion of loyalty and patriotism centred round the altar "to Rome and Augustus". But that was

* The other two were Julia's children Julia and Agrippa Postumus.—EDD.

obviously impossible in Rome itself. The only inspiring motive—
in addition to Stoicism, which could never be a popular creed—
had been, for the last two or three centuries, patriotism, the worship of the city and her glorious destinies. But even that had been
shattered by the civil wars. Augustus set himself deliberately to
the task of creating a new Rome and a new Roman culture. He
himself, like most of the nobles of his day, had received a Greek
education. It was what we should call a good classical education
in philosophy, literature, and rhetoric. Besides that he had been
initiated into the Eleusinian mysteries of Athens, and they were
a very powerful source of inspiration in the Mediterranean world,
for even eclectics like Cicero admitted that they carried with them
a hope of immortality. Augustus was himself deeply imbued with
Greek culture and like most Roman nobles had dabbled in literature. Thus it is not surprising that the type of civilisation which
he fostered in the new Rome was quite as much Greek as Italian.
The age of Augustus was in fact the culmination of Græco-Roman
culture alike in arts and letters because the fusion between the two
nations was now complete.

Elsewhere I have ventured to rebel against the practice in history of subordinating the arts to politics and declaring that artistic
production depends upon political facts. It is not so. Literary and
artistic results are due to literary and artistic causes. The Roman
literary language had only just attained perfection. Cicero had
perfected it for prose, and it only remained for poetry to acquire
a Virgil. Roman gentlemen from Augustus downwards were
busily writing hexameters in their spare time, and the recitals
which were given at dinner-parties formed one of the social inflic-
tions of the day. Just as Julius Cæsar and Cicero had thrown off
their epics, so the great men of the succeeding age were poets—
Augustus, Pollio, Mæcenas, Gallus, and all of them except
Agrippa. But alongside of these distinguished amateurs, professional literary men of humble birth were now coming to the
front. Virgil and Horace are not originally the products of the
Augustan Age, for they were both established poets before it began,
but from an early date they had enjoyed the protection and favour
of the Cæsarian party, even when it was uncertain whether the
future lay with Octavian or with Mark Antony. The conditions
of art at Rome were such that a professional man of letters depended very closely upon a patron. That was the tradition handed

on from the days of Plautus. Cicero, Cæsar, Lucretius, and Catullus had not been of the client class. They had flourished in that brief interval when it still seemed possible for Rome to develop a free literature of her own. But that possibility had been killed like so many other hopes by the civil wars, and now the choice lay mainly between distinguished scribblers and obsequious literary craftsmen. Thus we get a second courtly period of literature like that of the Ptolemies at Alexandria, like that of Louis XIV or of our own Stuart Age when poets wrote to please individual patrons. The patron, if he be a man of taste, generally demands a very high degree of finish, and thus it is the courtly ages that produce the finished craftsmanship. It may be remarked that the ages of private patronage have given the world much of its greatest literature.*

In the age of Augustus there was no censorship of letters such as generally prevailed under the stricter emperors of later days. Livy was permitted to publish his great history without curtailment of its strong republican tendency. When libels and pasquinades appeared against Augustus he was content to contradict them in a proclamation. Nevertheless he made his influence weightily felt in the world of letters. He gave 250,000 *denarii* to Varius for a tragedy which posterity has not taken care to preserve. He was himself a kindly and patient listener at the recitation of poems and history, speeches and dialogues, which formed the usual mode of first publication in those days. He only insisted that his own deeds should not form the subject of trivial composition by inferior authors. The authors most earnestly encouraged to write on behalf of the state and its ruler were Virgil and Horace. In this part of the work Mæcenas was the emperor's chief agent. Mæcenas, whose name has come to symbolise literary patronage, was a wealthy knight of an old Etruscan family who was content, like Cicero's friend Atticus, to pull the wires of state largely by keeping generous hospitality and knowing all the important characters of his day. Luxurious and effeminate in his tastes, he gathered a group of talented authors round his table, and very distinctly suggested to them the lines upon which he desired them to work. Virgil, Varius, Horace, and Propertius were members of his *salon*. Another gentleman of high lineage,

---

* The following pages on the literature of the Augustan age have been to a considerable degree rewritten.—EDD.

M. Valerius Messalla, maintained a rival coterie whose most prominent member was the elegiac poet Tibullus. Virgil, a native of the district of Mantua, who was perhaps not even a Roman citizen by birth, had sprung into fame with his *Bucolics,* a series of pastoral idylls in the style of Theocritus. But, though he was a provincial by birth, though he wrote of shepherds and produced the greatest of all ancient poems on country life, nothing is more untrue than to regard him as a son of the soil, or an inspired ploughboy after the manner of Robert Burns. On the contrary he had received an elaborate education in the style of the day under Greek masters at Cremona, Milan, and Rome. He was steeped in Greek philosophy and letters. His shepherds are not the unsophisticated rustics of the Mantuan plain. They are shepherds "à la Watteau", idealised like those of Theocritus, and though many a brilliant epithet displays the Italian's loving observation of nature, the background of the work is more artificial and literary than rustic or natural. His shepherds, like Sidney's, sometimes talk politics under a transparent disguise, which is occasionally somewhat incongruous, though, indeed, Milton's *Lycidas* shows how effectively the pastoral genre can embrace contemporary and personal references. We also find references to Gallus or Varius or Varus or Pollio, the young poet's friends or patrons. The success of the *Bucolics* led Mæcenas to choose Virgil for carrying out an important literary project. A poet was required to sing the praises of country life in such a manner as to encourage the movement "back to the land", which Augustus was trying to foster. In his *Georgics* Virgil frankly admits that he is fulfilling the "hard commands" of Mæcenas. The *Georgics* are a treatise on husbandry. We are informed that Virgil's poetry had regained him his paternal farm near Mantua. But the *Georgics* were not written on the farm. They were diligently composed in a library at Naples. They owed much to his study of Aratus and Hesiod, as well as to his experiences of Italian life, and even in those gorgeous passages where Virgil is praising country life, it is not only of the Italian farm that he is thinking, but also of literary hills and dells of Greece. He gladly digresses from the description of soils and mattocks to tell us a charming piece of Greek mythology or to introduce a literary reference. Octavian's divinity had been suggested already in the *Eclogues* before he became Augustus. Now the only question is which of the stars shall receive him after death.

"Already blazing Scorpion contracts his arms and has left thee more than a fair share of heaven." Virgil pauses to depict the victories of Augustus—Nile surging with war, Asia tamed, Niphates conquered, the Parthian in flight. No literary catchword was ever more absurd than the phrase "rustic of genius" applied to Virgil. As soon as he had the means, he turned his back upon his ancestral farm to devote himself to study and writing. Mæcenas was magnificently served. Virgil had already forged a weapon of matchless music and eloquence in his surging hexameters, and he used it to depict with unfaltering inspiration the joys and sorrows of rustic toil, the laborious tranquility of the farm, the beauty and interest of nature. Tennyson's poem *To Virgil*, itself of Virgilian majesty, felicitously describes the various beauties of Virgil's poetry as found both in the *Georgics* and in his other works. He was instantly recognised by Augustus as the destined laureate of the new Rome. Actually, many would agree with Dryden that in the *Georgics* Virgil's best work had been done. It is debatable whether Augustus' patronage was in fact a salutary influence in his life as a creative artist.

The *Aeneid* was solemnly devoted to the altar of Rome and Augustus. Homer was the Greek model here, as Theocritus had been for the *Bucolics* and Hesiod for the *Georgics*. The origin of Rome was to be linked on to the Trojan story as had already been done by the inventive Greeks. Aeneas had fled from Troy to Italy, and had left his son Iulus (the eponymous hero of the Julian house) to found a heroic kingdom in Italy long before the genuine Roman heroes. Piety was to be the great virtue honoured by this poem; for piety towards the memory of Julius Cæsar was the principal title upon which Augustus rested his claim to honour. There were other analogies, perhaps. Dido may have suggested Cleopatra to the Roman reader. But it is to the praise of Rome, to the glorification of that sense of filial duty which the Romans called "piety" that the great epic is mainly devoted. In spite of the splendour of its language, the majesty of its versification, and its innumerable and unfathomable profundities of thought and feeling, this work of a contemplative genius writing in a sophisticated age has not the fresh spontaneity of Homer nor his effortless felicity in characterization. The poet is not entirely successful with his plot. Aeneas himself, with all his piety, is a somewhat lifeless figure. The religious motives which led to his desertion of

Dido barely satisfy us, and Dido wins our sympathy, as she had won Virgil's. Aeneas is inhibited in action, and the gods intervene when danger or temptation threaten him. Our sympathies are often with the enemy, with Turnus or Camilla; for Virgil remembers that they are Italians. Aeneas is as chilly and statuesque as Augustus himself.

It is in the famous Sixth Book, which tells of the descent to Hades, that the praise of Rome is most eloquent and most explicit. Here we are shown the heroes of Roman history side by side with the heroes of the Greeks, and here the young Marcellus, lately dead, is introduced in those immortal and touching lines which caused Octavia his mother to swoon when the poet recited them. Here too the poet pronounces in very significant language the Roman idea of the destiny of his race :

> excudent alii spirantia mollius æra,
> credo equidem, uiuos ducent de marmore uoltus,
> orabunt causas melius, cælique meatus
> describent radio, et surgentia sidera dicent :
> tu regere imperio populos, Romane, memento;
> hæ tibi erunt artes, pacique imponere morem,
> parcere subiectis, et debellare superbos.

"Others shall mould, I doubt not, the breathing bronze more delicately and draw living features out of marble, others shall plead causes more eloquently, trace the motions of the heavens with a rod, and tell the risings of the stars. Thou, Roman, forget not to govern the nations under thy sway. These shall be thy arts : to crown peace with law, to spare the conquered, and to defeat the proud." In these lines we hear the proud Philistinism of an imperial people. This is the traditional Roman attitude towards the arts and sciences. They are for others to provide, for Greeks and Egyptians. Even oratory, the highest achievement of the Roman genius in literature, is thus surrendered to the foreigner. The Romans knew that they could buy or seize better statues than they could carve : their task was to conquer and govern—not an ignoble art.*

The Aeneid is explicitly a national laureate poem. The poet

---

* It is characteristic of Vigil that the four lines ostensibly dismissing the arts and sciences form one of the most impressive tributes to them to come out of antiquity. We observe the same phenomenon in *Georg.* II 475-82 and 490-2, where he renounces science and philosophy as poetic themes.—EDD.

seeks to enshrine all Roman life in his pages, to epitomise Roman history and to introduce allusions to characteristic pieces of myth and ritual. He inserts or adapts phrases of Ennius or Lucretius or other predecessors when they please him. They are superseded and replaced. Just like Dryden, he feels that he is the heir of the ages. The extraordinary popularity which Virgil attained even in his own lifetime grew in the course of a few centuries almost into a cult. His tomb became an object of pilgrimage; in early Christian times he became a prophet and in the Middle Ages a magician. The gentleness and purity of his personal life, the haunting rhythm and tender pathos of his hexameters, and a pervasive strain of mystery, even of Delphic obscurity, in his imagery and expression, played their part in the creation of this strange Virgilian legend.*

Horace was not from the beginning a Cæsarian and required winning to the imperial cause. As a young man, studying at Athens, he had with youthful enthusiasm for "liberty" taken a commission in the army of Brutus and Cassius and had fought against Antony and Augustus at Philippi. We have letters preserved in which Augustus good-humouredly confesses his disappointment that Horace, who had declined to become his secretary, has not sought his company. Horace was the son of a freedman, as he was not in the least ashamed to confess. But his father had managed to secure for Quintus the education of a gentleman under Greek teachers in Rome, himself attending the boy to school in place of the pedagogue slaves who usually undertook that office. Horace had further enjoyed what we should call a University education at Athens. He was, and remained, a Republican by instinct, but Mæcenas won him over to the cause of Cæsarism. He made his reputation with the *Satires* (*Sermones*), a species of composition which may be termed truly Italian. The satire is a conversational medley (*satura* is from Etrusc. *satir*, "speak") written in the language of prose with the rhythm of poetry. In this Horace was imitating the old Roman master Lucilius. †It is much to the credit of his critical discernment that Mæcenas was able to descry the brilliant abilities of Horace in

* No criticism or appreciation of the *Aeneid* should ignore the all-important fact that, when the poet died, three years' work on revision remained to be done.—EDD.

† *c.* 180-102 B.C. Less than 1300 lines of his voluminous work have survived.

this somewhat uninspiring medium. For though his *Satires* were sometimes bitterly satirical in the modern sense of the word, Horace's chief literary asset was the charm of a sunny, genial character. He had in addition a gift for composition and an industry which raised him to the level of original genius. It seems to have been Mæcenas who set him to the writing of lyrical odes. Biting satires might have been the most effective literary weapon in republican days, but the glorification of the new regime required something of a loftier strain. Virgil was engaged upon its epic, Horace was encouraged to write its occasional verse. The Greek lyrists of the older period had as yet remained unimitated in Latin. Accordingly Horace set himself to the task of celebrating the new Rome in the style of Sappho and Alcæus and Anacreon. That he accomplished his task so superbly is a proof of his energy and versatility. Sometimes he appears as a gentle valetudinarian whose idea of a banquet was a mess of cabbage and pot-herbs; at others he strikes the lyre of revelry and sings of wine and love. Lacking the spontaneous lyricism of his models, he had a faultless ear for the more solemn music of the Latin language and a perfect feeling for the right word in the right place. No writer has ever equalled his gift for making truisms sound memorable. No other writer has been able to assert that "it is joy and glory to die for the fatherland", or that "life is short" with an equal air of genuine wisdom. Latin with its terse precision is an ideal language for the expression of commonplaces. His patriotic eloquence is Roman rhetoric of the best kind. But perhaps his real strength lies in drama. It is strange that Latin of the classical period failed at producing a native drama. Perhaps it was because the writers of that age were so completely under Greek influences that their natural Italian genius for the theatre was stifled under the load of a classical convention. Certainly Horace had the gift, and in such passages as the dramatic duologue (Ode 9 of Book III), *Donec gratus eram tibi,* or the Epode of the witches (V), *At, o deorum,* or the still more famous Satire about the bore, he exhibits himself, like Browning, as a dramatist gone astray.* Regarded from the purely lyrical point of view, the Century Hymn, which he wrote to order as Rome's laureate, is not his least achievement. The Secular Games of 17 B.C. were intended to bring visibly before

* The dramatic element is marked in Horace's *Sermones,* as, in a greater or less degree, in all Roman Satire.—EDD.

66. OSTIA, the Port of Rome (Air View).

67. A STREET IN HERCULANEUM.

68. (*see next page*). A HOUSE IN HERCULANEUM.

69. (*opposite next page*). AIR VIEW OF POMPEII.

70. FORUM OF POMPEII with Vesuvius in background.

71.

STREET IN
POMPEII.

72.   A HOUSE AT POMPEII.

73. INTERIOR OF A HOUSE AT POMPEII.

74 (*see next page*). TRICLINIUM (dining room at Pompeii).

75 (*opposite next page*). FRESCO IN VILLA OF THE MYSTERIES showing initiation rites.

74.
*(see
previous
page).*

75.
(see
plate 73).

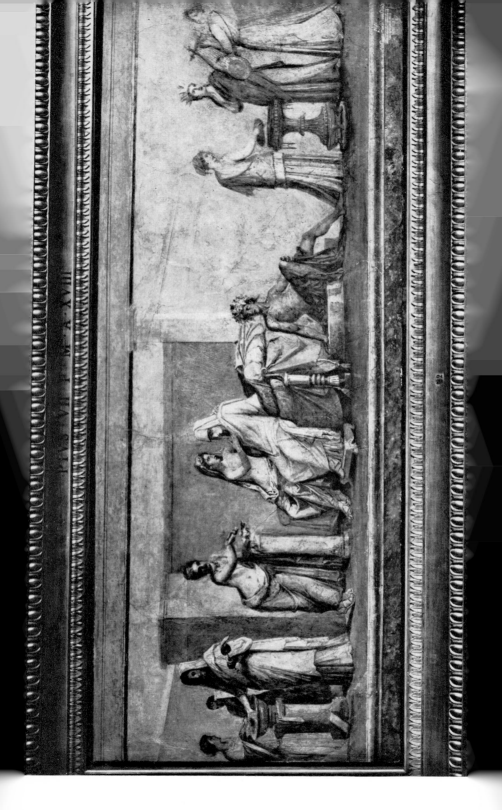

76 (*opposite*).
ALDOBRANDINI
MARRIAGE
SCENE.

77.
PERISTYLE
OF IMPERIAL
VILLA at
Piazza Armerina,
Sicily. (4th Cent. A.D.?).

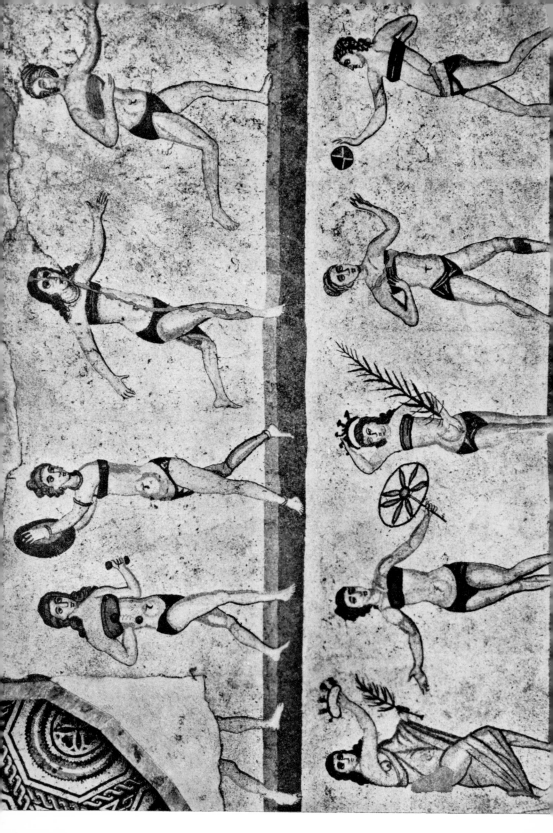

78-79.

MOSAICS
AT PIAZZA
ARMERINA
showing
sporting and
hunting
scenes.

80.
MAISON
CARREE,
NIMES
(Augustan
Age).

men's eyes the glories of the new monarchy and incidentally to carry in their train the salutary but unpopular measures of the Julian moral reform. So the choir of noble youths and maidens was taught to sing a prayer to Diana :

> diua, producas subolem patrumque
> prosperes decreta super iugandis
> feminis prolisque nouæ feraci
> lege marita,*

where the goddess is besought to increase the population of Rome and favour the senate's decrees about marriage. The fourth book of the *Odes* was added after a long interval at the direct request of Augustus. It is intended to bring the achievements of Augustus and his family, particularly the triumphs of Tiberius and Drusus, into favourable comparison with the heroic stories of republican history. It is most melancholy to observe that Mæcenas, to whom Horace was genuinely attached and whose name constantly occurs in his earlier writings, here drops out of the poet's verse. He had somewhat fallen out of Cæsar's favour.†

Although Horace is in his Odes as classical and conventional as all the Roman writers of his age, his *Satires* and Epistles are more intimate than any other Latin work of the great period. In them we get real glimpses of life at Rome, or on a country estate. We cannot fail to be struck with its idleness and emptiness. In the city he saunters from the forum to the baths, from the baths to the dinner-table with time and boredom for his only enemies. In the country he sometimes, it is true, toys with husbandry, or shows a faint interest in landscape-gardening, or loiters among his books, but the life is to a considerable degree super-civilised and unreal. The eyes of the literary Romans were too often turned behind them so that they could seldom see the greatness of the vista that was now opening for their countrymen in front.

Elegiac poetry is represented by Tibullus, Propertius, and Ovid, the work of Gallus and the other elegists of the period not having survived. These poets were mainly inspired by Alexandrian elegy, though it is doubtful whether the writers' love affairs, which are a main theme of Roman elegy, were at all prominent in Alexandrian

---

* *Carmen Sæculare*, 17-20.

† Mæcenas' last words to Augustus were *Horati Flacci ut mei esto memor.* The reader will draw his own conclusions.—EDD.

elegy. The elegiac couplet, consisting of hexameters alternating with pentameters, was, like the heroic couplet of Dryden and Pope, a metre that lent itself to punctilious artistry but tended to inhibit the natural movements of poetic genius.

Tibullus was perhaps the most successful of the elegiac poets in the sense that his talent was the best adapted to the elegiac medium. He is one of the most satisfactory of 'minor poets'. Lacking profundity of thought and intensity of feeling, he had a gracefully melancholic inspiration, not unlike that of Gray, and a faultless ear for the natural cadence of the elegiac couplet. His main subject is his sentimental attachment to the mistresses whom he calls by the Greek names of Delia and Nemesis, but he also reveals his love of the country, his freedom from materialistic ambitions, and his love of peace and hatred of war. On the spiritual side he was religious rather than philosophical, though in this, as in all else, sentiment rather than passion was his guiding force. He was a member of the artistic circle presided over by Messalla Corvinus, an interesting literary dilettante and man of affairs and a former republican, with whom Horace too had friendly relations dating from the time when they had been brother officers in the army of Brutus and Cassius. One of Tibullus' poems, I.7, is a birthday poem celebrating the triumph granted to Messalla in 27 B.C. for his reduction of an outbreak in Aquitania. The *Panegyricus Messallæ,* however, contained in the so-called *Corpus Tibullianum* (III.7), is not by Tibullus. Only the poems in Books I and II are by general consent his work. Book III is by various members of Messalla's circle, and their authorship is disputed. The most interesting ones are the six short elegies (III. 13-18) by the girl Sulpicia, a kinswoman of Messalla, on her love for a youth whose identity is concealed under the name Cerinthus. Among the poems in honour of this girl, III. 8, by an anonymous poet, is a charming description of her dressed up in dainty finery for a religious festival.

Propertius, upon whom the eccentric attentions of Ezra Pound have conferred a certain vogue, is in most respects strikingly different from Tibullus. Undoubtedly a greater poet, he is a less successful elegist. His genius, compounded of fiery passion, imagination, and lyricism, but lacking in the vigour that ensures equality of performance, renders him in some ways one of the most modern of Latin poets. "Sunt qui Propertium malint" is

Quintilian's cautious judgment, and it is the case that even today he is a favourite with some devotees of modern poetry with little taste for any other Latin poet. His ardent love for the mistress whom he calls Cynthia is the chief theme of his verse. At first he found this love, which he idealized, all-sufficient. Then the infidelities of his mistress shattered his illusions, quarrels and reconciliations followed one another, and at last, like Catullus, he brought his liaison to an end. In the Fourth Book we find a wide extension of interests in mythological and antiquarian directions. Whether this indicates growth or decline in his talents and inspiration is one of the questions on which critics do not agree. All are at least agreed in admiring the tender elegy on the death of Cornelia, daughter of Augustus' former wife Scribonia (IV.11). Mæcenas, of whose circle Propertius was a member, and Augustus have their share of notice from Propertius as from Horace. One of the curiosities of literary history is the apparent absence of friendship between these two poetic members of the same coterie. Apart from the fantasies of critics, the fact that Horace, who mentions every writer, great and small, of his acquaintance (see, e.g., *Serm.* I. 10. 81. ff.), is silent about Propertius is proof enough; and Propertius, who in II, 34 has a fine tribute to Virgil, is equally silent. The fact of their mutual repulsion is not surprising—Daudet and Verlaine were not more incompatible; but there may have been some deep cause of offence to account for the attitude of the usually friendly Horace. One thing that is easy to understand, because it is characteristic, is Horace's *silence,* which some ingenious but wrong-headed and indelicate commentators will not leave undisturbed. Even the "bore" of *Serm.* I.9 has been identified with Propertius! Critics of Propertius have often been troubled by his frequent use of mythological references and comparisons. They attribute this to Alexandrianism, as if Pindar and other Greek lyric poets had not used the same method, and they patronise the poet over this alleged error of artistic judgment. They forget that "Chacun à sa méthode de travail", and that this practice is one of Propertius' deliberate and necessary methods of achieving his artistic purpose. In brief, he is a poet with a strongly symbolistic cast of mind, and what may be called "mythological symbolism" was for him a necessary method of poetic expression. At its best it produces the most exquisite beautiees that we find in his always unpredictable verse.

It was perhaps an unlucky chance that made him an elegiac poet. His genius surges within the confining barriers of the elegiac couplet and often overflows them. Then one has the impression of a Coleridge or a Shelley trying to write in the rhymed couplets of Pope and Samuel Johnson.

Both these elegiac poets seem to have died fairly young. The third, Ovid, lived from 43 B.C. to about A.D. 18, but he would have been lucky to have died younger. Of provincial origin, like nearly all the Latin poets (he came from Sulmo, a town of the Pæligni), he lived the life of a gentleman of leisure at Rome for half a century. In A.D. 8 he was banished by Augustus and lived the rest of his life in miserable exile at Tomis on the Black Sea coast. At Rome he enjoyed the pleasures of polite society and neither practised nor professed virtuous behaviour. To the Muse, however, he remained always faithful, and his literary output was enormous in quantity, extremely varied in subject-matter, and, as is the way with prolific poets, unequal in quality. His *Amores,* dealing with a mistress called Corinna, are essays in the genre of erotic elegy rather than genuine love-poems like those of Tibullus and Propertius. They contain one memorable poem of a very different stamp, the tender and mournful elegy on Tibullus (*Amores* III. 9), who had died in 19 B.C. This is an appropriate point at which to consider that controversial question, Ovid's character as a man, not really separable from the question of his merit as a poet. We all know that he was flippant when he should have been serious, that his feelings were generally shallow and his principles lacking in elevation, that he brought to the business of life and of art cleverness instead of wisdom, and that neither his life nor his art show any development in adulthood or any capacity to benefit by experience. These deplorable shortcomings admitted, it remains our duty to reject uncompromisingly the darker picture that is sometimes painted. To an age that does not regard morality in terms of a single Commandment, the uncommendable attitude contained in the *Ars Amatoria* is no longer an insuperable stumbling-block; and in this connexion it should be remembered that Ovid goes out of his way to reject homosexuality, to which so many of the most respected Roman poets pay either personal or conventional tribute. In the *Ars Amatoria,* and in the behaviour that it implies, Ovid's fault, as mostly elsewhere, is levity and lack of moral responsibility, not cold viciousness or a desire to harm. He was like a naughty, but not malicious, child. Living in a society where courtesans were often fastidious semi-professionals or even amateurs, not to be won by gifts without personal graces, he teaches the art of winning their favours in a poem that is partly a witty mockery of all technical manuals and at times a satire on the whole course of such liaisons. Ovid would not have seduced your virtuous daughter, but his acquaintance would have led her into association with company that you would not have approved of. The allegation of cold-heartedness, based on his incorrigible flippancy in relating tragic tales like those of Dido, Niobe, and Philomela, is to be denied with emphasis. Even if we had not the testimony of the elder Seneca, a senior contemporary, to his genial and lovable disposition, we could see it for ourselves in such poems as the afore-mentioned elegy on Tibullus; in *Tristia* IV. 10, where his love for his parents, his brother, his fellow-poets, and the Muse is beautifully expressed in his hour of calamity; in *Tristia* III. 6, where he encourages his young friend and former pupil Perilla in her poetic efforts and speaks of his own hopes of lasting fame as outweighing all his afflictions; and in countless places in his *Heroides, Metamorphoses,* and *Fasti,* where pathos and imaginative sympathy abound, and virtue (e.g. Lucretia's) is praised with warmth and enthusiasm. It is Ovid's severer critics who are cold-hearted, not he. No Roman poet, not even Tibullus, is more free than Ovid from the Roman fault of cruelty. As a poet, he has the defects that arise from excessive facility and impetuosity :

> sponte sua carmen numeros ueniebat ad aptos,
> et quod temptabam dicere uersus erat.
> (*Trist.* IV. 10. 25-6)

But if he has the defects of his qualities, he has also the qualities of his defects, notably wit, polish, urbanity, and metrical skill. No Roman did more to transmit to Europe in an agreeable form the imaginative riches of Greek mythology (*Heroides, Metamorphoses*) and the attractive folklore of early Italy (*Fasti*). The *Metamorphoses* were written in hexameters of a sparkling vivacity that is utterly unlike the solemn grandeur of Virgil's hexameter. The rest of his extant work is in the elegiac metre, mostly adhering to the "Ovidian canon", to which Propertius' later work had pointed the way, requiring a dissyllabic termination of the elegiac cadence. It is interesting to note that Ovid, in contrast to Propertius, was moving away from this self-imposed restriction in his later work (*Tristia* and *Epistulæ ex Ponto*), written during his exile. Virgil and Horace likewise show, in the later parts of the *Aeneid* and the *Odes*, signs of dissatisfaction with Augustan canons of smooth perfection.

When we term the Golden Age of Roman literature "Augustan" we ought to remember that it began long before Augustus and ended before his death. Thus with all his patronage he may more justly be called the finisher than the author of it. Of all the great writers, only Ovid and Livy outlived Augustus. Summing up the characteristics of the literature of this day, we may say that on the whole polish and restraint were its most prominent characteristics. The freshness of Catullus, the stern conviction of Lucretius, the fire of Cicero were extinct. Nearly all that was native in Roman letters had yielded to Greek influence; only the crispness of epigram, the bite of satire and the dignified music of the language itself remained as the Italian heritage. Greece had quite definitely triumphed over Rome. Technical excellence united with richness of imagination fostered by Greek culture, widening human sympathies, and a warmth and delicacy of feeling that would have horrified Cato the Censor, go to make the literature of this period one of the greatest sources of joy and strength that antiquity has bequeathed to Christian civilisation. The efforts of the state to capture literature for its own service had on the whole failed. The horrors of the civil war outweighed the glories of the new regime, and with all his benevolence the emperor could never outlive the memory of his proscriptions. Literature never forgave the murder of Cicero though Varius might be loaded with treasure for his *Thyestes*. Indeed the widespread misery of those terrible days in 40 B.C. came home personally to most of our middle-class writers. Virgil, Horace, Tibullus, and Propertius had all received ineffaceable memories in the loss of their patrimonies. It was little wonder that even though they sang occasionally of wars and victories to gratify their patrons, their natural instinct was to compare Mars and Venus much to the disadvantage of the former.

When we turn to consider the art of the period, we must not forget to carry with us the light that we have obtained from the study of its literature. For Augustus* and his assistants were attempting similar ends in both regions. With temples, baths, circuses, amphitheatres, colonnades, libraries, and statues the new regime was to flourish its magnificence in the eyes of the world, and, above all, to dazzle the citizens of Rome, to win their whole-hearted support for the new regime and to reconcile them to the gradual disappearance of their voting rights. Money was lavished upon this object by the emperor and all his friends, and the building activity which transformed Rome from a city of brick into a city of marble must have given work and pay to vast numbers of the poor. But the magnificence has largely perished, as all magnificence must, and it is left for us by the study of a few ruined monuments, a few statues and busts, an altar here, a cornice there, to estimate the spirit of Rome in conformity with its literature.

Roman art supplied much inspiration to the artists of the Renaissance. Michael Angelo and Raphael learn their art by copying antiquities, and much of the Renaissance architecture was direct imitation of the Augustan Age. But with the birth of archæology as a science in the nineteenth century, scholars became accustomed to leap straight over the Roman era, or to regard it merely as a phase of the Hellenistic decline. From that view, undoubtedly erroneous and unjust, there has latterly been an attempt to escape. Wickhoff and Riegl, whose foremost interpreter in this country was Mrs Strong, argued that Roman art has an existence *per se*, not only possessing characteristic excellences of its own, but in many points transcending the limits of Greek art. To such pioneers we owe a deep debt of gratitude. They have undoubtedly drawn our attention to real merits and real steps of progress in the art of the Romans. But on the whole they have failed, as it seems to an onlooker, to prove their case. Partly it is in the long run a question of taste. A convinced Romanist like Mrs Strong displays for our admiration many works of art which trained eyes, accustomed to Greek and modern art, often refuse to admire. I would take as an instance the well-known "Tellus Group", a slab from the Augustan Altar of Peace,† preserved in the Uffizi Gallery at Florence. To me it seems a laborious composition, executed with care and skill, but wholly without inspira-

* Augustus and Mæcenas were tactful and genuinely liberal patrons who made surprisingly modest demands on the poets whom they supported—EDD.   † Plate 37.

tion or imagination. It is purely conventional allegory. How would the designer of an illuminated ticket for an agrictultural exhibition depict Mother Earth? He would design a group (would he not?) with a tall and richly bosomed lady for his central figure, he would put two naked babes upon her lap, at her feet would be a cow and a sheep, while the background would be filled with flowers and trees. The cornucopia would occupy a prominent position. If he were asked to fill his space with additional figures, he would throw in Air and Water, one on each side, designed on the same plan. There would be little motive in the group, little connection between the figures. The designer's aim would be that the spectator in a casual glance might observe the fitness of it all—Earth sitting between Air and Water—note it, and pass on. This is just what the Roman artist has done. He has earned his money. He has carved most skilfully and diligently, he has introduced all the conventional emblems. He has drawn his metaphor from stock. I cannot see that he has put any love or religion or indeed faith of any kind into his work. This then is the first point of criticism against the Romanists. I have put it as a mere subjective impression, which involves simply a question of taste. But in reality it is more. They are failing or have failed to make out their case, chiefly because the critical world of art-lovers declines to follow their expressions of enthusiasm, and can give reasons for its refusal.*

* In regard to what is said here and in the next few pages about Roman art, naturally tastes and views will vary. The reader will find it assessed differently and, we believe, with a deeper appreciation in e.g. *Cambridge Ancient History*, vol. X, ch. XVIII. It may, however, be worth remarking here in regard to the Ara Pacis that all the surviving fragments have been gathered together and the whole monument has been reconstructed near the Tiber, close to its original site. It is thus now easier to form a general impression of the monument as a whole, of which it has been written that it is "certainly the noblest of those storied public monuments, devoted to the pictorial record of contemporary history, which rank with the perfection of veristic portraiture and of three-dimensional painting as Roman Italy's signal contributions to classical art" (J. M. C. Toynbee). After a long absence in the provinces Augustus returned to Rome and in July 13 B.C. the site for the Altar was consecrated: to offer sacrifice went Augustus, accompanied by members of his family, priests, magistrates, senators and other public men, in solemn procession. That scene has now been preserved for posterity in the two magnificent processional friezes of the Altar itself. "It appeals to us", writes Professor J. M. C. Toynbee, "by its serene tranquillity, its unpretentious stateliness, its homely intimacy, its gracious informality, its delight in Nature, its purposeful unity, and not least by its modest dimensions." Symbolic of the "immense majesty of the Roman peace", it is a worthy memorial of the age.—EDD.

Secondly, we have a right to ask the apostles of Roman art what they mean by their claims. How justly may we call works like the Altar of Peace;* or even the Column of Trajan, "Roman Art"? Was any of it executed by Roman artists? We have just read the true Roman attitude towards art in Virgil's *excudent alii*. We may be sure that the Altar of Peace was executed by Greeks. The only named sculptors of the period are Greeks. This is indeed admitted, but then the Roman claim takes one of two forms, (1) that work executed in the Roman Empire may be called Roman, which is absurd, or (2) that apart from mere execution there are in the work certain characteristic innovations which are due to Roman inspiration. The latter claim is true, to some extent, and important.

Just as Mæcenas urged the poets to sing of kings and battles, so the patron of art gave instructions to the Greek artists. It is clear enough what instructions he gave. Like Cromwell he cried "Paint me as I am, warts and all. Leave your idealism, your perfect profiles, your serene gods in the tranquillity of Olympus, and depict men with the living emotions displayed in frown and wrinkle". That was excellent advice, no doubt, but he seems to have gone farther. He seems, like the good Dr Primrose, to have demanded value for his money by insisting upon so many portraits to the square yard of surface to be decorated. Is not this the explanation of the crowded figures in the new style of relief work, as exhibited at Rome from the Altar of Peace to the Column of Trajan? In the friezes of the Mausoleum, the fourth-century Greek sculptors had discovered the advantage of free spacing so that each figure has a value of its own. The florid taste of the millionaire Attalids of Pergamum had made a reactionary movement in the direction of crowded and tangled forms. Now these Roman friezes carry the demand a stage farther. In these processions we have a compact mass of faces, each admirably and no doubt faithfully portrayed, but ruining by their very numbers the artistic success of the whole. The spectator is not to admire a composition. As in Frith's "Derby Day" he is to pick out a face here and there and cry "That is Agrippa : that is Messalla : that is Germanicus". In its essence such a demand is not the mark of a people with any sense of art. On the contrary it is the measure of their crudity and Philistinism. Nevertheless this new demand

* Plates 34-37.

enabled the versatile Greek genius to win for itself fresh triumphs, especially in realistic portraiture and narrative relief-work.

Part of the claim which Wickhoff and his followers make for the originality of Roman art is based upon the belief that the limitations of Greek art are not self-imposed; for example, that the Greeks did not know how to express emotion in the plastic arts, that they could not make realistic portraits, that through ignorance they never perceived the beauty of a stark corpse, that Pheidias lacked the intelligence to find a dramatic centre for the Parthenon frieze, and so forth. Such assumptions as these are easily disproved. Greeks were capable of realism (witness the Ludovisi reliefs)* but they preferred to idealise. In portraying giants, barbarians, or slaves they could express transient emotions, but for Greeks and gods in statuary they deliberately preferred serenity. The Greeks sought to conceal their art rather than to display it, as we have learnt from the discovery of the subtle secrets of their architecture, and it is rash to assert of any principle of craftsmanship that the Greeks did not know it. Many of the claims of Rome to originality may be refuted by this consideration.

What I believe to be the true statement of the case is this: Greek art did not come to an end with the death of Praxiteles or the Roman conquest. Its central impulse passed over from the impoverished mainland to the still flourishing communities of the East, to Antioch on the Mæander where the Aphrodite of Melos was produced, to Rhodes where the Laocoön was carved, to Ephesus, and farther east still, even into Parthia and possibly India. It was by no means stereotyped but still producing new forms to meet fresh demands, as for sarcophagi in Sidon, or for paintings and mosaics in Egypt. In the course of this period the art of the Greeks was much influenced by the East. The Romans at first were content to take Greek art as they found it. In the days of Mummius they were merely like rich transatlantic collectors in search of beautiful, still more of precious and unique, commodities. They had no doubt some slaves of their own working in Rome at the arts and crafts. Some of these would be Greeks of inferior birth and capacity reproducing old Greek work for the Roman market. But some of them may well have been Italians, some Etruscans preserving the old artistic traditions of their race. This "collecting" era lasted down to the time of Augustus. We

* See *The Glory that was Greece*, Plates 34 and 35.

have seen it as late as Cicero and Atticus. There was little demand for new creations in those days. Few temples were being built. The artists were still scattered about the Levant. There was little to attract them to Rome.

But when Augustus decided to build a new Rome of marble, founding or restoring his eighty temples, with arches and theatres innumerable all over the Empire, there must have been a great influx of artists from Greece and Asia Minor. Now begins an art to which we may fairly apply the term Græco-Roman in the sense that it was the work of Greek artists supplying Roman demands. The new demands entailed still further artistic developments, some of them but not all to be regarded, by those who view the history of art as a whole, as improvements. One main effect of Roman conditions was that art largely ceased its service of religion and became devoted to secular purposes. Thus the limitations of Greek art of the best period, which were self-imposed and which had long broken down in Greece itself, were now definitely disregarded. The effect is seen especially in portraiture, where the Romans had a tradition of realism which was stimulated and nurtured by making wax images of the illustrious deceased. Hence in the decoration of the great Altar of Peace at Rome, the Greek artists, who would naturally have produced a frieze of gods or idealised worshippers, were asked for portraits of the men of the day. I think it is clear that enormous skill was devoted to the likenesses of men and very little care to the gods. The composition of the whole was of little account. A little later the demand for historical reliefs on arches and columns was met by the development of quite new features in the art of sculpture, namely, those spatial or tridimensional effects of perspective which are so remarkable on the Trajan column.* This art seems to have begun in Alexandrian times but Rome may claim the credit for its development. It was necessary, if sculpture was to do that for which it was surely never intended—to tell a story. The Parthenon frieze was religious ornament, the Trajan column is secular history. When the Romans required ornament they were content with mere decoration and the artists responded with the wonderful skill which they had probably learnt in Asia. Never have there been such exquisite natural designs in wreaths and festoons of flowers and fruit as in the sculpture of the Augustan

* Plates 57-60.

Age.* It is the same with the art of the goldsmith, as we see in the wonderful discoveries of silver-plate made at Hildesheim and Bosco Reale† or in the great imperial cameos wrought in sardonyx. Even the humble potters showed the same naturalistic skill, as we see in the famous vases of Arezzo,‡ or in the graceful terra-cotta and stucco reliefs intended for wall decoration. There was money and skill in plenty, but what was lacking was a spirit to animate it.

If we could be sure of our ground in setting down realism as the Roman contribution to the history of Art, it would be a great achievement for Rome. Realism is undoubtedly a fine thing though idealism is a finer. Unfortunately it seems that Hellenic art in the eastern centres was developing realism, or at least illusionism, for itself on its own soil. On the whole, in the controversy between the archæologists, Strzygowski, who claims the East as the inspiring force in Roman days, seems to have the best of it. The coins of Asia Minor present realistic portraiture quite distinct from that which was native on Roman soil. Thus the exquisite festoons of flowers, fruit, and birds, all botanically and anatomically correct to the last feather or stamen, are probably the product of Greece and the East.§ But we may well believe that the

---

* Plate 37.   † Plate 43.   ‡ Plate 42.

§ In the controversy, Rome or the East, agreement seems as far off as it was when these words were written; yet it may not be amiss to add that in the interval the champions of Rome have held their ground sturdily and have even scored points against Strzygowski. We hear less nowadays, for instance, of the view that Roman architecture is merely a continuation of Hellenistic, for this seems to have remained like the earlier architecture of Greece, a simple affair of columns and lintels; and if we inquire whence Rome derived its vaults and domes, it is still possible for Rivoira to argue that the Roman examples are older than their supposed prototypes in the East. In sculpture we are tending to seek the initial impulse of Roman portraiture in Etruria and not in Greece. Again in painting; the earlier, simpler styles of wall decoration at Pompeii (see p. 269) admittedly came from the East, but when we come to the more developed styles which for years past have been glibly derived from Antioch or Alexandria, we are confronted by the fact that at present we have no evidence that they were ever known outside Italy.

That Rome should be the heir of Greece was as inevitable as that Assyria should continue the traditions of Babylon. But in the Eastern Mediterranean in the first century B.C. art was sinking low as the result of years of war and turmoil. Augustus drew the embers together and fanned them to new flame, and the result was often something novel which it is only fair to credit to Rome. The sensationalism of the Laocoön and the cold dignity of the Ara Pacis are not far apart in time, but they belong

nature of the Roman patron's demands assisted this movement. The Roman, if we may judge by Pliny the Roman art-critic, was just the man to insist that an apple should not resemble a pear or to count the petals of a poppy. This sort of criticism affords excellent discipline for the artist. The statues of the period, such as the Orestes and Electra group by Stephanus at Naples,* are not very interesting works. They are plainly late-born issues of Greek sculpture, though in the latter there is an attempt at expression which seems to be derived from the influence of portraiture. The "Electra", for example, has the same look in her eyes, a frowning look as of one standing in strong sunlight, that we see in the portrait of Agrippa. Portraiture had taught the sculptor of this day new secrets about the setting of the human eye. They had learnt the effect produced by deepening the hollow under the brow and by making the direction of the glance diverge from that of the head and body. But much of this was a legacy from Scopas. In little things like the hang of Electra's robe there is visible degeneration. Here, as in the Tellus Group, the contour of the bosom is made to support the falling drapery, an unnatural and very unpleasing effect.

The architecture of the period is distinguished by similar characteristics. It is distinctly Græco-Roman with much of the subtle harmony of fine Greek work lost. The temples are, on the whole, the least interesting part of the work, for they are pale copies of Greek architecture not always very artistically adapted. A good many of the ruined monuments of Rome to which the pious traveller now directs his footsteps date from the Augustan period. Many of the temples of the Republic were now rebuilt on the old plan with more sumptuous materials, as, for example, the round shrine now thought to be the Temple of Portunus.† Technical innovations include the debasement of the Doric column by omitting those subtle flutings which gave it all the

---

to different worlds. Take a minor art—pottery; craftsmen from Asia Minor appear to have been the founders of the workshops at Arezzo in Etruria, but it is certain that neither before nor after did Asia Minor produce anything approaching in excellence the vases made in Italy. Nor must it be forgotten that the Roman Peace was the main factor in the rebirth of art in the East; later in the Empire schools of sculpture flourished again in Athens and in Asia and these in their turn reacted upon Italy.—F.N.P.

* Plate 21.
† Plate 40.

grace whereby its strength was saved from clumsiness, and by erecting it upon a pedestal. But the Romans preferred the more exuberant Corinthian order with its florid capital of acanthus foliage, a type which the Greeks had used very sparingly and seldom externally. Again, the Romans had discovered improved methods of construction which enabled them to use a wider span in roofing, but they made no artistic advantage out of this fact. On the contrary, by dispensing with the *peristyle* or surrounding colonnade they rendered the exterior of their temples much less interesting. The principal surviving relics of Augustan temples are eight columns of the Temple of Saturn which still stand in the Forum at Rome. The celebrated Pantheon* is now recognised to be a work of Hadrian's time though its portico may be that of the temple erected on the site by Agrippa. The finest extant example is undoubtedly not in Rome, the temple at Nîmes, known as the Maison Carrée,† a graceful erection of this period which exhibits the Corinthian style without undue extravagance.

As the Romans of this day showed few traces of genuine religious feeling, it is not surprising that they had little of their own to contribute to temple architecture except wealth and magnificence. But they were naturally devoted to building and that was the favourite extravagance of the rich. Little but a few pavements survives of all the handsome villas which dotted the hill-sides at Tibur and Præneste, or lined the coast at Baiæ, Naples, and Surrentum. But there are several secular buildings of Augustan date in which we can see a handsome Græco-Roman style of architecture wherein Greek columns and entablatures were used by Roman architects chiefly as ornament. The Theatre of Marcellus,‡ built in 13 B.C., still presents considerable remains, which though much defaced exhibit an appearance of bygone splendour. The lower story is Doric, the second is Ionic, and the third which has perished was probably in the Corinthian style. We may judge its effective appearance from the copy of its elevation which Michael Angelo produced in his design for the inner court of the Farnese Palace at Rome. The Renaissance learnt much of its architecture from Augustan Rome and these very designs may be seen around us to-day in the banks and town-halls of London. Thus Augustan Rome holds a supremacy for secular building even greater than Periclean Athens achieved for temples. Where

* Plate 61.   † Plate 80.   ‡ Plate 38.

magnificence and solidity—and it may be added cheapness—are the principal motives of construction, the Græco-Roman style of the first century B.C. is unmatched.

The most gorgeous of the architectural creations of Augustus was, however, the new Forum which formed the precinct of the Temple of Mars the Avenger which he vowed at Philippi to set up in memory of his punishment of the conspirators. The niches of the surrounding gallery were adorned with portrait-statues of the Roman heroes of history with biographical inscriptions on the bases. Further with Agrippa's help Augustus turned the Campus Martius into a great monumental zone : there were the Portico of Octavia, Agrippa's Baths, the Pantheon, the Theatres of Marcellus and Balbus, the Ara Pacis and the Mausoleum which Augustus built for himself and members of his family and on the entrance pillars on which were the bronze tablets inscribed with the Res Gestæ, the official record of his reign. In all the Augustan culture we see the impress of the prince's own Græco-Roman taste. It was all planned to achieve his object of dazzling the multitude and yet gaining over to his side the highest intellect and taste of his day. His own tastes were refined and fastidious : he hated extravagance, and utility was always before his eyes. "He read the classics in both tongues," says Suetonius, "principally in order to find salutary precepts and examples for public and private life. He would copy these out word for word and send them to his servants or to the governors of armies and provinces or to the magistrates of the city whenever they required his admonitions. He used to read whole volumes to the senate, and often publish them in an edict." We learn further that he always prepared his more important orations most carefully, writing them down and keeping the manuscript close at hand. This practice he followed even in his discourse with his wife. Augustan culture has just this quality : it takes immense pains and succeeds by virtue of them. It lacks a good deal in spontaneity but it makes up in excellence of technique.

THE GROWTH OF THE EMPIRE

Ambitionem scriptoris facile auerseris, obtrectatio et liuor pronis
auribus accipiuntur : quippe adulationi fœdum crimen seruitutis, mal-
ignitati falsa species libertatis inest.   TACITUS

IN these words, pregnant and terse as ever, Tacitus gives us
a key to the true reading of imperial Roman history. "We are
easily disgusted," he says, "with an historian's flattery, but his
malicious criticisms are greedily swallowed. For flattery bears the
odious stamp of servility, while malignity wears the false disguise
of independence." Thus out of his own mouth the foremost historian of the early Empire gives us the right to read the literary
sources in a spirit favourable to the emperors. So when the historians describe Tiberius as a bloodthirsty tyrant who hid himself
away in the island of Capri, and there (at the age of seventy!)
began to devote himself to disgusting orgies of lust and cruelty,
we shall prefer to reject that story as absurd, and to regard
Tiberius as a proud and reserved aristocrat who found it impossible to tolerate the mixture of adulation and spite with which he
was treated by the other nobles of Rome, and withdrew from the
capital in order to escape it. When Gaius (Caligula) is represented
as a lunatic, we recall that he was unpopular; when we are told
that he made his horse a consul, we recognise a satirist's humorous
exaggeration of his neglect of some noble family's claims to that
office; when we read that he set his army to collect oyster shells
on the Channel coast, we only conclude that his abandonment
of the projected invasion of Britain was a subject of ridicule
in Rome. Claudius is described as a stupid and clumsy pedant,
deformed and inarticulate: in reality he seems to have been a
scholar with a leaning towards antiquarian and republican traditions. Even in the case of Nero, the savage ferocity with which he

is charged is chiefly due to the fact that his hand lay heavy on the senators. He was undoubtedly popular with the commons, and his real offence was to possess more artistic leanings than were considered proper in a Roman noble, to be too fond of Greeks and art and music. Nevertheless it is impossible to write history in whitewash, and the only safe method of dealing with a period like this is to ignore the personalities on the throne of the Cæsars, and to attempt a broad treatment of the general tendency of these times.

But by neglecting the gossip and the personalities we do, I fear, run the risk of missing much of the interest of the period, and perhaps we lose an important part of the truth. We must not allow ourselves to be wholly deprived of that impression of purple and splendour which hangs about the Golden House of Nero, nor to forget the taint of crime which clings to the palaces of the Cæsars. The latter in particular is an essential part of imperial history. As we have seen, this Empire founded on compromise was and remained illegitimate. The succession was always open to question; there was no law of heredity. This fact was emphasised by the barrenness of the Roman aristocracy. For a hundred years no prince had a son to succeed him, so that the palace was always full of intrigue. Finally, the wickedness of the women is one of the most sinister features of the time. Though it was, indeed, no innovation of the Empire, it now gains a terrible significance in the dynastic conflicts which surrounded the throne. Every one of the early reigns is stained with murders and fearful crimes in the palace. No doubt much of this scandal is false and malicious. For example, it is by no means likely that Germanicus was poisoned. There were always scandal-mongers to hint at poison when any member of the ruling house died of disease.* But even with the most liberal discount for exaggeration, the record is a black one. Let us select two typical stories, in order to suggest the kind of satanic halo which surrounds the imperial houses as depicted by ancient historians.

Claudius, the conqueror of Britain, was in reality the most successful and best of the Claudian Cæsars who succeeded Augustus, but his wife Messalina, thirty-four years his junior, was a creature of shameless lust and remorseless cruelty. Valerius Asiaticus, a Gaul by birth but now the richest noble of his day, was in possession of the far-famed gardens of Lucullus. Messalina

* Contrast the author's attitude to Livia on p. 206.—EDD.

coveted the park and accused him to her husband, with the inevitable result. Asiaticus died like a gentleman. He took his usual exercise, he bathed and dined quite cheerfully, and then he opened his veins, "but not until he had inspected his funeral pyre and ordered its removal to another place, for fear that the smoke should injure the thick foliage of the trees". So died this lover of gardens. Messalina's sins grew more open, until at last she went through a public pantomime of marriage with one of her paramours, Silius, a consul-elect. The ceremony was performed before a number of witnesses duly invited. Claudius was at that time guided by the counsels of three Greek secretaries, and one of them determined to reveal the shameful truth to the emperor. Tacitus tells the story of her ruin in graphic language. She was celebrating the vintage feast in the gardens she had wickedly gained for herself. The presses were being trodden, the vats were overflowing, women girt with skins were dancing, as Bacchanals dance in their worship or their frenzy. Messalina with flowing hair shook the thyrsus, and Silius, at her side, crowned with ivy and wearing the buskin, moved his head in time with some lascivious chorus. One of the guests had climbed a tree in sport and reported a "hurricane from Ostia". It was truer than he knew, for just then messengers began to arrive with news that Claudius was on his way from Ostia, coming with vengeance. The revels ceased, the revellers fled in all directions, and Messalina, left deserted, mounted a garden cart to proceed along the road to meet her husband. Her appeal failed, though Claudius would undoubtedly have relented but for the interference of the freedman Narcissus. After dinner, warmed with the wine, he bade some one go and tell "that poor creature" to come before him on the morrow to plead her cause. But Narcissus had already sent soldiers to her, and she was despatched. "Claudius was still at the banquet when they told him that Messalina was dead, without mentioning whether it was by her own or another's hand. Nor did he ask the question, but called for his cup and finished the repast as usual."

Nero,* too, in the pages of Suetonius appears so incredible in his wickedness that some exaggeration is probable. Of his splendid new palace the Golden House we read: "The portico was so high that it could contain a colossal statue of himself a hundred and twenty feet in height; and the space it included was so vast that it

* Plate 45 (right)

had a triple colonnade, a mile in length, and a lake like a sea, surrounded with buildings that looked like a city. It had a park with cornfields, vineyards, pastures, and woods containing a vast number of animals of all kinds, wild and tame. Parts of it were entirely overlaid with gold, and incrusted with jewels and pearl. The supper-rooms were vaulted and the compartments of the ceilings, which were inlaid with ivory, were made to revolve and scatter flowers. They also contained pipes to shed scents upon the guests. The chief banqueting-room was circular and revolved perpetually day and night, according to the motion of the celestial bodies. The baths were supplied with water from the sea and the Albula". At the dedication of this magnificent building, all that he said in praise of it was : "Now at last I have begun to live like a gentleman". They charged Nero with the murder of all his relatives, and there is a grim sort of humour in the story of his frequent attempts upon his mother's life. His grievance against her was that she wished to rule. First, he deprived her of her body-guard, and suborned people to harass her with lawsuits which drove her out of the city. In her retirement he set others to follow her about by land and sea with abuse and scurrilous language. Three times he attempted her life by poison, but finding she had previously rendered herself immune by the use of antidotes, he next designed machinery to make the floor above her bed-chamber collapse while she was asleep. When this failed he constructed a special coffin-ship, which could be made to fall in pieces, and then sent her a loving invitation to visit him at Baiæ, a fashionable watering-place. The ships of her escort were likewise instructed to ram her by accident on the way home. He attended her to the vessel in a very cheerful spirit and kissed her bosom at parting with her. After which he sat up late at night waiting with great anxiety for the joyful news of her decease. But news arrived that the accident had miscarried, the dowager empress was swimming to shore. When her freedman came joyfully to narrate her escape, Nero pretended that the man had come to assassinate him and ordered her to be put to death. Suetonius adds "on good authority" that he went to view her corpse and criticised her blemishes to his followers, and then called for drink. After this he was haunted by her ghost.

The famous story of his death is told with a little restraint, and the latter part of it is not incredible. When the first bad news came of the revolt of Vindex with the legions of Gaul, Nero summoned his privy council and held a hasty consultation with them about the crisis, but spent the rest of the day in showing them a hydraulic organ and discoursing upon the intricacies of the invention. Then he composed a skit upon the rebels, and prepared a pathetic speech which was to make the mutineers return to his allegiance in tears. He sat down to compose the songs of triumph which should be sung upon that occasion. In preparing his expedition his first thought was to provide carriages for the band: he equipped all his concubines as Amazons with battle-axes and bucklers. But when he heard of the revolt of the Spanish army under Galba also, he fell into a temper and tore the dispatch to pieces. He broke his precious cups and put up a dose of Locusta's poison in a golden box. He ordered the prætorian guard to rally round him, but they only quoted Virgil to him:

Is death indeed so hard a lot?

At midnight he awoke and found that the guards had deserted his bedside. Even his bedding and his golden box of poison had been stolen. So he stumbled out into the night as if he would throw himself into the Tiber. But a few faithful slaves came to him and a freedman offered him his country villa for a refuge, and Nero rode thither in a shabby disguise. An earthquake shook the ground and a flash of lightning darted in his face; he heard the soldiers in the prætorian camp shouting for Galba. Skulking among bushes and briers, he crawled on all fours to a wretched outhouse of his freedman's villa. There he ordered them to dig a grave and line it with scraps of marble. The water and wood for his obsequies were prepared, while he uttered the famous words *"qualis artifex pereo!"* either meaning "What an artist the world is losing!" or (more probably) "What an artistic death!" A dispatch came to announce that he had been declared a public enemy by the senate, and was to be punished according to the ancient custom of the Romans. He asked what sort of death that meant, and was informed that the criminal was generally stripped naked and scourged to death with his head in a pillory. Then he took up daggers and tried the points, but still he dared not die. He begged one of his attendants to give him the example. At last he heard the horsemen coming, quoted a line of the *Iliad* very appropriately, and drove, with the help of his secretary, a dagger into his throat.

Now, even of this, much is pure rhetoric. For example, it was impossible that Nero should have heard the soldiers in the Esquiline Camp from the road which he took to his servant's villa. The details are the invention of malice or the attempt of a literary artist to improve his story. Even Suetonius admits that the populace continued to deck Nero's tomb with spring and summer flowers, that they dressed up his image and placed it on the rostra as if he were still alive, and that a pretender, who arose in his name twenty years later, was received with acclamation among the Parthians.

Having made this concession to the literary tradition which can be shown to be very exaggerated and biased, we may now endeavour to gather up the fragments of history and briefly trace the progress of the Empire during its first century. First, as to its geographical growth; although Augustus had bequeathed in his testament the advice not to enlarge the frontiers of the Empire, and Tiberius had observed the precept, yet conquest still remained an object of ambition in the heart of every emperor who sought military renown or fresh sources of revenue. Britain, the declined legacy of Julius, was obviously beckoning the Romans. Diplomatic relations with the many kings of that island had been frequent, and it was found that Britain was an inconvenient neighbour for a rapidly romanising Gaul. There was a continual coming and going across the water, for there were kindred peoples on each side. Especially, it was the last refuge of the anti-Roman force of Druidism, a religion which was already declining and was suppressed by Claudius in Gaul. The main course of the conquest of Britain is fairly certain. Aulus Plautius with four legions,* and with the future emperor Vespasian as one of his brigadiers, defeated Caratacus and Togodumnus south of the Thames; he then crossed the river and occupied Colchester (Camulodunum), which became the centre of government of the new province. This was in A.D. 43, and Claudius himself spent a fortnight in our island in order to receive the honours of victory. The emperor, though absent during the main fighting, named his son Britannicus. Plautius himself seems to have reached the line of the Wash and Severn. Ostorius Scapula, his successor, advanced as far as Gloucester and

---

* The base of the invading army seems to have been Richborough in Kent. where traces of a large camp have come to light in recent years.—
F.N.P

Worchester but was mainly occupied in tedious warfare with the Silures of the Welsh mountains, and in the conquest of the elusive prince Caratacus (Caradoc). The mercy shown to that defeated hero suggests that the Romans had advanced in humanity since the days of Jugurtha. Ostorius also planted a colony of veterans at Colchester. The two succeeding legates made no fresh advance, but Suetonius Paulinus in A.D. 61 renewed the offensive in North Wales. While he was engaged in the conquest of Anglesey, the centre of a large community of Druids, leaving only the Ninth Legion to hold the conquered province, there broke out the great rebellion under the heroic Boudicca (Boadicea). It was not so much the oppressive nature of the tribute as the vexatious methods of the Roman financiers, who still as in republican days swarmed in the wake of eagles, that stirred the Iceni and their queen in revolt. Camulodunum, Verulamium, and Londinium were taken and sacked and there was an immense slaughter of Roman civilians and romanised Britons. But vengeance followed : no barbarians could stand against the tactics and discipline of the legions.

For the next dozen years succeeding governors were mainly content to pacify and civilise the island.

One of the extraordinarily pungent chapters of Tacitus shows us the Roman method of empire-building in Britain.* "The following winter", he says of A.D. 79, "was spent in useful state-craft. To make a people which was scattered and barbarous, and therefore prone to warfare, grow accustomed by comfort to peace and quietness, Agricola urged them by private exhortations and public assistance to build temples, forums, and houses, with praise for the eager and admonitions for the laggard. Thus they could not help embarking on the rivalry for honour. Now he began to instruct the sons of chieftains in the liberal arts, to extol the natural abilities of the Britons above the plodding labours of Gaul, so that those who lately rejected even the Roman language now became zealous for oratory. So even our dress came into esteem, and the toga was commonly worn. The next step was towards the attractions of our vices, lounging in colonnades, baths, and stylish dinner-parties. They were too simple to see that what they called civilisation was really a form of slavery." There is no doubt that the Britons took as readily as their Gallic cousins to the Roman

* *Agricola* XXI.

civilisation. Many of them took Roman names and some became Roman citizens. They learnt the pleasures of the bath and the amphitheatre, their mines were exploited, arts and industries were introduced, agriculture was improved. The Druids hid themselves away in the unconquered fastnesses of Wales or crossed over to the Hibernian island which the Romans never had leisure to invade. Meanwhile the Britons were learning to worship the obsolete gods of Rome, and presently the Eastern deities who came in their train.

The advance was resumed about A.D. 71, when Cerialis advanced his legionary force from Lincoln to York and completed the subjection of the Brigantes of northern England. He was followed by Julius Frontinus, who moved his legionary base from Gloucester to Cærleon and succeeded in subduing the Welsh tribes which had baffled Ostorius Scapula. By A.D. 78 Roman garrisons were securely posted over the whole of Wales. Frontinus was succeeded as governor by the father-in-law of Tacitus, Julius Agricola, who finally defeated the tribes of North Wales. From his legionary base at York (Eburacum) he reduced northern England and then advanced into Scotland also, where he inflicted a bloody defeat upon the wild Caledonians. But Scotland remained unconquered, as did the neighbouring island upon which also Agricola had cast his ambitious eyes. The Roman army was wanted elsewhere, and the Emperor Domitian declined to countenance any further adventures. Little more of our island's story is recorded until the travelling Emperor Hadrian came to visit us in A.D. 122. It is possible that Roman arms suffered a heavy disaster prior to his visit. The legion at York, the Ninth, suddenly disappears from view—presumably annihilated—and its place is taken by the Sixth brought over from Germany. Hadrian saw that the wild north was only to be won by a gradual advance with more or less peaceful penetration northwards. The system of fortified frontiers was already established on the Rhine and Danube, and Hadrian drew his finger across the seventy miles between Bowness and Wallsend. Across this space, where the Tyne and Solway almost overlap, the Roman lines ran straight over hill and dale, and there they are to this day as a silent proof of the greatness of the Roman people.* This was more than a frontier: it was a vast elongated camp, which looked south as well as north and frowned

* Plate 85.

alike upon the Brigantes and the Caledonians. It was pierced at intervals by fortified gates, and great roads ran northwards through it. On the north there was first a ditch, and then a stone wall broad enough for two or three men to walk abreast along it and nearly twenty feet high. Built behind and into the wall were sixteen large posts. Between these at intervals of a mile were smaller "mile-castles", and between these again were sentry-posts. Southward was the so-called Vallum, a ditch with a mound on either side. South of this ran a military road, giving lateral communications; it had probably formed the Trajanic frontier. This labour, though it is small in comparison with Roman works elsewhere, was achieved by the Roman legionaries and their "auxiliaries", who came from Gaul, Spain, the Danube, and even the Orient. It seems to have been completed in an astonishingly short space of time, although in the existing remains traces of alteration and repair at various periods of its stormy history can be observed. There were detached forts both north and south of the wall of Hadrian. It was Antoninus Pius who made the next step twenty years later. He built a turf wall from the Forth to Clyde, which was only about half as long and of inferior strength. But it eventually proved too advanced a position to be held in comfort and after forty years it was abandoned. Thenceforward, until the latter part of the fourth century, the wall of Hadrian formed the frontier.

Gaul meanwhile was becoming as civilised as Italy herself. Numbers of the Gauls who had acquired the Latin speech received the *ius Latinum*, which was almost equivalent to full citizenship. Claudius admitted the chiefs of the Aedui into the Roman senate, and part of the speech in which he justified the admission of Gauls is preserved on a bronze tablet at Lyons.* Twice in the course of the century there were interesting attempts to give political expression to the Gallic sense of nationality. The revolt of Vindex at the close of Nero's reign was little more than a mutiny, but the projected "Empire of the Gauls", which was set up during the confusion that followed the fall of Vitellius, came near success. Jealousy between the Gauls and Germans wrecked it.

In the case of Germany, it looked for a time as if Tiberius, who, of course, had personal knowledge of the difficulties and advantages of further conquest, meant to break his step-father's

* See also Tacitus, *Annals* XI. 24.—EDD.

precept and annex more territory. But probably the annual expeditions of Germanicus were not intended to be more than punitive and demonstrative. Blood enough was shed, and acres enough laid waste, to appease the ghosts of Varus and his unburied legions. But though the great battle of Idistavisus was hailed as a Roman victory, Arminius himself continually eluded the Romans and the legions were more than once in peril of ambush. When Tiberius cried halt, it was open to the critics to find a malevolent explanation in his jealousy of Germanicus, but it is much more likely to have been the deliberate policy of an emperor who had knowledge of Germany. Thus, although Arminius presently fell a victim to his own ambition, and perished by the dagger of a tyrannicide kinsman, he had done his work and saved the liberty of Germany. Henceforth the Romans confined themselves to the Rhine frontier, though they had posts and summer camps beyond it. By degrees the generals of the Upper and Lower Armies in Germany developed into governors of two German provinces, but Germany was unconquered. There was a great military road along the left bank of the Rhine joining the garrison towns where the legions were quartered. Mogontiacum (Mainz) and Vetera Castra (Xanten) remained as the headquarters. Claudius founded a colony at Cologne (Colonia Agrippinensis); Trier (Augusta Treverorum), another foundation of about the same date, grew into an important centre of Roman civilisation, as its majestic Roman gate* and fine amphitheatre still bear witness. Under Claudius also the great Via Claudia over the Brenner Pass was completed, and the canal joining the Maas to the Rhine. This was better work for Roman soldiers than slaughtering Chatti and Chauci in their native forests. The re-entrant angle of the Rhine and Danube about the Black Forest, where the rivers run small, was recognised as a danger-point. Since the Marcomanni had migrated from this area to Bohemia about 9 B.C., it had been occupied by a body of Gallic emigrants. The region was known as the *Agri Decumates,* but it is uncertain whether this means that the Gallic settlers paid a tithe of their produce as rent and undertook their own defence, which was a frontier policy adopted by Rome in later times.

It was the Flavian emperors, Vespasian and Domitian, who advanced a step further beyond the Rhine. Vespasian annexed the Agri Decumates in 73-4; Domitian defeated the Chatti and

* Plate 84a.

encircled the Taunus region. Here he established a line of watch towers and small forts on the hills, with larger forts in the plain below, all relying on the legionary fortress at Mainz in the rear. From this area, which encircled the west part of the Maine, he ran a defence line southwards across the Odenwald, then on along the river Nekkar via Stuttgart; from near here it turned eastward to join the Danube at Faimingen. Thus the whole area of south-west Germany was protected and Roman communications be-tween Rhine and Danube were greatly shortened and simplified. Under Hadrian this frontier line in Upper Germany and Rætia was strengthened by a continuous palisade and ditch, but Antoninus in about A.D. 140 advanced the central portion of the line still farther east, so that it branched off from the Maine at Obenburg, ran through Lorch, and joined the Danube at Hein-heim. This double line, resembling the two walls of Hadrian and Antoninus in Britain, was held for about forty years, after which the inner line was evacuated, many of its forts becoming towns. This policy of setting up immobile defences like the Great Wall of China is always a dangerous one. Useful at first and visibly strong, it tends to lull the defenders into a false security. The camps and forts grew into towns, the armies into peaceful citizens living with their wives and children and devoting themselves to trade and husbandry. Meanwhile the barbarians on the other side were growing stronger and learning the art of war as fast as the Romans were forgetting it.

Roman *Limes*

After this the danger-point for the Empire shifted gradually eastwards down the Danube. Claudius had converted Thrace from an allied kingdom into a Roman province in A.D. 46. Much difficulty was caused by the Dacians,* who lived just across the Danube on the north bank opposite the Roman province of Mœsia and in the modern Roumania. As the Danube was apt to become frozen in winter it ceased to offer a satisfactory frontier so long as there were powerful enemies on the other side. At first the Romans tried the system of transplanting them, 50,000 under Augustus and 100,000 under Nero, and settling them in the province of Mœsia. But it was a stupid policy, for it meant constant intrigues between the free barbarians and their enslaved kinsfolk. Vespasian accordingly moved two legions down from Dalmatia to reinforce the two already stationed in Mœsia. But presently there arose an able and heroic king called Decebalus, who welded the Dacians into a compact and organised kingdom, and began to menace the security of the Empire. Like Maroboduus of Bohemia, he drilled his barbarians on the Roman model. In A.D. 85 he invaded Mœsia, won victories and did great damage. Domitian, called upon to face this peril, fought several campaigns with considerable success and was then content with accepting Decebalus as a client prince. He gave him Roman engineers and artillerymen, and even sent gifts of money which the barbarians were pleased to regard as tribute. This has been set down as cowardice, and it was certainly imprudence in Domitian, for Decebalus grew stronger and more dangerous. It was left for Trajan, the greatest soldier of all the early emperors, to face this thorny problem in the two great Dacian Wars of A.D. 101 and 105. The war is depicted for us by pictures in stone. The spiral reliefs which cover the Column of Trajan in Rome record many details of the history of the two Dacian Wars. We see the embarkation of the Roman army, we see it on the march with its scouts in advance, we see the solemn purifications, sacrifices, and harangues which preceded battle. We see the battles themselves, in which the Romans with sword and *pilum* defeat the Dacians and their mail-clad Sarmatian cavalry. The great bridge built across the Danube at Drobetae by the Green architect Apollodorus is faithfully depicted. We can watch the siege of the Dacian capital, Sarmizegethusa, and observe the construction of the siege-engines. Scenes of pathos are most graphically portrayed, the torturing of Roman prisoners by the barbarian women, the suicide of the Dacian chiefs by poison, and the death of the heroic Decebalus.

* Plates 56-60.

At intervals throughout the story there appears and reappears the calm and stately figure of Trajan, steering his ship, sacrificing for victory, leading the march or the charge, haranguing his troops, directing the labour of engineering, consulting with his officers, or receiving the submission of the foe.*

The result of the two wars was that Dacia was annexed and became a province of the Empire. Here, as elsewhere, Trajan showed his contempt of natural frontiers. As a gallant soldier himself, he believed in the invincibility of the Roman arms, and preferred to put his trust in legions rather than in walls. For this he has been condemned by modern historians, but history is on his side. More than anything else it was reliance on natural frontiers and artificial ramparts, with the consequent loss of military instincts, which was to be the undoing of the Roman Empire. Think of unwalled Sparta and the Maginot Line.

The eastern frontier had remained quiet for nearly half a century thanks to the reorganisation carried out by the Flavian emperors. After the destruction of Jerusalem, which was placed under a legate in command of a legion (see below), the province of Syria was extended northwards to include Commagene and the crossings of the Euphrates, while Cappadocia and Lesser Armenia were put under the administration of the governor of Galatia. Through this reorganisation an unbroken line of Roman provinces faced any menace from Armenia or Parthia. For a long time there was a game of tug-of-war between Rome and Parthia, the rope being supplied by the kingdom of Armenia. The Augustan policy of filling the oriental thrones with princes trained at Rome was not a great success. You might learn bad lessons at court; you might even learn to know Rome without learning to love or fear her. The princes sent to Armenia or Parthia were unstable allies and the ordinary course of events was for the Romans to send out a king to Armenia and for the Parthians to depose him. Again it was left for Trajan to attack this problem in the old Roman fashion; when the usual submissive embassy arrived, Trajan answered, as a Metellus might have done, that he wanted deeds not words, and he led his army on. Trajan found the Eastern legions, whose headquarters were at Antioch, already civilianised and orientalised so that they had become useless for fighting. At this time there were three legions in Syria, one in Judæa and two

* Plates 56-60.

in the reorganised province of Cappadocia. The first task was to restore discipline and energy to these troops. Then, without bloodshed, in A.D. 114 Armenia was declared a province. Parthia, distracted by civil war, was overrun, its capital Ctesiphon easily taken by siege. Mesopotamia was made a province, and to Parthia was given a new king. The client kingdom of Adiabene became a third new province under the name of Assyria. This meant that the Tigris became the eastern frontier instead of the Euphrates. Unfortunately these conquests had been too easily achieved, largely through the temporary dissensions of the Parthians, who accordingly failed to experience the salutary discipline of real defeat. Trajan died on his way home, and Hadrian, who was more of a statesman than a warrior, reversed his predecessor's policy. He surrendered the three new provinces and even acquiesced in the Parthians' choice of a king of their own in place of the Roman nominee. The only new provinces of Trajan's creation which Hadrian retained were Dacia, Transjordania and Arabia Petræa, the land of the Nabatæans.

Although their military force was contemptible, their spiritual zeal made the Jews the most difficult people to govern in the whole Empire. Worshipping their Jealous God with fierce ardour, they could not join in the Cæsar-worship which was the outward sign of loyalty and patriotism throughout the Roman world. Moreover the Semitic question had already begun to vex the soul of Europe. Throughout the East and especially in the trade centres such as Antioch, Alexandria, and Cyrene there were already large communities of Jews who lived on the usual terms of deep-rooted racial animosity with their neighbours. It is only fair to the Roman government to admit that it tried to conciliate its difficult subjects. Though the vanity of Caligula led him to accept the suggestion of erecting a colossal statue of himself in the Temple at Jerusalem, yet, when the philosopher Philo and his fellow-ambassadors came over to plead against the outrage, the emperor good-humouredly remarked that if people refused to worship him it was more their misfortune than their fault. As a rule the Roman procurators who administered Judæa were almost too tolerant of Jewish fanaticism. The Jews were exempt from military service: their Sabbaths were respected. A Roman soldier who tore a book of the law was put to death. It was useless to argue with such sects as the Zealots and Sicarii (assassins). The anti-Semite

spirit broke out into massacres. In Cæsarea, Damascus, and elsewhere the Gentiles slew the Jews; in Alexandria and Cyrene the
Jews slaughtered the Gentiles. In Jerusalem the Romans had to
face violent discord between the rival factions, and naturally they
sided with the more tolerant and moderate Sadducees against
the stern Pharisees and the smaller sects of extremists. In A.D. 66
matters came to a crisis. A Roman garrison was attacked and
destroyed : the army which came from Syria to avenge them was
repulsed with slaughter. This occurred while the Emperor Nero
was on one of his theatrical tours in Greece, and in the next year
Vespasian was sent with an army of three legions and auxiliaries
which increased its numbers to over 50,000. During the last days
of Nero and the short reigns of his three successors, Vespasian was
gradually subduing Palestine and driving the irreconcilables before
him into Jerusalem. Vespasian himself became emperor and it
was left to his son Titus to finish the tragedy. The siege of
Jerusalem (A.D. 70) was one of the most difficult tasks which the
Romans ever had to face. In addition to its natural strength there
were six lines of fortification to be overcome one by one, and each
was defended with all the grim tenacity of which the Semite race
is capable when it is on the defensive. Five months the great siege
lasted, and at the end Jerusalem was a heap of ruins. Some of the
Temple treasures were saved for the Roman triumph, and the
Arch of Titus still shows us the famous seven-branched golden
candlestick being carried up to the Temple of Capitoline Jove.*
It is said that one million Jews perished in the war and 100,000
more were sold into slavery. Jerusalem became merely the camp
of the Tenth Legion. All Judæa became one province, and the
scattered Jews were only allowed to keep their privileges on condition of registering their names and paying a fee of two denarii
every year for their licence.

But this awful lesson had not quenched the fire of Jewish
patriotism nor killed their hopes of an earthly Messiah who should
restore the kingdom of David. At the end of Trajan's reign there
was a widespread rising of the Jews in Palestine co-ordinated with
that of the Jews of the Dispersion in Babylonia, Cyprus, Cyrene
and Egypt. It was suppressed so successfully that the Jews of the
Dispersion gave the Roman government little trouble in the future.
But once again in Palestine under Hadrian there was a Jewish

* Plate 52.

rebellion stimulated by the fact that the emperor forbade the rite of circumcision and decreed the foundation of the Roman colony at Jerusalem with a temple to Jupiter on Mount Zion. The rebels, under a leader named Bar-Koseba, held out for four years and sorely taxed the military resources of the Empire; even far-off Britain was called upon to supply reinforcements.* In the end the revolt was stamped out with merciless severity (in 134) and the Jews were scattered for ever. They were forbidden to enter Jerusalem (Aelia Capitolina) except once a year, but Hadrian's measures against this law were relaxed under Antoninus.

The only other noteworthy addition to the Roman Empire was Mauretania (Morocco). When Caligula had its king Ptolemy murdered, a rebellion broke out which was crushed under Claudius, who annexed the country and organised it in two new provinces.

On the whole, then, we can see that the Roman Empire had almost reached its natural limits. It had seized as much as it could govern, and now, with the exception of the Parthian kingdom, all that lay outside its frontiers was naked barbarism. So the centre grew more and more unwarlike, while the legions had little to occupy their minds except the speculation whether their particular general had a chance of the purple. For this reason alone the Cæsars were loth to embark on conquests, unless like Trajan they were willing to undertake the campaigns in person. A victorious general was always to be dreaded by his master.

THE PRINCIPATE

At first sight the position of the princeps is one of immense and terrible power. But earthly power has its natural limits in human weakness. Weak or wicked emperors were generally the servants of their favourites, male or female, or they lived under fear of the legions. Without their bureaux they were helpless, and the bureaux in the skilled hands of Roman knights or Greek freedmen were acquiring real power. But it is astonishing how much actual work was done by the more conscientious Cæsars. In Pliny's letters we see what minute details were referred by a provincial governor to his master and how minutely they were ans-

---

* Among the now famous "Dead Sea Scrolls" there has recently been found at least one military despatch signed by Bar-Koseba himself and sent to a subordinate officer.—EDD.

wered. The answers may be, and no doubt sometimes are, the composition of secretaries, but there is a personal note in them which often suggests the emperor's own dictation. Probably Trajan was exceptionally industrious and Pliny exceptionally punctilious. Nevertheless it looks as if a strong emperor actually ruled this vast domain. It is one of the merits of despotism that the monarch's power increases automatically with his virtues and capacity. A Caligula could not do so much harm : an Augustus, a Claudius, a Trajan, or a Hadrian might benefit millions of mankind. I think it is clear that they did so. The insane work of slaughter had almost ceased. All over the world the markets were full, the workshops were noisy with hammers, the seas were thronged with ships, the great highways busy with travellers. Justice was strong and even-handed. Taxes were low and equitably assessed. For the most part men had liberty to go their own ways and worship their own gods. From the accession of Augustus to the death of Antoninus Pius—and with a few intervals one might safely go farther—the world was enjoying one of its golden periods of prosperity. It is unhistorical to look ahead and pronounce this happy world to be already doomed.

Yet, on the other hand, it is idle to deny the unsound spots in this imposing fabric of empire. The weakness was at the centre. The aristocracy of Rome was gay and splendid, but not happy or secure. The ghost of the Republic still haunted her streets. To make a necessary repetition : if Augustus had been succeeded by a son as wise and tactful as himself, and if the throne had then passed to a third generation with the soldierly qualities of Trajan and the statesmanship of Diocletian, the Empire might have taken shape as a strong hereditary monarchy with a senate co-operating heartily, and an army obeying loyally. But that was not fated so. Tiberius was too proud to play the comedy as Augustus had done : instead, he made enemies of the aristocracy and became suspicious and tyrannical. When they lampooned and abused him, he turned into a despot. Cremutius Cordus the historian was prosecuted for calling Cassius "the last of the Romans" and, despairing of acquittal, ended his own life. At last Tiberius withdrew himself in gloomy despair and left the government in the hands of an unscrupulous intriguer, the knight Sejanus, who still further harried and alienated the nobles. It is hard to know the truth about Caligula, so palpably is his story written by satirists. He may have been mad. The adulation which surrounded the Cæsars was enough to turn the head of a vain youth. He was certainly extravagant and increased his unpopularity by taxes upon litigants and prostitutes. It was the officers of the prætorian guard who conspired to assassinate him.

Claudius was chosen by the bodyguard who had murdered his predecessor and he bought their allegiance with less than 4000 *denarii* apiece. He was the uncle of Caligula, but no process of adoption had lifted him into the royal house. Still he was the grandson of Livia and his assumption of the name "Cæsar" passed without comment. Claudius set Augustus before him as his model and in all things he was careful to return to republican precedents. He took the office of censor for the revision of the senate-roll. He increased the patriciate, encouraged the state religion and by personal attention improved the administration of justice. Much trouble had been caused by the practice of "delation". Even under the Republic criminal prosecutions had been the easiest method of obtaining political notoriety. Tiberius had added the motive of pecuniary gain. But under Claudius delation was discouraged. On the other hand the power of the bureaucracy was greatly increased, and the affairs of the Empire were principally conducted by the three powerful Greek secretaries.

On the death of Claudius who is alleged to have been poisoned Nero succeeded almost as a matter of course. His mother Agrippina had secured his succession by having him raised to honour just as had been done for Tiberius by Augustus. He had already been styled "Prince of the Youth", designated for the consulship and endowed with the proconsular power. There was, however, a possible rival in the young Britannicus, and Nero was chosen by the prætorian guard just as clearly as Claudius. During the first five years, when the young prince was under the guidance of the philosopher Seneca, the senate had less to fear, and the Roman state enjoyed some liberty, but when Tigellinus, the wicked prefect of the guard, gained his evil ascendancy over the mind of Nero, there were some prosecutions of influential senators which made the whole senate tremble. Yet, even in these worst days of the worst of emperors, good administration proceeded. Nero himself made an interesting proposal for the abolition of customs in the Empire and, indeed, may fairly be called "The Father of Free Trade". But the capitalist class succeeded in suppressing the proposal. The duties on corn were, however, reduced and the collection of taxes carefully regulated. Charges of extortion against tax-collectors were given precedence in the law courts, a notable measure of justice. It was much more the dancing and singing of the *princeps* than the extortions of Tigellinus and the judicial murders of noblemen that caused the unpopularity which brought Nero to his doom. Among the many who fell victims to the ferocity of Tigellinus were two honest Republicans of the old school, men who were genuine believers in the Stoic faith and who kept the birthdays of Brutus and Cassius as annual feasts. It is probable that serious opposition of this sort was far from rare among the aristocracy of the Empire. Writers like Lucan and Tacitus were evidently in sympathy with it, and though Thrasea Pætus and Barea Soranus are famous for the Stoic deaths they died, yet they were only two out of many who lived wholly on the memory of the Republic.

Nero's fall was due to his undisguised autocracy and cruelty, which alienated the senatorial aristocracy, the army, and the people alike; it was brought about through the defection of the prætorian guards, whose allegiance had been bought in the name of Galba. Nero was the last member of the Julio-Claudian family, and at his death the last shadow of dynastic claim died away. The succession of the principate became a mere scramble in which the strongest or the luckiest or the heaviest briber won the day. Pretenders sprang up against Galba, several of the armies put forward their generals as competitors for the throne; and Galba himself had not even enough generosity to pay the bribes by which he had secured the throne. Thus the year 69 was a year of incessant civil war. Galba was murdered in the streets of Rome; Otho was defeated in battle near Bedriacum and committed suicide; Vitellius, the choice of the legions in Germany, reigned from April to December, when Rome was once more occupied by an army. The legions of Syria, seeing that their fellow-soldiers of Spain and Germany had already made their generals into emperors, had determined to take a hand in the game, and now Vespasian came as the fourth Cæsar in the space of a single year.

It speaks well for the solidity of the imperial system as organised by Augustus that it survived the shock of such events as these. It proves that the system was everything and the man little or nothing.

The new emperor, Vespasian,* who succeeded after all this turmoil, was different from his predecessors in that he had two grown-up sons ready to succeed him. It is said that Mucianus, a still more powerful general and legate of Syria, had surrendered his claims because he was childless. If so, it was nobly and wisely done. Vespasian was able and willing to restore the machinery of the Augustan principate. He was himself a humble Sabine with no claims of birth. He was firm but not oppressive towards the senate, which needed replenishing. Many of the older aristocratic families had died out, and Vespasian drew on the municipal aristocracy of Italy for his new senators. The tapping of this new source had a good moral and social effect on court life in Rome, while the officials gradually formed a new aristocracy of service. Vespasian kept control over the prætorian guard by appointing Titus, his son, to its command. He also established the succession beyond doubt by making Titus his consort. Vespasian and Titus were elected consuls nearly every year. Vespasian's principal work was to restore the financial credit of the government. Unfortunately the two sons, Titus, and then Domitian, who followed him upon the throne and with him make up the "Flavian" dynasty, were scarcely worthy of their father. Titus was "the darling of the human race", generous and mild to the senators, but too fond of his popularity to be a strong ruler, and Domitian† developed into a genuine tyrant. With his autocratic system of rule he was naturally oppressive to the aristocracy, and his name is in consequence written on the pages of history as that of a monster of cruelty. Domitian certainly made constitutional changes which rendered the monarchy a more open fact. He held the consulship for seven years continuously, he became censor for life and drew up the senate-roll to suit his fancy, he refused the usual request of the senators that the emperor should admit that he had no power to condemn a senator to death. Also he openly spurned the proud senators and permitted the servile modes of address which Augustus and other emperors had forbidden.

These high-handed proceedings made the senators hate and plot against him. Plots were followed by executions, and Domitian gradually became more and more tyrannical. More of the Stoic

* Plate 46 (left)
† Plate 46 (right)

Republican party were executed, and the odious practice of delation came once more into vogue. At last there was a successful plot
organised in the palace, and Domitian fell to the dagger. It should
be added that as an administrator he seems to rank high in the
roll of Roman emperors; his personal unpopularity seems to have
blinded ancient writers to his undoubted abilities.

With the three succeeding emperors, Nerva (96-98), Trajan
(98-117), and Hadrian (117-138), we have a series of genuine
constitutional rulers who show the system of the principate at its
best. The excellent figure which these rulers cut on the page of
history is not wholly unconnected with the fact that we have now
passed beyond the region illuminated by the satire of Tacitus and
the tittle-tattle of Suetonius. Their deeds speak for them. In Nerva
we have the senate's choice of a ruler, elderly, blameless, but weak.
Had he not died in less than two years, he might have brought
the throne of the Cæsars down to the ground. Knowing his own
weakness, Nerva adopted the foremost soldier of his day as his
heir, and Trajan,* beloved of the soldiers and ready to purchase
the love of the Roman rabble, succeeded without a murmur. He
spent most of his reign in the camp. In the camp he died, and the
succession was by no means clear when Hadrian,† a kinsman
though a distant one, had the courage to seize and the luck to
hold the imperial power. All these three emperors granted the
senate's claim that the emperor should not have the power to
condemn a senator to death, and in some aspects the senate
seemed to have regained much of its old prestige. But Trajan was
too masterful and Hadrian too ubiquitous to leave any real scope
for senatorial initiative. It was really under these benevolent despots that the Dyarchy ceased to have any significance. As usual
the benevolence of the despot was the most fatal enemy to liberty.
Not only in Rome but even in the municipalities of Italy politics
were ceasing to have any real meaning, and men of standing had
to be coerced into taking part in the comedy. The bureaucracy
of the imperial palace now governed the world, and the better it
governed the more quickly did the life-blood of the Roman world
run dry in its veins. We now find imperial "curators" and
accountants going up and down the provinces to set their finances
in order. Whenever there is trouble in any corner of the earth, an

* Plate 47 (right)
† Plate 48a.

imperial "corrector" travels down from Rome by the admirable system of imperial posts to set it right. Where, of old, a local squire, the *patronus* of the municipality, would leave a charitable legacy for the maintenance and education of poor children, the state with its admirable system of *alimenta* was beginning to assume the responsibility. The state had its Development Fund which made loans on mortgage at very low interest, generally 5 but sometimes 2½ per cent., to small farmers, and the interest was applied to orphanages and the education of the poor. Nerva has the credit for introducing this splendid system of public charity and Trajan developed it. It was Hadrian who gave the finishing touches to the organisation of the civil service as a close bureaucracy entirely divorced from the military profession. This service was chiefly in the hands of the knights, and it ranged in a carefully graded hierarchy of officialdom down from the three principal Secretaries of State, the Finance Minister, the Chief Secretary, and the Minister of Petitions, down to the Fiscal Advocates who looked after local revenue. Though the Roman Empire is often represented as groaning under the weight of taxation, and no doubt the more extravagant emperors did amass heavy liabilities, yet Hadrian, despite Trajan's expenses in warfare and building, was able to remit about 225 million *denarii* of arrears due to the fisc. He also introduced a system of periodical reassessments and gave the fullest liberty for his tenants-in-chief to appeal against the collectors. Hadrian it was, also, who really introduced the system of installing a junior colleague in the Empire, a plan which Augustus had foreshadowed in his elevation of Tiberius. This plan produced one of the firmest dynasties that ever held the imperial throne, namely, the Antonines, Antoninus Pius, Marcus Aurelius, and Commodus, who ruled from Hadrian's death in 138 to 192. The age of the first two Antonines is considered by Gibbon and many others to be the culmination of the Roman imperial system.

Two facts of very great importance stand out from this hasty review of the principate during its first two centuries. In the first place, it is still, in the strict constitutional sense, a compromise. The theory of the constitution had not changed since Augustus. It is still a Republic—*Respublica Romana*—governed by senate, consuls, tribunes, and an intermittent public assembly. There is, as there nearly always had been, a *princeps,* that is, leading citizen, a man raised by personal eminence and prestige far above his colleagues. Certain powers are delegated to him by the state. Above all he is master of the legions because he has consular or proconsular authority over all the provinces where troops are stationed. There still remained certain theoretical limitations to his power. He could not, for example, impose a tax on Rome or Italy by his own authority. But the feebleness and sycophancy of the senate and magistracy made him actually omnipotent. It is true that this sycophancy was not altogether the fault of the senate. Under the tyrannical emperors like Tiberius, Nero, and Domitian, when the "delator" flourished, no senator's life was secure. At a frown from Cæsar it was customary to go home and open one's veins after writing a complimentary will in which one bequeathed everything to that best of rulers. This sort of behaviour led inevitably to the growth of autocracy. The emperor was the one person who dared to act, and the more capable and well-intentioned the ruler, the more closely were the fetters riveted around the necks of the Roman People. The silent growth of bureaucracy, of which the historians have little to tell us, but which we can gather from the inscriptions of the period, is both the symptom and the cause of this increasing power of the principate.

In the second place, it is important to notice that, although the city of Rome was growing marvellously in riches and splendour, she was losing her old domination in the world and becoming the capital instead of the mistress of the Empire. The magistracies of the city had almost ceased to have any importance except as grades on the road to proconsulships. Italy herself was sinking into the position of one among the provinces of the Empire, and with the growth of Hadrian's centralised system of imperial administration even the provinces were losing their significance as units of government. It seems impossible that almost the whole of Europe and large parts of Asia and Africa could ever have been governed by one man or even one bureau. Yet it was almost achieved by the Roman Empire. The world-state was almost a fact, and a few more Trajans and Hadrians would have accomplished it. The city-state idea, as a unit of patriotism, still flourished. But with the great roads stretching like railways to the four corners of the earth, and the imperial officers travelling along them, with the legions massed along the frontiers and men recruited in Spain sent to serve in Britain, the sense of territory, from which the modern state was to arise, began to develop itself.

IMPERIAL ROME

If the external history of the Empire has suffered by being so largely written by the opposition, the intimate life of the city has been still more distorted through being written for us by satirists. The humorous or venomous descriptions of Juvenal, Martial, and Petronius form our principal source of information, and Pliny, who gives us a very different picture of tranquil and cultivated leisure or of useful activity carried on in refined and elegant surroundings, has commonly been regarded as a remarkable exception. Yet the material remains are on the side of Pliny; and we owe a great debt to modern writers, like Sir Samuel Dill, who have been able to emphasise this point. Romances such as those of Lytton, Melville, and Sienkiewicz have embroidered the theme of Juvenal, and everybody nowadays has his vision of Imperial Rome based upon such fairy-tales. It is probably vain to attempt a refutation of the popular view which pictures the Roman of the Empire as exclusively spending his time in the amphitheatre watching the lions devour the Christians, except when he was supping on nightingales' tongues from plates of gold. Moreover these things are a not unimportant part of the truth. Imperial Rome remained as bloody and brutal in its amusements as Republican Rome. In fact, as the emperors were not only richer than the old senators, but also much more carefully watched and bitterly lampooned, so the number of wild beasts slain at a *venatio* of Trajan exceeded the slaughters exhibited by Pompeius. Doubtless the imperial epicure Apicius excelled his republican predecessor Lucullus in the variety of his menu, and the lascivious entertainments of Petronius Arbiter and his master Nero certainly dwarfed the attempts of Sulla. At heart it was the same Roman people, enjoying the same stupid pleasures and violent sensations under circumstances of greater magnificence and refinement. It was a society founded on slavery, acknowledging no limits to the free indulgence of pleasure. But one misconception must be combated. The whole imperial period of five centuries should not be regarded as one slippery Gadarene slope down which the Romans were hurrying to destruction. Fashions came and went. Extravagance was at its height under Nero: there was a reaction towards greater simplicity under Vespasian. Under Trajan and Hadrian life was orderly and refined. Under Marcus Aurelius philosophy was even more fashionable than vice. Nor was bloodshed the only form of public enjoyment; the amphitheatres often presented spectacles quite as inoffensive and much more splendid than our modern hippodromes and circuses. Chariot-racing, in particular, though a good deal more dangerous than the modern steeplechase, took its place along with gladiators and beast-baiting as the popular sport, and the Romans showed as much enthusiasm for Coryphæus and Hirpinus as we do for our Derby winners. The charioteer Lacerna had as much vogue with them as had Steve Donoghue with our fathers, and they took sides with the Greens and the Blues even more seriously than we do with Light or Dark Blue oarsmen. The Romans had an inherited taste for blood. There were philosophers who condemned gladiatorial shows, but the comparative rarity of such protests illustrates the powerful moral effect of convention.

On the whole, apart from its follies, material civilisation was steadily advancing during the whole period at present under review. In such matters as transit, public health, police, water-supply, engineering, building, and so forth, Rome of the second century left off pretty much where the reign of Queen Victoria was to resume. The modern city of Rome is obtaining its drinking-water out of about three of the nine great aqueducts which ministered to the imperial city. The hot-air system which warms the hotels of modern Europe and America was in general use in every comfortable villa of the first century A.D. Education was more general and more accessible to the poor in A.D. 200 than in A.D. 1850. The siege artillery employed by Trajan was as effective, probably, as the cannon of Vauban.

The city of Rome must have been a wonderful spectacle under the emperors. One of our modern international exhibitions might faintly recall a little of its splendours, with gilt and stucco for gold and marble. Northward from the slope of the Aventine Hill there was a succession of majestic public buildings, temple beyond temple, forum beyond forum, as each of the great emperors had added to the work of his predecessor and endeavoured to eclipse it. At your feet would be the Circus Maximus, where the chariot-races were held, and beyond it the Palatine Hill crowded

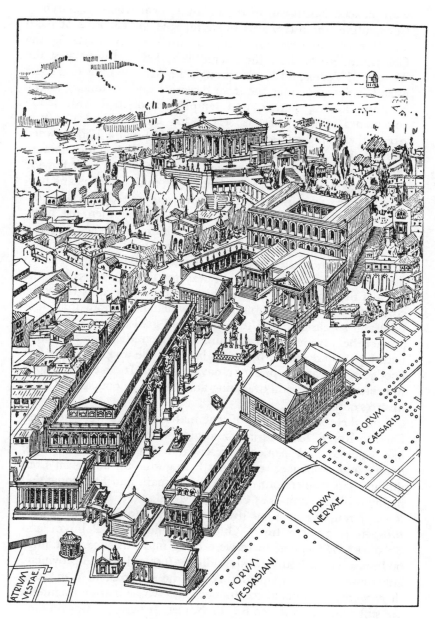

The Roman Forum in the early Empire

with palaces. North-east of the Palatine, near where the Arch of
Constantine was afterwards to stand, rose the Colossus of Nero
and the mighty Flavian Amphitheatre known to us as the
Colosseum. From there the Sacred Way led northwest past the
Temple of Venus and Rome through the Arch of Titus to a series
of stately *fora,* opening one from the other and containing altars,
columns, arches, statues, and temples surrounded with shady
colonnades, whose cloisters served for business and pleasure.
Above them on the west rose the ancient Capitoline Hill crowned
with its great Temple of Jupiter and immemorial citadel. Picture
these magnificent spaces filled with grave citizens in their flowing
white togas, hurrying slaves in their bright tunics, visitors and barbarians from all corners of the earth, trousered Gauls, skin-clad
Sarmatians, mitred Parthians. Every now and then the burly
gladiators swagger through the crowd admired by every one, or a
procession of the shaven begging priests of Isis passes by with
strange cries and gestures. Perhaps the lictors come swinging down
the hill bidding every one make way for the slaves carrying the
litter of the emperor, who is on his way to sacrifice. Or fancy the
crowd in the Great Amphitheatre, which held more than fifty
thousand spectators, with the purple and gold awnings spread to
protect them from the blazing sunshine, the auditorium perfumed
with scents and cooled by fountains, and the arena at their feet
flooded with water to present a naval combat. It is a city wrapped
in profound peace, still dreaming amid its splendours that it is the
mistress of the world.

And these signs of magnificent material riches were not confined to Rome. Alexandria would almost rival her. Asiatic towns
like Ephesus and Antioch presented a similar appearance of
luxury and opulence. In the north Lugudunum and even Londinium had a splendour of their own. Spain had handsome and
highly civilised capitals at Cordova, Merida, and Tarragona. The
Roman remains at Trier dwarf the comfortable erections of a
prosperous modern town. Out in the desert at Palmyra and
Ba'albek* (Heliopolis) there were rising into existence those huge
buildings which testify to the industry fostered by the provincial
government of the emperors. Along the sea-coast of Campania
there were sea-fronts of continuous villas whose marble fragments
are still washed up in the Bay of Naples. It tasks the imagination

* Plate 84b.

of genius to conjure up that glowing world of the past out of the ruined foundations that remain. Turner's famous picture of Baiae represents a successful attempt to do so. Pompeii, wonderful as it is, was only a small and obscure country town. Yet it was lavishly provided with temples, baths, theatre, and amphitheatre.

In North Africa, where nothing but man's labour organised under a good government is required to make the desert blossom as a rose, there was a teeming population which prospered on agriculture. Timgad (Thamugadi), in Numidia, was founded in the year 100 as a colony by Trajan. Here, in the blank desert of to-day, the French explorers have revealed porticoes and colonnades, a forum, a municipal senate-house, a theatre, a capitol, rostra, a triumphal arch, baths, shrines, and temples, together with the aqueduct and fountains which alone made all this splendour possible. Even the barracks of the Third Legion at Lambæsis, not far from Thamugadi, show architectural splendour and comfort. For public munificence this age is unequalled in history. It must have been a very powerful sense of patriotism that impelled rich men to devote so large a part of their fortunes to the embellishment of their native towns. The benefactions of the modern millionaire seem miserly in comparison. Pliny, who was not a very rich man as wealth was accounted in his day, presented his native town of Como with a library at a cost of nearly 250,000 *denarii*, and maintained it with an annual endowment of more than 25,000. He offered to contribute one-third to the cost of a secondary school, and made the wise provision that the parents of the boys should contribute the rest, in order that they might feel an interest in the school and take pains in the choice of suitable teachers. He gave 125,000 *denarii* more for the support of poor children. He bequeathed money for public baths, and 125,000 *denarii* for their adornment and upkeep, and nearly 470,000 to his freedmen and for public feasts. And, as Dill has pointed out, the inscriptions of every municipal town prove that this princely generosity and patriotism were by no means the exception. "There was in those days an immense civic ardour, an almost passionate rivalry, to make the mother city a more pleasant and a more splendid home." Among the most princely of these benefactors was the Athenian Professor of Rhetoric, Herodes Atticus, who added a new quarter to Athens in the reign of Hadrian.

Perhaps the most remarkable feature of life in the Roman

Empire under the good emperors of the second century is the growth of a lower class with occupations and ideals of its own. We have already remarked that the poor free Roman of republican days scarcely emerges into the light except as a soldier. But now the inscriptions show us a happy and industrious class of artisans and humble tradesmen, grading down through the freedmen to the slaves, many of whom now lived and worked under quite tolerable conditions of life. Especially noteworthy is the social tendency of the day. Every occupation and craft was forming its guilds or *collegia,* about which the inscriptions give us full and most interesting details. The *collegia* were not quite Friendly Societies, and still less Trade Unions, though they undoubtedly claimed political privileges and perhaps even made some attempt at collective bargaining with the public. Sometimes they obtained exemption from taxation. They dined together, they had their chapels and festivals, their colours and processions. They had officers modelled on the old Roman magistracy, with *decuriones* as committee and a quæstor as treasurer. They had their list of patrons who were expected to earn the honour by generosity. In the main they were burial clubs. Even slaves and gladiators had their guilds and fraternities : of course they were regulated by the state.

As yet, in spite of its growing centralisation and spirit of paternal despotism, the Roman government was true to its ancient principle of allowing full local autonomy. The municipal life of a small Campanian town like Pompeii afforded scope for local ambition and a political ardour to which the election posters and the inscriptions scratched or scribbled on the walls bear eloquent witness. Sometimes the name of the candidate is written with the laconic addition *v.b.,* "a good man", or it may be "Please make P. Furius *duumvir,* he's a good man". But occasionally the commendations are more explicit : "a most modest young man", "he will look after the treasury", "worthy of public office", and so forth. Sometimes a trade-guild supports its candidate. Thus the liquor interest in politics is already noticeable before A.D. 79. The humour of the opposition is seen in such a poster as "the pickpockets request the election of Vatia as ædile". And the intrusion of the feminine element is to be observed in *"Claudium IIvir. animula facit"* ("His little darling is working for Claudius as *duumvir"*). The wit of the Pompeian wall-scribe was brighter, though not always cleaner, than that of his modern counterpart.

There is the proud inscription "Restitutus has often deceived many girls", but there are also testimonies of conjugal affection like "Hirtia, the Dewdrop, always and everywhere sends hearty greeting to C. Hostilius, the Gnat, her husband, shepherd and gentle counsellor". There is also an interesting account from a bakery:

1 lb. of oil	6*d.*	bran	9*d.*
straw	7½*d.*	a neck-wreath	4½*d.*
hay	2*s.*	oil	9*d.*
a day's wages	7½*d.*		

We find advertisements like "Scaurus' tunny jelly, Blossom Brand, put up by Eutyches, slave of Scaurus".

EDUCATION AND LITERATURE

A noticeable feature of the times was the wide diffusion of education. Everyone, it seems, could read and write, even the slaves, even the humble British workman. Many a Pompeian schoolboy has scribbled a line from Virgil, or Ovid, or Propertius. Many an adult has added his or her original compositions. We have seen in the case of Pliny how the rich men interested themselves in the foundation of schools, both primary and secondary, for their native towns. In the Greek world, as may be expected, education was most highly developed and thoroughly graded from the elementary to the university stage. For elementary schools the voluntary system was in vogue, but it was under careful public supervision, and, as we have seen, the state undertook the maintenance of poor children, girls as well as boys. In contrast to the present day, the teachers were often held in such high honour, that many a public inscription testifies to the gratitude of a town towards its schoolmasters. That they also received more substantial recognition is proved by the fact that they were often able to leave handsome benefactions themselves. They were elected, sometimes after an examination or after giving specimen lessons, by the local education committees, with religious ceremonies, and they took an oath of office on entering upon their duties. They had their unions and associations like other professions. In one inscription found in Callipolis, "The young men and the lads and the boys and their teachers" unite to confer a wreath of honour upon one of the mathematical masters. The teachers seem to have been subject to annual election or re-election. There were also visiting masters of special subjects. The Greek secondary school tended to lay much stress upon athletics, but it gave more attention to music and religion than similar institutions of to-day. Reading, writing, and arithmetic together with music, dancing, and drill were the staple subjects of the elementary school. "Rhetoric", which meant the study of literature on the technical side, as well as the practice of declamations, was the main occupation in the high schools and the universities. But philosophy, moral and physical, was also carefully studied. University professors often rose to real affluence.

In the polite world of Rome, literature was extremely fashionable. Everybody was writing and insisting upon reading his compositions to his friends. These literary labours were often pursued with amazing diligence. Both Pliny and his uncle devoted themselves to reading and writing almost from morning to night, and Pliny the Younger tells how he was laughed at for carrying his notebooks with him even when he was out boar-hunting. By the time he was fourteen he had written a Greek tragedy. His sketch of a day's doings at his country villa shows the literary perseverance of a Roman gentleman. He rose at six and began to compose in his bedroom. Then he would summon his secretary to take down the result from dictation. At ten or eleven he would continue his work in some shady colonnade, or under the trees in the garden, after which he drove out, still reading. "A short siesta, a walk, declamation in Greek and Latin, after the habit of Cicero, gymnastic exercise, and the bath, filled the space until dinner-time arrived." Even during dinner a book was read aloud and the evening was enlivened by acting or music or conversation. Many of Pliny's friends, such as Suetonius and Silius Italicus, emulated this studious existence, and his uncle even surpassed it. The elder Pliny consulted two thousand volumes in the writing of his Natural History alone, and he left one hundred and sixty volumes of closely written notes and excerpts. Nor was this an unimportant circle of literary bookworms. On the contrary, it was the highest society of the day. The elder Pliny was on terms of daily intercourse with the Emperor Vespasian, and the younger Pliny, besides being governor of Bithynia, was intimate with Trajan.

At first sight we may find it strange that all this strenuous devotion to study produced so little in the way of first-rate original literature. It is of course customary to ascribe the decline—assuming that it was a decline—of the Golden Age of Augustan literature into the Silver Latin of Tacitus and Juvenal to the tyranny of emperors like Tiberius and Nero. It is perfectly true that Tiberius made it dangerous for senatorial historians to praise the murderers of a Cæsar. But that is a ludicrously inadequate explanation for the eclipse of literature. The experience of Virgil showed that it was possible for a great loyalist to win fortune and glory amounting to idolisation. The senators who wanted to continue their school declamations against tyranny were certainly discouraged, but there was still plenty of room for literary activity. The truth is, as we have seen, that Augustan literature was not the work of a young Rome, but of an old and perhaps already declining Græco-Roman culture. Again it was literary, not political, causes which led to literary decline. Tacitus, who had for his themes the conquest of Britain and the wars in Germany and the East, the Siege of Jerusalem, the burning of Rome, the tragic Year of the Four Emperors, the crimes and follies of Nero, and the development of the great imperial system, complains of the lack of interest in the history of his own times compared with those of the heroic past. The tyranny that depressed literature was of its own making, the tyranny of convention, classicism and erudition. To take poetry, though so many noble writers were toying with the epic, the best they could produce was the *Thebaid* of Statius, the *Argonautica* of Valerius Flaccus, more promising but unfinished, the *Punica* of Silius Italicus, longest and feeblest of all these imitations of Homer, and the *Bellum Ciuile* of Lucan, which, though it contains many a brilliant epigram and memorable phrase, lacks simplicity and naturalness. The *Bellum Ciuile* is often declamation, rhetoric shouting at top pitch on page after page. Virgil had brought the literary epic to perfection: to carry it any farther in the same direction was to incur tediousness. Above all, both Lucan and Silius lacked the greatest of all Virgil's gifts, his wonderful ear for verbal music. Virgil, like Milton, presented his epic diluted for mortal ears with music and human nature. It was not in the spirit that Lucan failed. He admired the republican cause and Pompeius, its champion, quite as sincerely as Virgil admired Augustus or Milton Cromwell. Thus it was not politics, but the literary tradition that caused his failure, at least his failure to hold the ear of to-day. Past generations have esteemed him high among the world's poets. Dante owed not a little to Lucan and Statius as well as to Virgil.*

It was only in its lighter forms that poetry continued to make progress. The *Silvæ* of Statius, which were shorter occasional poems in elegiac or lyric measures thrown off at odd moments with ease and rapidity, are far more interesting than his frigid epic. Martial, the Spanish writer of *vers de société,* has a pretty wit that is often surprisingly modern in its tone. Certainly Juvenal towers over all others who have attempted satire. Horace had been content with an easy familiarity of tone which might wheedle a friend into the path of good sense by poking fun at his follies. Juvenal thunders his denunciations of wickedness with a moral heat which is surprising in an age often accused of feebleness. He does, however, resemble Lucan in spoiling some of his effects by want of light and shade, by a too persistent flow of rhetoric. He seems unable to distinguish between harmless follies like playing the lute and real delinquencies like murdering one's mother. He clearly draws far too black a picture of the men and morals of his day. But the pulpit from which he preaches is a high one. If Juvenal is supreme over the poets of his time, Tacitus is as clearly monarch of the prose-writers. He was continuing the work of Livy and writing from the same republican stand-point. But for history-writing he had certainly discovered a finer style of rhetoric. Both are rhetoricians first and historians a long way after, but the packed epigrams of Tacitus often say as much in a line as Livy is capable of conveying in a chapter. In describing a battle, a riot, or a panic, or in painting some tragic scene, such as the death of Vitellius, Tacitus is unequalled. The freedom that was permitted to him and Suetonius in depicting the crimes and follies of the earlier Cæsars affords remarkable evidence of the freedom of letters under Nerva, Trajan, and Hadrian. Here, again, it is necessary, as in the case of Juvenal, to beware of accepting too literally the truth of harsh criticisms upon the preceding generation. To praise the past at the expense of the present was one of the traditions of Roman literature.

All the erudition of the age added little to the real advance of learning except in the domain of law. Industrious compilers like Pliny the Elder have preserved a great deal of ancient lore for our

* For a more sympathetic presentation of Lucan, see W. B. Anderson in the *Oxford Classical Dictionary*, p. 514. EDD.

81.
MAUSOLEUM
OF PLACIDIA,
RAVENNA
(5th Century
A.D.).

82-83.   AMPHITHEATRE AT NIMES (probably Augustan Age)

84.   (*overpage*) (a) PORTA NIGRA AT TRIER (*c.* 300 A.D.) (b) TEMPLE OF BACCHUS AT BA'ALBEK, SYRIA. (2nd-3rd Century A.D.)

85.   (*opposite next page*) SECTION OF HADRIAN'S ROMAN WALL IN NORTHUMBERLAND.   (Early 2nd Century A.D.)

84.

(a)

86. *(Opposite)* CATACOMB OF ST. DOMITILLA, ROME.   87. *(above)* PORTA
MAGGIORE SANCTUARY, ROME (1st Century A.D.)

88.
A MITHRAEUM
AT OSTIA

89.   STATUE OF MITHRAS, sacrificing a bull in the
Mithraeum at Ostia.

90-91. **THE PONT DU GARD IN PROVENCE.** Perhaps of
the Augustan Age.

92-93.
ARCH OF
CONSTANTINE,
beside the
Colosseum.
A.D. 312.

94.

SCULPTURE
FROM THE
ARCH OF
CONSTANTINE.

95. COLOSSAL BRONZE STATUE AT BARLETTA
representing a late Roman Emperor.

96. (*over page*). ROMAN BRIDGE AT ARIMINUM
(Rimini) built by Augustus and Tiberius

36
(See
previous
page)

study, but they are for the most part utterly uncritical and un-scientific. There were no scientific thinkers like Aristotle in the Roman world. Still, some text-books, in Greek or in Latin, which served the middle Ages for instruction were produced under the principate, such as Vitruvius on architecture, Strabo and Pom-ponius Mela on geography, Columella on agriculture, Quintilian on rhetoric, and Galen on medicine. The last was state-physician to Marcus Aurelius and was employed by him to study and com-bat the terrible plague which the Roman army brought back from the East. But for medical science he added little to his Greek master Hippocrates. In just the same way, the philosophers came no nearer to the core of reality than their masters of the fourth and third centuries before Christ, hard though they toiled and much as they spoke and wrote. They were indeed learning, what the old Greeks had failed or scorned to learn, how to apply doc-trines to life, but in depth of thought they were so far behind that they ceased even to be able to comprehend Aristotle. Even Philo, the profound and learned Jewish philosopher, is doing little more than to attempt an application of Platonic and other Greek ideas to the teaching of Moses. Such originality as there was in the world of letters still proceeded mainly from the provinces. Greece was still putting forth original contributors to literature like the novelist Lucian, the biographer and moralist Plutarch, Pausanias the guide-book writer, Dio Chrysostom and Apollonius the preachers. Africa produced a novelist in the mysterious quack-magician Apuleius. Spain sent forth a whole galaxy of talent in the two Senecas, Lucan, Quintilian and Martial. The younger Seneca, Nero's complacent tutor, is perhaps the most typical figure in the literature of the principate. Based on the usual rhetorical training of his day, his literary work consists of rhetori-cal drama and rhetorical philosophy, including some rhetorical science. No writer has ever attained to such a position of wealth and honour by the exercise of his pen. It cannot be said that Seneca's position was gained without defilement, or that it brought him happiness. He was partly responsible by his weak compliance for the deterioration of character in his imperial pupil. If so, it brought its own retribution, for Nero drove him to suicide. Though Seneca's tragedies are neglected to-day, they formed the connecting-link between Euripides and the stage of the Renaissance.

It will be seen that the principal defect of thought and literature under the Empire was its lack of originality. But, after all, that had always been the deficiency of Roman writers. It was due very largely to the overwhelming incubus of Greek civilisation, from whose leading-strings the Romans, to the end of time, never escaped. That in its turn arose chiefly through the nature of their education, which turned all their attention to *style* as the end of literary endeavour. Lacking the intellectual powers and ambitions of the Greeks and of such native giants as Cicero and Virgil, the majority of Roman writers were no less inhibited than inspired by their models; and under the imperial despotism opportunities for new developments in subject-matter and in speculation were severely limited.

ART

With art it is much the same story; for the decoration of their villas and colonnades the Romans of the Empire continued to prefer their statues imported from Greece. Pausanias shows us that Greece, even in the second century A.D., was still teeming with works of art of every kind. Impoverished and shrunken as the old Greek cities were at this period, it shows some high-mindedness that they still retained treasures which would have fetched millions in the trans-Adriatic markets. There was, however, a brisk trade in copies and imitations of the masterpieces. For statues, then, the Greek work of the fifth and fourth centuries almost destroyed any attempt at originality by the Romans. Only in portraiture was there much progress, and here work of great power and vigour was produced. It reaches the zenith perhaps under the Flavian emperors, but their successors of the Antonine period and later are often depicted on their busts with triumphant but unsparing realism. The bust of Philip the Arabian in the Vatican is one of the most striking. Sometimes it almost seems as if there was a malicious spirit of caricature in these too faithful portraits. Can Marcus Aurelius, the philosopher prince, have presented to the world a visage so weak and so tonsorially perfect? Can Caracalla have borne his bloody mind so visibly written on his face? In portraiture there is certainly progress and not decay.

Otherwise, to judge by the remains, sculptors were almost confined to bas-relief. This was the medium chosen by emperor after

emperor for the narration of his exploits, and advances were unquestionably made in the art of pictorial or narrative sculpture.
That this is a high art in itself may, I think, be contested. If we
look for the end to which this art of narrative relief was tending,
we shall find it on the base of the Column of Antoninus Pius preserved in the Vatican garden. These cavalrymen placidly gyrat-
ing round the group of standard-bearers, each on his own little
shelf, are so extremely life-like as to recall nothing in the world so
much as pieces of gingerbread. We begin to perceive that Madame
Tussaud would have been hailed as a great creative artist in
Imperial Rome. Nevertheless, without subscribing to all the super-
latives of Mrs Strong, we may admit that art was still alive and
vigorous and still scoring fresh technical triumphs in the Antonine
period and even later.

Roman archæologists have worked out the history of imperial
art with some precision. The severe classicism of the Ara Pacis
and of the portraits of Augustus grew softer in the succeeding
reigns—the spirit of Ovid replacing the Virgilian; the "Clytie" of
the British Museum, probably Antonia the younger daughter of
Mark Antony, illustrates this tendency. Under Claudius there
was great constructional activity, mainly of a utilitarian character.
The Claudian aqueduct, whose immense arches in brick still
break the level horizon of the Campagna, is one of the greatest
works of this period.* Nero's was an age of Greek curio-hunting;
much of Rome was rebuilt after the great fire in his reign and the
Golden House must have been a stupendous sight. But on his
death the Romans made haste to obliterate all traces of his work.
The Flavian epoch saw a reaction against classicism—a return to
Italian tradition with its greater realism, coupled with a willing-
ness to experiment with new forms, which have led some critics
to style this the culminating point of Roman art. Vespasian destroyed Nero's Golden House and restored the Capitol. He and
his sons built the Baths of Titus, the Arch of Titus† with the celebrated Jewish relief, and the mighty Flavian Amphitheatre, the
Colosseum.‡ This was built in the style already noticed in the
Theatre of Marcellus, namely, with the three Greek orders of
architecture, Doric, Ionic, and Corinthian, adorning the three

* Plate 49.
† Plates 50-52.
‡ Plates 53 and 54

stories of the façade; but here, as so often, the Greek façade is a mere shell to hide the solid Roman masonry of which the building is really constructed. It is noteworthy that the monuments of this age refute the historians who allege among Domitian's other sins that he tried to destroy the works and the memory of Titus, his more popular brother. In the technical language of Wickhoff, this Flavian Age shows us "illusionism" at its height in art. Under Trajan, and in his famous column, the art of continuous narration in low relief is fully developed.* Hadrian, the cultured, travelling Philhellene, encouraged a reversion to the classical traditions of Greek art. The art of his period was profoundly influenced by the type of Antinous, a beautiful youth beloved by the emperor, whose romantic death by drowning in the Nile made a powerful impression upon the whole Roman world, because he was believed to have sacrificed his life for his emperor's in obedience to an oracle. This type is preserved for us in many forms, as in the colossal Mondragone bust in the Louvre.† His features were utilised to represent all the young male gods on Olympus. In their tragic beauty we see a mirror of Greece tinged by the Orient, as if Dionysus had wedded Isis and this were the offspring. The Antonine period, as exhibited on the panels in the Palazzo dei Conservatori, is gifted with immense technical fluency and, as Mrs Strong remarks, a new spiritual seriousness. As compositions they are superb, but the weakness of expression in the face of Marcus Aurelius himself quite spoils their effect for some spectators.

Architecture was still mainly designed in the three Greek modes variously combined, in spite of the fact that Rome had progressed far beyond Greek limits in constructional ability. Roman builders could manage a roof-span far in excess of the Greeks. The Roman arch gave a strength in concrete vaulting which expensive marble was unable to attain. Roman brickwork denuded of the marble incrustations which generally covered it of old is probably more impressive in its ruins than it was when it was draped with Hellenism, and, to me at least, remains like the aqueduct at Pont du Gard‡ and the Bridge of Alcántara seem truer witnesses of the grandeur of Rome than all the marbles in all the museums. The celebrated Castle of St Angelo, which still keeps watch and

* Plates 56-60.
† Plate 48b.
‡ Plates 90 and 91.

ward over the Tiber, is nothing but the core of Hadrian's tomb—the *Moles Hadriani*—once clad in a vestment of Greek marbles and covered with Greek ornament.* The Pantheon, in spite of the inscription which ascribes it to Agrippa, is proved by the stamps on its bricks to be a building of Hadrian's time. The plan is that of a dome so constructed that if the sphere were complete it would rest upon the earth. It is not, however, a true dome, since the roof was built as a cap upon a solid core afterwards removed. The magnificent interior has lost little of its ancient splendour.†

For temple architecture, although the Romans had adopted the forms of Greek art they had wholly deserted the spirit of austere self-restraint upon which that art had rested. Thus they readily adopted the luxuriance of the East when it came to hand. In the splendid ruins of Heliopolis (Ba'albek) and Palmyra we see a riotous luxuriance of ornament which would have shocked the religious sense of Ictinus, but which fitly enshrined the ritual and

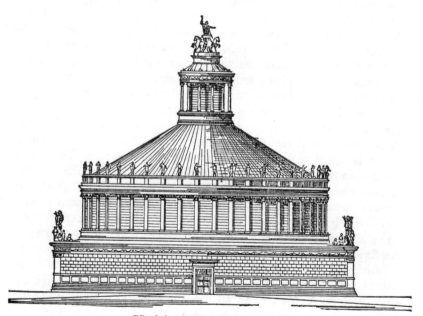

Hadrian's Tomb: restored

* Plate 63.
† Plate 61.

mysteries of the Sun-god. This craze for the colossal would have made the reverential Greeks tremble in fear of provoking the Nemesis of a jealous Heaven, but in its ruins it has left us superb and awful reminders of the riches and grandeur of its authors, and of the end of all riches and grandeur.

In domestic building the Romans had almost as little regard as the Greeks for the exterior elevation of their villas and palaces. The Roman gentleman still made it his favourite hobby to collect villas, and Pliny had almost as many as Cicero. But the main idea of the villa was comfort, and the main idea of Roman comfort was coolness, quiet, and beautiful scenery. Thus the wealthy man's house consisted of a series of marble courts and cloisters spread over the ground regardless of space. Landscape and landscape-gardening were the most charming features. The Roman appreciated the scenery of Como or Sermione, Tivoli or Naples, quite as keenly as the tourist of to-day. He thought much of fresh air and good water. Nearly all Roman gentlemen were agreed in considering Rome itself, with its smells, its noise, and its perils by fire, as a pestilent place of abode, and they gladly fled to their country estates at Præneste or Baiæ. Hadrian's villa at Tivoli* comprised an enormous complex of courtyards, colonnades, baths, theatres, libraries and garden enclosures, to many of which he gave the name of buildings famous in antiquity or places he had seen on his travels. This was a favourite affectation of wealthy Romans; we saw (p. 121) Cicero constructing a Platonic Academy. The decoration of these villas encouraged two minor arts which figure prominently among their remains. The floors were commonly adorned with marble mosaic, of which we still have some charming examples. The interior walls were either incrusted with marble, in the wealthier houses, or stuccoed and painted. Hence, it results that the art of painting is represented to us almost solely by mosaics, wall-frescoes,† and a few portraits on Egyptian mummy-cases. Nothing remains of the great masters of antiquity, Polygnotus, Zeuxis, and Apelles. But there may be faint echoes of their work on the frescoes of Pompeii executed by unnamed decorators. Even so there is great charm in much of this work. Mau, the great authority on Pompeii, distinguished four successive phases of painting in that city. At first the aim was to

* Plate 62.
† Plates 41, 75 and 76.

imitate the marble slabs used to cover the walls of the rich man's house. Then growing bolder the painter imitates various forms of architectural treatment dividing up his wall space into panels and portraying cornices, columns, pilasters, and so forth. This is roughly the style of the first century B.C., and it is found in the so-called house of Livia on the Palatine Hill at Rome. The third style, which Mau terms the "ornate", was prevalent until about A.D. 50. The architectural features now make no pretence at illusion. The columns have become mere bands of colour, and there is profuse ornament everywhere. The colours are somewhat cold. The fourth or "intricate" style once more emphasises the architectural character of the decoration, but the patterns are too intricate to present any appearance of reality. The whole wall space shows a riot of fantastic ornament often extremely graceful and effective. Flying goddesses and cupids impart a sense of airy lightness, and floral forms festoon themselves in charming curves. The pictures are smaller and the spaces wider. No more pleasing treatment of the interior walls of a house has ever been devised, at any rate for warm climates. The subjects of the pictures are almost exclusively mythological. The destruction of Pompeii by the eruption of Vesuvius in A.D. 79 makes it impossible to study the further development of ancient painting in such detail. The scanty traces of later work that remain reveal few new features—on the contrary a return to the soberer early styles.

The minor arts of the jeweller, the gem-engraver, the goldsmith reach a high state of technical perfection, but they do not improve in spirit or artistic feeling with the progress of the ages. Much of the furniture found at Pompeii and Herculaneum, especially the bronze-work, exhibits most graceful forms, always Greek in inspiration.

LAW

The greatest intellectual achievement of the Roman people was in the domain of law. The spiritual endowment of the typical Roman included all the qualities of the lawyer—a sense of equity that was quite devoid of sentimentalism, an instinct for order, discipline, and business, a language of great clarity and precision, and above all, a devotion to ceremonies and formulæ which sternly rejected abstract casuistry. Their law took its rise in a series of religious formulæ known only to priests and to the king as chief priest. The Twelve Tables put some of the most ancient principles into words, and, partly from their use as a text-book of education, were regarded almost with as much veneration as the Two Tables of Moses. They were, in fact, sometimes considered as the sole fountain of jurisprudence, or at any rate as the sole code of written law. The legislative enactments of the state were on a far lower plane and no ancient people ever considered its legislature capable of turning out a daily quota of legislation as modern parliaments are supposed to do. In the main the fabric of Roman jurisprudence consisted of "case law" made by the judges on the tribunals. The *prætor urbanus* made the Civil Law of Rome, and this became permanent by means of the system of Perpetual Edicts. Religion continued to control the international law of the Roman world, an affair of ceremonies in the hands of the priestly college of heralds—the *jus fetiale*. But, meanwhile, the *prætor peregrinus*, who had to decide cases between non-citizens, was gradually accumulating a body of law, wrongly termed international, in the *jus gentium*. It was observed that there was a great deal in common between the various codes of the Italian and other Mediterranean states, and this was put together in the foreign prætor's edict. The more philosophical jurists, inspired with the Stoic doctrines about following nature, evolved the theory that this common element of various nations was nothing but the Natural Law, *jus naturæ*. It was a fruitful error, and it lies at the base of much of the modern "international law" as expounded by Grotius and other seventeenth-century jurists.

The Civil Law of Rome was in the main, then, a series of precedents handed down by prætor to prætor from times beyond record. To it was added a large body of "counsel's opinions" which drew their validity largely from the eminence of their authors. It was Hadrian who set about the systematisation of these. He organised the *jurisprudentes* into a regular profession. He appointed his "counsellors" from the leading barristers of the day, and he gave to the whole body of *responsa prudentium*, "the opinions of the learned", the validity of statutory law. The justice and precision of the civil law was the most attractive feature of Roman civilisation to the barbarian world. Gallic and British communities made haste to learn Latin in order that they might gain the "Latin right" which admitted them to the privilege of enjoying Roman law. In A.D. 212, Caracalla, who did little else to deserve the gratitude of posterity, uttered a single edict called the "Antonine Constitution" which admitted the whole Empire to the privileges of Roman citizenship. Now a single code ran throughout the whole Western world. Hadrian had set his most distinguished lawyers, under the leadership of Salvius Julianus, to codify the "perpetual edict" of the prætors. It was under the Antonines that some citizen from the East, only known to us by the common prænomen of Gaius, wrote those learned "Institutes of Roman Law" which are still the nursery of our lawyers. But it was the great Eastern emperor Justinian (A.D. 527-565) who codi- fied the whole body of civil law in a series of immense documents. Roman law had already conquered its barbarian conquerors, the Goths, and almost every European legal system except our own is based upon that ancient law which arose from the Twelve Tables and the prætor's edict. The canon law of the Church was Roman law in its essence.

PHILOSOPHY AND RELIGION

Much attention has been paid in recent years to the religious development of the Romans under the Empire and to the momen- tous conflict of religions which was going on from the age of Hadrian until the final triumph of Christianity. Humanly speak- ing, it was "touch and go" between several religions competing for the vacant place in the faith of the Empire, and at the last the strife was practically narrowed down to a duel between two oriental monotheistic systems, Mithraism* and Christianity, with Neoplatonism as a third contestant. The subject is too vast for anything like adequate treatment here. But I would emphasise one point of view which is often overlooked.

The Roman state is too often regarded merely as the enemy and persecutor of the Christian religion. It is forgotten how large a share Rome may claim in its establishment. Not only did the Romans adopt Christianity, but they organised it and sent it forth conquering and to conquer in the wake of the legions. It is not a case of a wicked and corrupt people suddenly converted in the midst of its sins. On the contrary it is easy to show that the thinkers of the Roman Empire were tending towards philosophic and reli-

* Plates 88 and 89.

gious ideas which made them ready to accept both the ethical teaching and the theological revelations of the Son of God. It is unnecessary to remind the modern reader how large a part the Greek philosophy of Stoicism with its Roman modifications had played in shaping the thoughts of one Roman citizen, Paul of Tarsus. Philo, the Alexandrian Platonist, had developed a doctrine of the Divine *Logos*, which may be counted among the philosophical influences that conditioned the thought of the fourth Evangelist, and through him the whole course of Christian teaching.

The Romans may have added little to abstract philosophy or to metaphysics, but they made the somewhat barren abstractions of Zeno and Stoic into something more than a philosophy, into a faith which had a power to influence conduct far beyond the power of the state system of half-Greek Olympian gods. If the power and the sincerity of a religion may be tested rather by its martyrs than by its proselytes, Stoicism had a worthy record. Stoics like Thrasea Pætus, Barea Soranus, and Helvidius Priscus faced a tyrant's frown for duty's sake just as truly as Peter and Polycarp.

The attitude of the Roman government towards Christianity has been too often explained to need more than a brief recapitulation. At first Christianity was confounded with Judaism, which had already begun to make converts at Rome without seeking for them. The Roman government was extraordinarily tolerant towards creed, but it demanded an external compliance with the Cæsar-worship which it was imposing on the provinces as a test of loyalty. But the Christians did not take the divine command "render unto Cæsar the things that are Cæsar's" to include scattering incense on his altars. Too many of them had been brought up in the punctilious exclusiveness of the Jewish tradition for them to display on such points the laxity which is sometimes called broadmindedness. Even in the private intercourse of social life the Christians were unpleasantly apt to insist upon their scruples. The meat in the butchers' shops had often been slain in sacrifice, and the Christian conscience revolted at "meat offered to idols". The libation with which the wine-cup started on its rounds was another offence to the tender monotheistic conscience. These things made the Christians unpopular. Their close associations, their secret meetings and love-feasts, the communism which they practised, all aroused the suspicions which are begotten of mystery. Lastly, their conviction that the Second Coming and the Day of Judgment were at hand made them ardent proselytes. It made them utter prognostications of death and damnation to all around them, and to see apocalyptic visions of the fall of the kingdoms of this earth. Such prophecies were sometimes misunderstood as involving treasonable designs. The first persecution under Nero was largely the result of such suspicions.

But the official attitude of the permanent Roman government is probably revealed in the famous correspondence between Pliny and his emperor, Trajan. Imperial Rome is not to set up an inquisition. No man is to be punished for his faith, but if he is accused to the governor and is obstinate in refusing to pay the obeisance demanded by the state he is to be punished for his contumacy. That is precisely the attitude which the humane and enlightened Christian states have adopted towards heresy. Later, when the Faith grew in importance, and when it even reached the point where soldiers refused the military oaths, some emperors, often the better emperors, strove to fight against it. Then there were sometimes inquisitions and wholesale martyrdoms as under Decius and Diocletian. But no martyrdom, however public or agonising, could quench the faith of those who saw the heavens opening and the Angels of God descending with their crowns of glory. The publicity of the scenes and the constancy of the victims increased the number of the converts. Foolish magistrates sought to encounter obstinacy with further severity, and the Faith only grew the more abundantly. It was not so much his personal conversion—for that was tardy and half-hearted—as the motive of policy, that induced Constantine to promulgate what is commonly called the Edict of Milan in 313, by which toleration was extended to the Christian faith throughout the Roman Empire.

We must not be surprised that the best emperors, including the saintly philosopher, Marcus Aurelius, were the most bitterly hostile to Christianity. Stoic philosophers were teaching doctrines that had much in common with Christian philosophy, but that renders it all the less likely that Stoic philosophers should be among the converts. Nevertheless Christian doctrine, especially in the Græco-Jewish communities of Asia Minor, was falling in prepared soil. The Stoic paradoxes had undoubtedly prepared the way for the Christian paradoxes. The doctrines of humility and asceticism were a common-place of the Cynics. "No cross, no Crown", "He who would save his life must lose it"—such sayings as these might gain ready assent from thoughtful Romans. Epictetus, a pagan slave of Domitian's day, wrote his answer to the tyrant : "No man hath power over me. I have been set free by God. I know His Commandments; henceforth no man can lead me captive". The Stoics were daily teaching that it is hard for a rich man to enter the Kingdom of God. This is the creed of Marcus Aurelius : "To venerate the gods and bless them, and to do good to men, and to practise tolerance and self-restraint". The horrors of the amphitheatre are one side of imperial society. But on the other side Musonius Rufus, a Stoic who stood high in the favour of Vespasian and Titus, went among the soldiers to preach against militarism. Slave-drivers as the Romans were, they were beginning to feel a sense of the brotherhood of man. Seneca was calling the slaves "humble friends". "Man is a holy thing to man", he says; and such teaching was reflected even in the legislation of the day. Juvenal pleads passionately for kindness to slaves and for moral purity in the home. Seneca not only feels that men are brothers, but that God is the Father of us all. We have seen how public charity was finding expression in the *alimenta* and the free schools. "Love them that hate you" would not strike the Romans of the second century as anything more than a strong expression of the truth they had already begun to recognise. Thus the practical side of Christian ethics found its harmonies in the conduct as well as the theory of the more enlightened pagans. Peace and humanitarianism were in the air of the Antonine Age.

As for religious dogma, the whole tendency of thought was towards monotheism. "God is a Spirit" would find an instant acquiescence among educated Romans, even though they frequented the temples of a hundred different gods. Philosophy among Greeks and Romans alike had always been monotheistic. On the subject of immortality the philosophers were divided. Marcus Aurelius and Seneca are on the whole not hopeful. Probably the beliefs of the common folk—as testified in the epitaphs of their cemeteries—were equally divided. The laconic epitaph : "I was not, I was : I am not, I care not", is common. But other epitaphs equally common express the hope of reunions in the other world or even of being "received among the number of the gods". But on the whole the commonest view of Death was as a happy release and an unending sleep. The immediate hope of eternal bliss was the greatest thing Christianity had to offer to the pagan world.

Rome, then, was in many ways prepared for the reception of Christianity, whose doctrines found an echo in the aspirations of the day. She did much to give to Christian theology its Western form, and of course the ritual and practice of the Roman Church was in many ways merely a continuation of old pagan rites and ceremonies. Ancient deities became Christian saints with little change of rite or cult; images were often adapted and even names were sometimes scarcely altered. But, in fact, the whole conception of that mighty Church which conquered the world, including the barbarian invaders, was the offspring of the Roman political system. It was her genius for statecraft that made Rome the Eternal City. In one form or another she has governed the world for twenty centuries.

EPILOGUE

Musae, quid facimus? τί κεναῖσιν ἐν ἐλπίσιν αὔτως
ludimus ἀφραδίῃσιν ἐν ἤματι γηράσκοντες;
Σαντονικοῖς κάμποισιν, ὅπου κρύος ἄξενόν ἐστιν,
erramus gelido—τρομεροὶ καὶ *frigido*—πηκτοί
AUSONIUS

I S H O U L D have preferred to leave the Roman world at the height of its grandeur, when the whole vast territory was enjoying prosperity, if not peace, under the virtuous and benevolent Antonines. In that way this book would best create the true impression of Rome, not as a lamentable failure, but as the conspicuous success which it assuredly was. But as the reader will probably follow the old Greek maxim and desire to see the end before recording a judgment, a few pages are added containing a very brief summary of the closing scenes. It is necessary to notice that even the closing scenes cover a period of two hundred years, and that this progress is not even yet entirely downhill. They include good and bad reigns, periods of prosperity as well as disaster.

Here again the impression of pessimism which we get from reading the account of the Empire is due to the historians as much as to the history. The author or authors of the *Augustan History* are small-minded writers who label the various princes as good or bad largely according to their treatment of the senate. These historians are trained in the school of Suetonius; they dwell upon gossip and can form no large political judgments. Very little of the gossip is authentic. If they have decided to revile an emperor they repeat the scandals narrated by Suetonius about Tiberius or Nero. In some cases they show a good knowledge of public administration and of military action : this in part may create a false preponderance of warfare in the annals of the period.

The succession of the imperial throne continued to be the weak point of the whole system. The succession of good emperors was

276

abruptly broken when the saintly Marcus Aurelius gave place to his worthless son Commodus, who was murdered after a dozen years of debauchery, and thereafter the throne itself passed through unspeakable degradations. The guards who murdered Pertinax formally put the succession up to auction in the prætorian camp. Septimius Severus (193-211) gave a brief respite of strong government which almost destroyed the fiction of senatorial authority, for Severus enhanced the military aspect of the Principate at the expense of the civil. Severus' son, Caracalla, was probably the worst of all the emperors in personal vice and brutality, but he was the author of that famous decree which conferred the citizenship on the free inhabitants of all the provinces. In Elagabalus (218-222) Rome had for master the vile and effeminate priest of the Sun-god, who brought the fetish-stone of Emesa into the city and attempted to make all the gods bow down to it. Alexander Severus was a blameless prince, and Maximin the Thracian drove the barbarians back behind the *limites* of the Rhine and Danube. After the Gordians the senate enjoyed the privilege of nominating an emperor Pupienus, but the disorders of the period may be gauged from the fact that in the eighteen years following Alexander Severus, who died in 235, twelve persons wore the purple, all made and unmade by the armies. Then Gallienus assumed it, having for his colleague at first Valerian, his father, who was the first of Roman emperors to be taken prisoner by the enemy. Strange and horrible tales hung about his mysterious fate when taken captive by Shapur, the Persian king. In the latter years of Gallienus the Empire was practically divided, for his rebellious general Postumus was recognised as emperor throughout Gaul, Spain, and Britain. In this period, too, Palmyra rose for a moment into independent power as the meeting-place of the caravan routes across the Syrian plains. Under the famous Queen Zenobia it practically ruled over the eastern parts of the Empire, and its splendid ruins prove its wealth and magnificence. Gallienus brought the Empire through the crisis without complete disaster and the tide was turned by his successors. Claudius Gothicus (268) was an efficient soldier. He smote the Goths and might have restored the Empire in full, but the plague, which had never wholly disappeared since the time of Marcus Aurelius, carried him off in the third year of his reign. The task was left for Aurelian, that Pannonian peasant whose brilliant generalship hurled back the enemy on every side, while his statesmanship restored the authority of the emperor and even the financial credit of the Empire. The mighty wall with which he surrounded Rome is, however, a sad testimony of the dark days upon which the imperial city had fallen. The Palmyrene kingdom was defeated and the rich city plundered. The rebel Empire of the Gauls was destroyed for ever. The grandest triumph ever witnessed in Rome was that of Aurelian in 274. It is thus described in the *Augustan History*:

There were three royal chariots. One was that of Odenathus, brilliant with jewellery in gold, silver, and gems; the second, similarly constructed, was the gift of the Persian king to Aurelian; the third was the design of Zenobia herself, who hoped to visit Rome in it. Wherein she was not deceived, for she entered the city in it after her defeat. There was another chariot yoked to four stags, which is said to have belonged to the king of the Goths. On this Aurelian rode to the Capitol, there to sacrifice the stags which he had vowed to Jupiter the Highest and Mightiest. Twenty elephants went before, tamed beasts of Libya and two hundred different beasts from Palestine, which Aurelian immediately presented to private individuals in order that the Treasury might not be burdened with their maintainence. Four tigers, giraffes, elks, and other creatures were led in procession. Eight hundred pairs of gladiators, as well as captives from the barbarian tribes, Blemyes, Axiomitæ, Arabs, Eudæmones, Ludians, Bactrians, Hiberi, Saracens, Persians, all with their various treasures; Goths, Alani, Roxolani, Sarmatians, Franks, Suevi, Vandals, Germans advanced as captives with their hands bound. Among them also were the Palmyrene chiefs who survived, and the Egyptian rebels. Ten women whom Aurelian had taken fighting in male attire among the Goths were in the procession, while many of these "Amazons" had been slain. In front of each contingent a placard bearing the name of the tribe was carried. Among them was Tetricus (the "emperor" of the Gallic Empire) in a scarlet cloak, a yellow tunic, and Gallic breeches. There walked Zenobia too, laden with jewels and chained with gold chains which others carried. In front of the conquered princes their crowns were borne along labelled with their names. And next the Roman People followed; the banners of the guilds and camps, the mailed soldiers, the royal spoils, the whole army and the senate (although it was saddened to see that some members of its body were among the captives) added much to the splendour of the show. It was not until the ninth hour that the Capitol was reached, and the palace much later.

Aurelian endeavoured to establish the Persian worship of the unconquered sun as a state religion, and earned the gratitude of the vulgar by supplementing the free supply of corn with a daily ration of pork. Oil and salt were distributed gratuitously, and he even prepared to supply free wine. The three emperors who succeeded Aurelian, Tacitus, Probus, and Carus, were men of good character, and the first two were, once more, the nominees of the senate.

Throughout this troubled age the causes of confusion were twofold. On the one hand the Empire itself was so vast and scattered that it tended now to fall to pieces of its own momentum, as the seedbox opens to scatter its seeds. Britain, Gaul, Germany, Palmyra—each in its turn began to feel a unity of its own. Rome was far away, and the government was often weak and negligent. Here was an opportunity for the local generals to carve out empires for themselves. While the emperor hurried this way and that, fresh rebellions broke out in his rear. It was no one's fault in particular. The world-state was now impossible. When the provinces became civilised and self-conscious they were bound to feel their natural unity.

In the second place, the barbarians were now grown to full stature. They were no longer quarrelsome tribes which could be turned against one another by adroit statecraft, but nations much less barbarous than of old, with some organisation and a purpose above that of mere plunder. No artificial ramparts could hold them. It is very doubtful whether even the legions of Rome at their best could have resisted these repeated assaults on all sides. The first great inroad across the Danube took place in the reign of M. Aurelius. It was crushed, as the column of that emperor depicts, and Sarmatia and Marcomannia were added as shortlived provinces. From the third century onwards we begin to hear of the greater barbarian nations, or groups of tribes, of the Alemanni, the Franks, the Saxons, the Goths, and the Vandals. Battle after battle was fought and triumph after triumph won against them, but they still pressed on. The weaker emperors essayed to buy them off with gold, the wiser with land, and the craftier set them to slay one another; but still they moved forward resistlessly, wave after wave, like the sea. This again was nobody's fault. It may have been the movement of Tartar savages in the Far East that set the Wandering of the Nations in motion. Whatever it was, all eastern and northern Europe was seething with restless movement and the tide rolled on irresistibly against the bulwarks of civilisation. Triumphs as great and glorious as those of Scipio and Marius were gained by Roman armies even in the fourth century. But the enemy was ubiquitous, the task impossible.

It is, however, true that those bulwarks were weaker than they should have been, partly by reason of the internal disorganisation caused by perpetual struggles for the succession, and partly through certain visible errors in Roman statesmanship. For one thing, the spirit of peace and humanity which was ripening in the securer central parts of the Empire had probably impaired its instincts of defence. The modern world is trying just now to believe that you can retain the power of defence when you have given up all thoughts of aggression. It may be so. The Roman world failed in the attempt. Rome's statesmen were now no longer soldiers, but lawyers and financiers. Even the prefects of the prætorian guard were lawyers. The army was a profession apart. Moreover, even the army had become so civilised that it had lost many of its martial qualities. Hadrian more than any other ruler is responsible for allowing the *cannabæ* or "booths" which had sprung up around the camps to grow into towns and even cities. The legions were now permanently established in their quarters, the soldiers married wives and occupied their leisure in business or husbandry. From the time of Septimius Severus the marriage of a soldier was officially permitted. Hadrian it was, too, who in his large cosmopolitan spirit had introduced many and doubtless useful barbarian methods of fighting, so that the old Roman military traditions had fallen into desuetude. A legion was now no better than its auxiliaries. The auxiliaries were often barbarians and soon the legions themselves became half barbarised. It was only a step further when barbarians were recruited in tribes to fight Rome's battles under their own commanders.

Secondly, the whole Roman world was being slowly strangled with good intentions. The bureaucracy had grown so highly organised and efficient, so nicely ordered through its various grades of official life, that everybody walked in leading-strings to the music of official proclamations. Paternalism regulated everything

with its watchful and benignant eye. The triumph of the system
may be seen in the famous Edict of Prices issued by Diocletian in
A.D. 301. Here we find scheduled a maximum price for every possible commodity of trade and a maximum wage for every kind of
service. Death is the penalty for any trader who asks, or any purchaser who pays, a higher price. No difference of locality or season
is permitted. Trade is forbidden to fluctuate, under penalty of
death. This delightful scheme, which was engraved on stone in
every market in Europe, was evidently the product of a highly
efficient Board of Trade, which had sat late of nights over the study
of statistics and political economy. Benevolent officials of this type
swarmed all over the Empire, spying and reporting on one another
as well as on the general public.

The same system of blear-eyed officialism had found a still
more ingenious method of throttling the society which it was
endeavouring to nurse back into infancy. It was under Alexander
Severus (about A.D. 230) that the various *collegia* or guilds were
incorporated by charter, so that every industry became a close
corporation. This rendered the task of administration much simpler, but it meant that every occupation tended to become hereditary. There was, for example, a guild of the *coloni* or tillers of
the soil. The most benevolent of the emperors, Marcus Aurelius
and the two Severi, had planted barbarians on Roman soil under
condition of military service in lieu of rent. This service became
hereditary also. Before long each piece of ground had to supply a
recruit. The *decuriones,* moreover, or municipal senators, who
had once been the honoured magistrates of their townships, also
became a caste. As they were made responsible for the collection
of property tax in their boroughs, and as wealth began to decline
and taxation to increase, they were reduced to a condition of
penury and misery. The exemption from taxation of whole classes
of society, such as the soldiers and eventually the Christian clergy,
added to their burdens. Then, since many of them attempted to
evade the distresses entailed upon their rank by joining the army
or even selling themselves into slavery, a decree was issued which
made their office hereditary. It became a form of punishment to
enrol an offender among these *curiales.* A decree of Constantine
bound all the tillers of the soil in hereditary bondage for ever. In
these ways Roman society fell into stagnation. Since the progress
of the Manchurian Empire in China proceeded on very similar

lines, it looks as if the benevolent despotism engendered by highly centralised government of very large areas is one of the methods by which Providence is accustomed to bring great empires low.

At the close of the third century Diocletian endeavoured to save the state by a bold revolution. He swept away the hollow pretence of republicanism and frankly surrounded the throne with every circumstance of majesty and ceremony. The free access which had generally been granted by the most despotic princes was replaced by an elaborate system of intermediaries. To meet the obvious needs of devolution in government, as well as to stop the incessant struggles for the succession, he invented an ingenious divison of responsibility. Henceforth there were to be two Augusti, one taking the East and one the West. The Empire was not actually divided, for the joint writ of the two colleagues was to run all over it. Moreover each Augustus was to have a junior colleague, a "Cæsar", acting as his lieutenant and prepared to step into his place. Ties of marriage were to unite all four into one close family alliance. The provinces had by now been so subdivided that they numbered one hundred and sixteen, and Diocletian grouped them into twelve "dioceses" each under a "vicar", directly responsible to one of four "prætorian prefects", who shared the administration of the whole. The troops were no longer subject to the provincial governors, but each army had a "duke" (*dux*) of its own. Each frontier—and these were still further fortified—was under its own "duke". At the same time steps were taken to organise a central striking force—the *comitatus* of the emperors. The four Prefectures and twelve Dioceses were as follows :

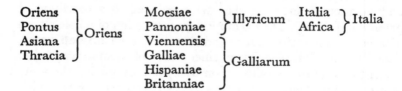

Italy, it will be observed, has now definitely declined into the status of a province among many, and Rome itself was not sufficiently near the frontier armies to be a convenient capital. Diocletian preferred to make his residence at Nicomedia. The senate, as a necessary consequence, receded into the background, and remained little more than a title of dignity. The emperor's Consistory, a privy council composed of the heads of departments, took its place for practical purposes. The new hierarchy of officials rejoiced in barbaric titles which would have shocked the ears of a genuine Roman.

Naturally these advances in the direction of more and stronger government proved no alleviation of the woes which sprang from too much supervision. One improvement there was. In the general economic collapse of the mid-third century the monetary system broke down through inflation and devaluation, so that there was widespread reversion to the natural economy of barter. But a fresh start was made under Diocletian and Constantine: a new gold coin, the *solidus*, was issued and the mints throughout the empire were re-organised. Thus the general economy of the empire was strengthened.

Constantine signalised Diocletian's plan of dividing the responsibility of government by founding a new capital at Byzantium. His motives were probably mixed. In the first place he would be free of the awkward republican traditions which still kept re-asserting themselves, and in the second place Constantinople was a more central and a much more defensible situation. But, more than all, in this new Rome he could break away from the old religion. Constantine's plan for restoring the tired and afflicted world was the adoption of Christianity. The Edict of Milan (313) granted Christians complete freedom of worship and recognised Christian churches as legal corporations. It was already the religion of the court—ever since Constantine had seen his famous vision of a cross of light superimposed on the sun, and heard the words ἐν τούτῳ νίκα—"hoc signo uinces". Still half-pagan, the emperor had made the Cross his mascot, and in the strength of it had defeated his rival Maxentius at the Mulvian Bridge just outside Rome.* Constantine himself was by no means a saint; in murdering kinsmen he was, in fact, among the worst of the emperors, but unwittingly he saved the world by his conversion. Meanwhile the extravagance with which he adorned his new city afflicted the whole Empire with the burdens of fresh taxations.

The scheme of a divided Empire failed, although it gave the groaning world a spell of comparative tranquillity; after the

* Plate 94.

anarchy of the third century, the Constantinian dynasty must have seemed an era of peace and security. After Theodosius (395) the division became permanent. The Eastern throne remained secure for another thousand years, protected by the admirable strategic position of Constantinople. The contempt with which it was long treated by historians has now broken down, and it is seen that the Byzantine Empire not only stood as the bulwark for the West against the East but preserved for us the inestimable treasures of Greek intellect. The Roman tradition, now inextricably mingled with the Greek, lingered on there unchanged, even to the very chariot-races which still threw society into a ferment. Even in modern times the inhabitants of Greece and Roumania distinguish themselves from their oriental neighbours by the proud title of "Romans".

But in the West a series of phantoms succeeded one another upon the throne. The floodgates of the Rhine and Danube frontiers broke down completely and the new nations streamed into their heritage. Then it was found how truly Constantine's policy had saved the world. Though the Goths took and plundered Rome (410), they came in not as pagan destroyers, but as Christian immigrants, and it was Gothic generals and Gothic armies who saved Europe from destruction. About 447 the Mongolian Huns under their terrible Attila came riding into western Europe from the steppes of Russia. They crossed the Rhine half a million strong, destroying and burning as they came. The Roman emperor's sister Honoria proposed marriage to Attila, and the proud barbarian offered her a place in his harem if she would bring half the Western Empire as her dowry. The Roman general Aëtius with a half-barbarian army in alliance with the Visigoths checked them at the Battle of the Campi Catalauni (Châlons-sur-Marne) and the peril drifted away. Aëtius who had saved Rome was stabbed by his ungrateful emperor.

The Vandals had already overrun Spain and streamed across to Africa, whence they issued forth to make a second sack of Rome (455). Britain had been deserted rather by the choice of its army than by command of any emperor, and left a prey to the pagans of the north in 409. Italy itself was wholly in the hands of the barbarians, who lived on terms of apparent equality with the Romans. Puppets wore the imperial purple and did the behests of barbarian "Patricians", Ricimer the Suevian, Gundobald his nephew, and finally Odoacer, a tribeless barbarian from the north. By this time the Western Empire was dismembered for ever, and western Europe was merely a series of barbarian principalities. In 476 Odoacer removed the last puppet-emperor of Rome, who by coincidence bore the significant name of Romulus Augustulus. The seat of the Western Empire had long been removed from the twice-sacked city of Rome, and the later princes had ruled from Ravenna, where the little mausoleum of the Empress Placidia, sister of Honorius, still stands as a type of the shrunken glories of the last successors of Augustus.*

In theory the Western Empire did not come to an end in 476. The Eastern emperors now claimed authority over the whole Roman world and exercised it so far as they could obtain obedience. Strong Cæsars like Justinian made their rule respected far and wide. Geographically and politically, the West had now begun its mediæval existence as a congeries of small kingdoms generally of uncertain extent.

But in a far truer sense Rome continued to rule the world as before. Her two great legacies, the Roman Law and the Roman Church, ruled it as completely as ever the legions had done. Even in politics, the grand conception of the Christian Republic, Church and State in one, with the Pope as the successor of St Peter bearing the keys of Heaven and Hell, while the Emperor as the successor of Augustus wielded its sword, continued for another thousand years to dominate Europe. It was under the ægis of this great idea that the young nations grew up and came into their own.

Thus the true history of Rome from this point is the history of the Church, and this is no place to relate it. But it may be contended here that the visible Church was as truly a creation of the Roman spirit as was the Empire itself. Rome had seized upon the teaching of One who lived in poverty and obscurity among slaves and outcasts, who preached against worldliness, formality, and ambition, who sent out His disciples to beg their way, and out of this, with her wonderful genius for government, she had created a powerful monarchy which could humble kings, and an organised ecclesiastical state which spread like a network over the earth and tamed the fury of the barbarians.

In the same way the culture of these latter days is to be found in Church History. Tertullian, St John Chrysostom, and Augus-

* Plate 81.

tine are its representative writers and thinkers, more truly than Ausonius or Claudian who, though Ausonius was nominally a Christian, continue the pagan tradition. In secular art we have still magnificent portraits* with a new tendency towards hieratic majesty and grim frontality; the Arch of Constantine† was partly compiled out of earlier remains, but some of its friezes reflect the contemporary style which was carried unchanged on to early Christian sarcophagi. But the art of the age finds its best expression in the sacred mosaics of Rome and, later, of Ravenna, or in ivories such as the famous Barberini panel, showing Constantine as the establisher of the Christian Faith. Architecture continues to show remarkable developments, and in the wonderful palace which Diocletian constructed for his retirement at Spalato on the Dalmatian coast there are new combinations of the Roman arch with Greek columns, which are full of promise for the birth of Gothic art. In Rome itself the mighty vaults of the Basilica of Maxentius illustrate with what splendour the Empire, which seems to us to be dying, could still clothe its public life; and here we place the first appearance on a monumental scale of Christian architecture with its wealth of promise for the future. The great basilicas and the domed mausoleums of Rome, as well as the cruciform churches of the Eastern Empire, warn us that we are passing from the ancient to the mediæval world.

* Plate 95.
† Plates 92-94.

CHRONOLOGICAL SUMMARY

YEAR B.C.	DOMESTIC EVENTS	EXTERNAL EVENTS
753	Legendary date for the foundation of Rome	
575	Approximate date for unification of Rome into a city	
510	Traditional date of the expulsion of Tarquin and establishment of the Republic	Probable date of first treaty between Rome and Carthage
508	Traditional date of the Etruscan invasion under Lars Porsena	
494	Traditional date of the First Secession of the Plebeians	
493		First treaty between Rome and the Latins, drawn up by Sp. Cassius
474		Defeat of the Etruscans by Syracuse
450	The Twelve Tables	
390	Conquest of Rome by the Gauls	
367	Licinian Laws: (1) forbid large holdings of public land; (2) enact that one consul shall be a plebeian	
351		Conquest of South Etruria by Rome. Cære becomes the first *ciuitas sine suffragio*
348		Treaty of commerce between Rome and Carthage

287

YEAR B.C.	DOMESTIC EVENTS	EXTERNAL EVENTS
343 to 266		Samnite Wars, involving subjugation of the Latins, and eventually of all Central Italy
321		Great defeat of the Romans at the Caudine Pass
312	Censorship of Appius Claudius including construction of Via Appia	
281 to 275		War with Tarentum and Pyrrhus involving conquest of South Italy
268	First coinage of silver	
264 to 241		First Punic War, involving conquest of Sicily, Sardinia, and Corsica—first transmarine provinces
264	First gladiatorial games at Rome	
240	Livius Andronicus. Beginning of Roman literature	
222		Defeat of the Cisalpine Gauls
220	Via Flaminia to Ariminum	
218 to 201		Second Punic War
218	Lex Claudia forbids Senators to engage in commerce	
216		Romans severely defeated at Cannæ
205	Introduction of Phrygian worship of Magna Mater	
202		Victory of Scipio at Zama
201		Peace with Carthage involving cession of Spain
200 to 194		Second Macedonian War
196		Flamininus proclaims the liberty of Greece

YEAR B.C.	DOMESTIC EVENTS	EXTERNAL EVENTS
190		Defeat of Antiochus the Great of Syria at Magnesia
186	The Bacchanalian "conspiracy"	
184	Censorship of Cato the Elder. Death of Plautus. Basilica of Cato constructed	
171 to 168		Third Macedonian War
167	1000 Greeks, including Polybius the historian, brought to Italy as hostages	
161	Greek orators and philosophers expelled (vainly)	
160	*Adelphi* of Terence performed	
148		Macedonia becomes a province
146		On destruction of Carthage, Africa becomes a province
	Great influx of Greek Art	Corinth destroyed
133	Tribunate and agrarian programme of Tiberius Gracchus	Kingdom of Attalus bequeathed to Rome, becomes province of Asia
123	Tribunate and agrarian programme of Gaius Gracchus. Establishment of the *Equites* as a political power	
121		Province of Gallia Narbonensis, formed by conquest of South Gaul
112 to 106		War with Jugurtha; triumph of Marius
113 to 101	Army reforms and political power of Marius	War with Cimbri and Teutons
96		Cyrene bequeathed to Rome

YEAR B.C.	DOMESTIC EVENTS	EXTERNAL EVENTS
91		War against the Italian allies (Social War)
88	Conquest of Rome by Sulla, and restoration of the Senate	War with Mithridates of Pontus. Massacre of Romans
87	Revolution of Cinna and Marius with great massacre of nobles	
82	Return of Sulla and proscription of the democrats	Defeat of the Samnites at the Colline Gate of Rome
81	Sulla dictator. Cornelian Laws improve the judicial system. Cicero's first speech	Cisalpine Gaul becomes a province
74		Bithynia bequeathed to Rome
73	Insurrection of slaves under Spartacus	
67		Pompeius defeats the pirates
63	Consulship of Cicero, who crushes the conspiracy of Catiline	Pompeius ends the Mithridatic War. New provinces organised : Cilicia, Bithynia with Pontus, Syria, and Crete
60	Union of Pompeius, Cæsar, and Crassus, the "First Triumvirate"	
59	Consulship of Cæsar, and grant of the province of Gaul	
58	Banishment of Cicero	Cæsar defeats the Helvetians
57	Recall of Cicero	Cæsar defeats the Nervii
56	Renewal of the "Triumvirate" at Lucca	Cæsar defeats the Veneti by sea
55	Dedication of Theatre of Pompeius	Cæsar invades Britain
54		Second invasion of Britain
53		Defeat of Crassus by the Parthians. Cæsar subdues the Treveri, and crosses the Rhine

YEAR B.C.	DOMESTIC EVENTS	EXTERNAL EVENTS
52	Senate-house burnt in a riot. Pompeius passes l a w s against Cæsar	Great revolt of Gaul under Vercingetorix crushed at Alesia
51		Final subjugation of Gaul. Cicero governor of Cilicia
49	Cæsar begins the Civil War	
48	Battle of Pharsalus, defeat of Pompeius	Cæsar regulates Egypt, leaving Cleopatra as queen
46	Defeat of Pompeians at Thapsus in Africa. Cæsar dictator. Dedication of new Forum Julium, and Temple of Venus Genetrix	
45	Cæsar enlarges the senate and regulates the municipal constitutions of the Italian towns	
44	Assassination of Cæsar. M. Antonius in command of Rome. Cicero's *Philippics*	
43	Octavian, Cæsar's heir, with the consuls defeats Antony at Mutina, and is elected consul. "Second Triumvirate" formed, Antony, Octavian, and Lepidus. Proscription of the tyrannicide party, including Cicero	
42	Battles of Philippi. Defeat of Brutus a n d Cassius. Temple of Saturn rebuilt	
41	War at Perusia, in which Octavian crushes the revolt of L. Antonius	M. Antonius with Cleopatra in Egypt
37	Library of Pollio founded. Octavian marries Livia	
36	Sextus Pompeius defeated. Lepidus deprived of his army	Antony defeated in Parthia

YEAR B.C.	DOMESTIC EVENTS	EXTERNAL EVENTS
31		Defeat of Antony and Cleopatra at Actium by Octavian
29	Triumph of Cæsar Octavianus	Conquest of Egypt
28	Census and restoration of senate. Dedication of temple and library of Palatine Apollo; eighty - two temples restored	Moesia made a province
27	"Restoration of the Republic", really the beginning of the Empire. Octavian receives the title of *Augustus*. Pantheon of M. Agrippa built	Provinces divided between Augustus and senate. Augustus takes Spain, Gaul, Syria, and keeps Egypt
23	Augustus resigns the consulship. Death of Marcellus	Failure of expedition to Arabia
20		Augustus in Asia. Submission of Parthians
19	Death of Virgil and Tibullus	Conquest of North Spain
17	Social legislation. Secular games. Horace as laureate. Augustus adopts Gaius and Lucius his grandsons	
16		German invasion of Gaul. Defeat of Lollius. Drusus
13		in Gaul for conquest of Germany
12	Dedication of Ara Pacis Augustæ	
11	Theatre of Marcellus built	
9	End of Livy's *History*	Death of Drusus after four campaigns in Germany
8	Deaths of Horace and Mæcenas	Tiberius in Germany

YEAR B.C.	DOMESTIC EVENTS	EXTERNAL EVENTS
4		Death of Herod. Probable date of birth of Christ
2	Banishment of Julia	
A.D.		
2	Death of Lucius Cæsar.	
2	Death of Gaius Cæsar. Tiberius adopted	
4	Building of "Maison Carrée" at Nîmes	Tiberius' annual campaigns in Germany
6	Establishment of military chest at Rome. Temple of Castor rebuilt	Judæa becomes a province (census of Quirinius) Great revolt in Pannonia
8	Banishment of Ovid	
9		Subjection of Pannonia Defeat of Varus by Arminius in Germany
14	Death of Augustus. Succession of *Tiberius*. Political extinction of the *comitia*. Extension of law of treason and growth of informing (*delatio*)	Revolt of Rhine and Danube armies quelled by Germanicus and Drusus
16		Germanicus defeats the Germans under Arminius at Idistavisus
27	Tiberius retires to Capri. Sejanus in command of Rome	
37	Death of Tiberius; accession of Gaius (*Caligula*)	Futile expedition towards Britain
41	Caligula murdered by prætorian guard; accession of *Claudius*	New provinces incorporated : Mauretania, Lycia, Thracia (46), and Judæa. Conquest of Britain begun (43)
54	*Nero*	
55	Poisoning of Britannicus	
61		Revolt of Boudicca in Britain

YEAR A.D.	DOMESTIC EVENTS	EXTERNAL EVENTS
64	Fire at Rome, and first persecution of the Christians	
68		Revolt of Vindex in Gaul and Galba in Spain
68 to 69	Year of the Four Emperors : *Galba,* June-Jan. 69 *Otho,* Jan.-April *Vitellius,* April-Dec.	
69	*Vespasian,* "The Flavian Dynasty"	Revolt of Batavians under Civilis
70 to 78	Erection of Colosseum, Arch of Titus, and Baths of Titus	Siege and destruction of Jerusalem
79	*Titus.* Eruption of Vesuvius. Herculaneum buried in mud and Pompeii in ashes. Death of elder Pliny	
81	*Domitian*	Progress of Agricola in Scotland. Construction of German *limes*
86		Wars against the Dacians
96	Murder of Domitian *Nerva,* repealed law of treason and reduced taxes	
98	*Trajan,* built Forum Traiani, Basilica Ulpia, and Column of Trajan	(101-102) First Dacian War. (105-106) Second Dacian War. Dacia becomes a province. (114-116) Invasion of Parthia, capture of Ctesiphon. New provinces : Armenia, Mesopotamia, Assyria, and Arabia
118	*Hadrian,* built *Moles Hadriani,* Temple of Venus and Rome, Pantheon, Villa at Tivoli, and Temple of Olympian Zeus at Athens	Abandoned Armenia, Mesopotamia and Assyria. Grand tour of the Empire. Hadrian's wall in Britain. Revolt and destruction of the Jewish nation
138	*Antoninus Pius.* "The Antonine Dynasty." Built Temple of Antoninus and Faustina	

YEAR A.D.	DOMESTIC EVENTS	EXTERNAL EVENTS
161	*Marcus Aurelius.* Plague in Italy. Statue and column of M. Aurelius	War against Parthia. War with Marcomanni and Quadi. Emperor died at Vienna
180	*Commodus*	
193	*Pertinax* murdered by soldiers. *Didius Julianus* bought the throne. *Septimius Severus* proclaimed by the Illyrian legions. Great jurist Papinian flourishes	Expedition to Britain. Emperor died at York. Strengthening of walls
211	*Caracalla*	All inhabitants of provinces (except Egypt) become citizens
217	Baths of Caracalla finished	
218	*Elagabalus.* Attempt to introduce Sun-worship	
222	*Severus Alexander.* The jurist Ulpian and the historian Dio Cassius flourished	New Persian Empire of the Sassanidæ begun
235	*Maximinus Thrax*	
238	*Gordianus I and II and III*	
244	*Philippus the Arabian*	
249	*Decius.* Persecution of Christians	Defeat of the Goths in Thrace. Decius fell in the fighting
251	*Gallus*	
253	*Aemilianus,* then *Valerianus*	Wars against German invaders, Franks, Alemanni, and Goths. Expedition to Persia. Emperor captured
260	*Gallienus.* Time of great confusion owing to pretenders. "The thirty tyrants"	Tetricus sets up a rival empire in Gaul and Spain. Odenathus sets up an independent kingdom at Palmyra in Syria
268	*Claudius Gothicus*	Defeats German invaders

YEAR A.D.	DOMESTIC EVENTS	EXTERNAL EVENTS
270	*Aurelian* (*Restitutor Orbis*). Wall round Rome	Sacrifices Dacia across the Danube to the Goths. Repulses Alemanni and Marcomanni from Italian soil. Defeats Zenobia and destroys Palmyra. Defeats Tetricus
273		Temple of the Sun constructed at Heliopolis Ba'albek)
275	*Tacitus* (choice of the senate)	
276	*Probus*	Drives back the Barbarians and restores the defences
282	*Carus*, then *Numerianus*, then *Carinus*	
284 to 305	*Diocletian* resided chiefly at Nicomedia in Asia Minor, leaving the west to Maximian. Constantius and Galerius appointed Cæsars. Persecution of Christians	Persians defeated, Egyptian and British revolts crushed
307	Six "Augusti" claiming the purple, Constantine of Britain among them	
323 to 337	*Constantine the Great* (sole emperor). Christianity recognised by the State	
325	Arian conflict, Council of Nicæa	
330	Building of Constantinople	
361 to 363	*Julian the Apostate* endeavours to revive Paganism	
375		Beginning of the great German folk-wanderings
379 to 395	*Theodosius*. After Theodosius the division of the Empire becomes permanent	Visigoths received in Mœsia if Christians. Massacre of Thessalonica. St Ambrose of Milan

YEAR   DOMESTIC EVENTS   EXTERNAL EVENTS
A.D.

395   Arcadius rules the East :
      Honorius rules the West

WEST   EAST

400   Alaric invades Italy
404   Imperial residence trans-
      ferred from Rome to
      Ravenna
409   Abandonment of Britain by
      Rome
410   Capture and sack of Rome
      by Alaric
415   Visigoths found a kingdom
      at Toulouse
429   Vandals found a kingdom in
      Africa
449   Anglo-Saxons begin to settle
      in Britain
451   Attila and the Huns defeated
      by Aëtius and the Goths
      near Châlons
452   Foundation of Venice
455   Sack of Rome by the
      Vandals
476   Odoacer, barbarian general,
      deposes the last Western
      emperor, Romulus Augus-
      tulus
527   Justinian emperor. Victories
                                       of Belisarius. Codification
                                       of law

BIBLIOGRAPHY

(This selective list of books, designed as a guide to the reader who wishes to enquire farther on any special point, includes only works written in English.)

General Works of Reference

Oxford Classical Dictionary (Clarendon Press. 1949).

SANDYS. Companion to Latin Studies (Cambridge University Press. 3rd. edit. 1921).

SMITH & MARINDIN. Classical Dictionary (Murray. 1894).

STUART JONES. Companion to Roman History (Clarendon Press. 1912).

General Histories of Rome

BOAK. A History of Rome (Macmillan. New York. 4th. edit. 1955).

CAMBRIDGE ANCIENT HISTORY. vols. iv, vi-xii (Cambridge University Press 1924-39).

CARY. A History of Rome (Macmillan. 2nd. edit. 1954).

FRANK. A History of Rome (Holt. 1924).

METHUEN'S HISTORY of the Greek and Roman World:

    SCULLARD. A History of the Roman World 753-146 B.C. (3rd. edit. 1961).

    MARSH. A History of the Roman World 146-30 B.C. (2nd. edit. 1953).

    SALMON. A History of the Roman World 30 B.C.-A.D. 138 (3rd. edit. 1959).

    PARKER. A History of the Roman World A.D. 138-337 (2nd. edit. 1958).

PELHAM. Outlines of Roman History (Rivington. 5th. edit. 1926).

ROSTOVTZEFF. A History of the Ancient World, vol. 2 Rome (Clarendon Press, 1927).

SCULLARD. From the Gracchi to Nero (Methuen. 1959).

General Histories of the Republic and Empire

Republic:

HEITLAND. The Roman Republic. 3 vols. (Cambridge University Press. 1909).

MOMMSEN. A History of Rome 4 vols. (Everyman's Library. Dent).

ROBINSON. A History of the Roman Republic (Methuen).

WARDE FOWLER. Rome (2nd edit. by M. P. Charlesworth, Oxford University Press).

Empire:

BURY. The Student's Roman Empire (to the death of Marcus Aurelius) (Murray. 1913).

CHARLESWORTH. The Roman Empire (Oxford University Press. 1951).

GIBBON. Decline and Fall of the Roman Empire. Edit. Bury, 7 vols. (Methuen, 1896-1900).

MATTINGLY. Roman Imperial Civilisation (Arnold. 1957).

STEVENSON. The Roman Empire (Nelson. 1930).

WELLS AND BARROW. A Short History of the Roman Empire to the Death of Marcus Aurelius (Methuen. 1931).

Earliest Antiquities

BLOCH. The Origins of Rome (Thames and Hudson. 1960).

FELL. Rome and Etruria (Cambridge University Press. 1924).

PALLOTTINO. The Etruscans (Penguin Books. 1955).

RANDALL-MACIVER. Italy Before the Romans (Clarendon Press. 1928).

—— The Etruscans (Clarendon Press. 1927).

ROSE. Primitive Culture in Italy (Methuen. 1926).

WHATMOUGH. The Foundations of Roman Italy (Methuen. 1937).

Special Periods and Biographies

BADIAN. Foreign Clientelæ, 264-70 B.C. (Clarendon Press. 1958).

BOISSIER. Cicero and his Friends (Innes. 1897).

BUCHAN. Augustus (Hodder & Stoughton. 1927).

COWELL. Cicero and the Roman Republic (Pitman. 1948).

FERRERO. Greatness and Decline of Rome. 5 vols. (Heinemann. 1909).

FRANK. Roman Imperialism (Macmillan. 1914).

GREENIDGE. A History of Rome B.C. 133-104. (Methuen. 1904).

HILL. The Roman Middle Class in the Republican Period (Blackwell. 1952).

HENDERSON. Life and Principate of the Emperor Nero (Methuen. 1903).

—— Five Roman Emperors (Cambridge University Press. 1927).

—— Life and Principate of the Emperor Hadrian (Methuen. 1923).

JEANS. The Life and Letters of Cicero. (Macmillan).

JONES. Constantine and the Conversion of Europe (Hodder & Stoughton. 1948).

MARSH. The Founding of the Roman Empire. (Oxford University Press. 2nd. edit. 1927).

—— The Reign of Tiberius (Oxford University Press. 1931).

MOMIGLIANO. Claudius (Clarendon Press. 2nd. edit. 1961).

OMAN. Seven Roman Statesmen (Arnold. 1934).

RICE HOLMES. The Roman Republic 70-44 B.C. 3 vols. (Clarendon Press. 1923).

—— The Architect of the Roman Empire. 2 vols. (Clarendon Press. 1928-31).

SCRAMUZZA. The Emperor Claudius (Harvard University Press. 1940).

SCULLARD. Roman Politics, 220-150 B.C. (Clarendon Press. 1951).

STARR. Civilisation and the Cæsars (Cornell. 1955).

STRACHAN-DAVIDSON. Cicero (Putnams. 1925).

SYME. The Roman Revolution (Clarendon Press. 1939).

TAYLOR. Party Politics in the Age of Cæsar (California University Press. 1949).

VOLKMANN. Cleopatra (Elek. 1958).

WARDE-FOWLER. Cæsar. (Putnams. 1892).

WARMINGTON. Carthage (Hale. 1960).

Constitution, Administration and the Provinces

ADCOCK. Roman Political Ideas and Practice (Ann Arbor. 1959).

BROGAN. Roman Gaul. (Bell. 1953).

CHAPOT. The Roman World (Paul. 1928).

COLLINGWOOD AND MYRES. Roman Britain (Clarendon Press. 1937).

GREENIDGE. Roman Public Life (Macmillan. 1901).

HAVERFIELD. The Romanisation of Roman Britain (Clarendon Press. 4th edit. 1923).

HOMO. Roman Political Institutions (Paul. 1929).

MOMMSEN. The Provinces of the Roman Empire. 2 vols. (Macmillan. 1909).

RICHMOND. Roman Britain (Penguin Books. 1955).

RIVET. Town and Country in Roman Britain (Hutchinson. 1958).

STEVENSON. Roman Provincial Administration. (Blackwell 1939).

Social and Economic

ABBOTT. The Common People of Ancient Rome. (Routledge. 1911).

BARROW. Slavery in the Roman Empire (Methuen. 1928).

CARCOPINO. Daily Life in Ancient Rome (Routledge. 1941).

CHARLESWORTH. Trade-routes and Commerce in the Roman Empire (Cambridge University Press. 2nd edit. 1926).

CARY & HAARHOFF. Life and Thought in the Greek and Roman World (Methuen. 1940).

FRANK. Economic History of Rome (John Hopkins University Press. 2nd. edit. 1927).

—— Some Aspects of Social Behaviour in Ancient Rome (Harvard University Press. 1932).

DILL. Roman Society from Nero to Marcus Aurelius (Macmillan. 1905).

—— Roman Society in the Last Century of the Western Empire (Macmillan. 1899).

FRIEDLÄNDER. Roman Life and Manners (Routledge. 4 vols. 1908-37).

GRANT. The World of Rome (Weidenfeld and Nicolson. 1960).

GROSE-HODGE. Roman Panorama (Cambridge University Press. 1944).

HEITLAND. Agricola : a study in Agriculture in the Ancient World (Cambridge University Press. 1921).

LEWIS & REINHOLD. Roman Civilisation, I, II. (Columbia University Press. 1951 and 1955).

MOORE. The Roman Commonwealth (English Universities Press. 1942).

TUCKER. Roman Life in the Roman World of Nero and St. Paul (Macmillan. 1918).

ROSTOVTZEFF. Social and Economic History of the Roman Empire (Clarendon Press. 2nd. edit. 1957).

Religion and Philosophy

ALTHEIM. Roman Religion (Methuen. 1938).

ARNOLD. Roman Stoicism (Cambridge University Press. 1911).

BAILEY. Phases in the Religion of Ancient Rome (Oxford University Press. 1932).

GLOVER. Conflict of Religions in the Early Roman Empire (Methuen. 11th edit. 1927).

HALLIDAY. Lectures on the History of Roman Religion (Liverpool University Press. 1922).

—— The Pagan Background of Early Christianity (Liverpool University Press. 1925).

HICKS. Stoic and Epicurean (Longmans. 1910).

RAMSAY. The Church in the Roman Empire before A.D. 170 (Putnams. 10th. edit. 1913).

ROSE. Ancient Roman Religion (Hutchinson. 1948).

WARDE FOWLER. The Religious Experience of the Roman People (Macmillan. 1911).

—— The Roman Festivals (Macmillan. 1899).

Literature and Language

ADCOCK. Cæsar as Man of Letters (Cambridge University Press 1956).

BEARE. The Roman Stage (Methuen. 2nd edn. 1955).

—— Latin Verse and European Song (Methuen. 1957).

BONNER. Roman Declamation (Liverpool University Press. 1949)

CAMPBELL. Horace : a New Interpretation (Methuen. 1924).

CLARKE. Rhetoric at Rome (Cohen and West. 1953).

CRUTTWELL. History of Roman Literature (Griffin. 7th edn. 1910)

D'ALTON. Horace and his Age (Longmans, Green & Co. 1917).

—— Roman Literary Theory and Criticism (Methuen. 1931).

DUFF. Literary History of Rome from the Origins to the Close of the Golden Age (Benn. New edn. 1953).

——Literary History of Rome in the Silver Age (Benn. New edn. 1960).

—— Roman Satire (C.U.P. 1937).

FRAENKEL. Horace (Clarendon Press. 1957).

FRANK. Catullus and Horace : two poets in their Environment (Henry Holt and Company. 1928).

—— Vergil, a Biography (Henry Holt and Company. 1922).

—— Life and Literature in the Roman Republic (C.U.P. 1930).

GLOVER. Life and Letters in the Fourth Century A.D. (C.U.P. 1901).

—— Virgil (C.U.P. 7th edn. 1942).

HIGHET. Juvenal the Satirist (Clarendon Press. 1954).

KNIGHT. Roman Vergil (Faber and Faber. 2nd. edn. 1944).

LAIDLAW. Latin Literature (Methuen. 1951).

LAISTNER. The Greater Roman Historians (University of California Press. 1947).

LINDSAY. The Latin Language (Clarendon Press. 1894).

LÖFSTEDT. Roman Literary Portraits (Clarendon Press. 1958).

LUCK. The Latin Love Elegy. (Methuen. 1959).

MACKAIL. Latin Literature (Murray. 1895).

MASSON. Lucretius, Epicurean and Poet (Murray. 1907 and 1909).

NORWOOD. Plautus and Terence (Harrap. 1932).

PALMER. The Latin Language (Faber and Faber. 1954).

ROSE. Handbook of Latin Literature (Methuen. 2nd edn. 1949).

RUSHFORTH. Latin Historical Inscriptions (Clarendon Press. 2nd. edn. 1930).

SELLAR. Roman Poets of the Republic (Clarendon Press. 3rd edn. 1889).

—— Roman Poets of the Augustan Age (Clarendon Press. Vol. I, 3rd. end. 1897. Vol. II, 2nd. edn. 1899).

SIKES. Lucretius, Poet and Philosopher (C.U.P. 1936).

—— Roman Poetry (Methuen. 1923).

SUMMERS. The Silver Age of Latin Literature (Methuen. 1920)

SYME. Tacitus (Clarendon Press. 1958).

TYRRELL. Lectures on Latin Poetry (Macmillan. 1895).

WALKER. The Annals of Tacitus, a Study in the writing of History (Manchester University Press. 1952).

WILKINSON. Horace and his Lyric Poetry (Cambridge University Press. 1945).

—— Ovid Recalled (Cambridge University Press. 1955).

Art and Archæology

ASHBY. Architecture of Ancient Rome (Batsford).

CARRINGTON. Pompeii (Clarendon Press. 1936).

CHARLESTON. Roman Pottery (Faber and Faber. 1955).

MAIURI. Roman Painting (Zwemmer. 1953).

MATTINGLY. Roman Coins (Methuen. 2nd. edit. 1960).

RIIS. Introduction to Etruscan Art (Munksgaard. 1953).

RIVOIRA. Roman Architecture (Clarendon Press. 1927).

ROBERTSON. Greek and Roman Architecture (Cambridge University Press. 2nd. edit. 1943).

STRONG. Art in Ancient Rome. 2 vols. (Heinemann. 1929).

TOYNBEE. The Hadrianic School (Cambridge University Press. 1934).

WALTERS. The Art of the Romans (Methuen. 2nd. edit. 1928).

WICKHOFF. Roman Art (Macmillan. 1900).

Law

BUCKLAND. Textbook of Roman Law (Cambridge University Press 2nd. edit. 1950).

JOLOWICZ. Historical Introduction to the Study of Roman Law (Cambridge University Press. 2nd. edit. 1952).

ROBY. Roman Private Law (Cambridge University Press. 1902).

SCHULZ. History of Roman Legal Science (Clarendon Press. 1946).

—— Principles of Roman Law (Cambridge University Press. 1936).

—— Roman Classical Law (Clarendon Press. 1952).

STRACHAN-DAVIDSON. Some Problems of Roman Criminal Law (Clarendon Press. 1912).

Geography and Topography

CARY. The Geographic Background of Greek and Roman History (Clarendon Press. 1949).

MURRAY. Classical Atlas for Schools (Murray. 2nd. edit. 1917).

PLATNER & ASHBY. Topographical Dictionary of Rome (Clarendon Press. 1929).

ROBATHAN. The Monuments of Ancient Rome (Bretschneider. 1950).

Atlas of the Classical World. Ed. Van der Heyden & Scullard (Nelson. 1959).

INDEX

305